CONTEMPORARY DRIFT

LITERATURE NOW

Literature Now

Matthew Hart, David James, and Rebecca L. Walkowitz, Series Editors

Literature Now offers a distinct vision of late-twentieth- and early-twenty-first-century literary culture. Addressing contemporary literature and the ways we understand its meaning, the series includes books that are comparative and transnational in scope as well as those that focus on national and regional literary cultures.

# Contemporary Drift

GENRE, HISTORICISM, AND THE PROBLEM
OF THE PRESENT

## Theodore Martin

Columbia University Press
*New York*

Columbia University Press
*Publishers Since 1893*
New York   Chichester, West Sussex
cup.columbia.edu

Library of Congress Cataloging-in-Publication Data

Names: Martin, Theodore, author.
Title: Contemporary drift : genre, historicism, and the problem of
the present / Theodore Martin.
Description: New York : Columbia University Press, [2017] | Series:
Literature now | Includes bibliographical references and index.
Identifiers: LCCN 2016058572 (print) | LCCN 2017020167 (ebook) |
ISBN 978-0-231-54389-7 (e-book) | ISBN 978-0-231-18192-1 (cloth) |
ISBN 978-0-231-18193-8 (pbk.)
Subjects: LCSH: Contemporary, The, in literature. | American fiction—
20th century—History and criticism. | American fiction—21st century—
History and criticism. | Contemporary, The, in motion pictures.
Classification: LCC PS374.C596 (ebook) | LCC PS374.C596 M37 2017 (print) |
DDC 813/.609—dc23
LC record available at https://lccn.loc.gov/2016058572

Cover design: Kimberly Glyder

*Seventeen years later, this book is dedicated to the memory of my dad.*

# CONTENTS

# ACKNOWLEDGMENTS

Given the many years that have gone into writing it, *Contemporary Drift* is, in a certain sense, not very contemporary. That's fine by me. For how else would I have had the time to benefit from the good sense, great intelligence, and endless generosity of so many friends, teachers, and colleagues over the years? Above all, this book owes an immeasurable debt to Colleen Lye and Kent Puckett, who have looked out for me since the very first day I set foot at Berkeley. I could not have completed this project without the immense and implausible amount of faith they've shown in it, and still less without the towering intellectual and scholarly example they set. Stephen Best and Carol Clover were equally indispensable guides to working through many of the ideas that would form the foundation for this book. The early days of developing this project were survived with no little help from Jasper Bernes, Erin Beeghly, Ben Boudreaux, Natalia Cecire, Chris Chen, Amanda Goldstein, Tim Kreiner, Cody Marrs, Swati Rana, and Jill Richards.

At the University of Wisconsin, Milwaukee, it was my absurd good fortune to have Jane Gallop, Richard Grusin, and Jason Puskar as generous mentors as well as cherished friends. My wonderful colleagues in English made UWM a lively, supportive, and collegial place to work and write. I owe a special thanks to department chairs Liam Callanan and Mark Netzloff, who offered extensive support both institutionally and personally.

Meanwhile, a great many irreplaceable friends made Milwaukee home: Dick Blau, Carolyn Eichner, Christine Evans, Elena Gorfinkel, Kennan Ferguson, Nick Fleisher, Greg Jay, Jennifer Jordan, Andrew Kincaid, Richard Leson, Aline Lo, Patrick Mundt, Erin O'Donnell, Alex Pickett, Rick Popp, Shannon Popp, and Jocelyn Szczepaniak-Gillece.

In simplest terms, this book could not have been written without Margaret Ronda, Tobias Menely, Tom McEnaney, and Josh Gang. Sean Goudie and Priscilla Wald have been amazing advisers and formidable interlocutors; I really can't imagine what I did to deserve them. I'm immensely grateful to the numerous friends and colleagues who have been generous enough to read, listen to, or discuss parts of this project over the years: Jennifer Ashton, Adrienne Brown, Todd Carmody, Joshua Clover, Thom Dancer, Susan Stanford Friedman, Mark Goble, Eric Hayot, Danielle Heard, Matt Hooley, Sarah Juliet Lauro, Andrew Leong, Samaine Lockwood, Kate Marshall, Walter Benn Michaels, Christopher Miller, Christen Mucher, Mary Mullen, Jeff Nealon, Julie Orlemanski, Sonya Posmentier, Namwali Serpell, Rebekah Sheldon, Richard So, and Aarthi Vadde. I'm also deeply grateful to the editors who supported my work at early and impressionable stages of my career: Nancy Armstrong and Marshall Brown. Special thanks to Kate, Tobias, Namwali, and Walter for invitations to present parts of this book, and to audiences at Notre Dame, UC Davis, UC Berkeley, and the Newberry Library for listening.

Support for the writing of this book was provided by the Doreen B. Townsend Center for the Humanities at Berkeley, the Center for 21st-Century Studies at UWM, the First Book Institute and the Center for American Literary Studies at Penn State, the Institute for Research in the Humanities at UW Madison, the National Humanities Center, and the University of California, Irvine, Humanities Commons.

I owe a great deal of gratitude to the editors of the Literature Now series: Matt Hart, David James, and Rebecca Walkowitz. They thought this book could be better, and—luckily for me—they pushed me to make it so. I am especially, incalculably indebted to Matt, who believed in this book, went to bat for it, and tirelessly guided me through every step of the editorial process. I have been extremely lucky to have the opportunity to work with the wonderful people at Columbia University Press. Philip Leventhal has been a patient and expert editor. Miriam Grossman has offered cheerful and timely assistance. I also want to thank Andy Hoberek and an anonymous reader for responding to this manuscript with incredible care and showing me countless ways to improve it.

A few parts of this book have appeared previously in substantially different form. Portions of chapter 1 have been adapted from "The Privilege of Contemporary Life: Periodization in the Bret Easton Ellis Decades," *Modern Language Quarterly* 71, no. 2 (2010): 153–74; and portions of chapter 3 have been adapted from "The Long Wait: Timely Secrets of the Contemporary Detective Novel," *Novel: A Forum on Fiction* 45, no. 2 (2012): 165–83.

Solon Barocas and Ben Petrosky will always be family. So will my family. Fran Martin is the most inspiring person I know; however much I have figured out how to live is because of her. Jon Martin and Hannah Martin Herrington have loved, tolerated, and laughed with me more than I could hope for. Rick Martin has influenced me more than I imagine he realizes. Cia White has shown me what it really means to be a reader, a writer, and a teacher. This book is dedicated to the memory of Ken Martin, my dad, whom we all miss as much now as then.

Lastly, my two true loves. Lulu McClanahan is a world inside the world. And Annie McClanahan is just the world. She is my condition of possibility, my realm of necessity, my first and last instance, and every word I've ever written and will write is for her and because of her.

CONTEMPORARY DRIFT

# THESES ON THE CONCEPT OF
# THE CONTEMPORARY

This book is a study of contemporary literature and film. It is also a study of what it means to call things like literature and film "contemporary." Perhaps your first thought is that this will be a book devoted to novels and movies of just the past five, ten, or fifteen years; that certainly sounds contempo-rary. Or perhaps your expectations are looser, and you assume that I will be talking about art and culture since roughly the 1980s. Or perhaps you take the long view and expect to read a broad study of cultural production after 1945. These all are reasonable assumptions. The more persuasive this book is, however, the less it will satisfy them. That's because the aim of *Contemporary Drift* is not to settle once and for all the question of which framework for defining the contemporary is the right one but to explore the consequences—for contemporary arts, contemporary thought, and con-temporary politics—of how difficult the question is to settle. Despite the new and welcome burst of scholarly attention given to contemporary culture over the past fifteen years, surprisingly little thought has been given to the meanings and implications of the contemporary as a critical category.[1] This book is an attempt to correct that. *Contemporary Drift* is a survey of the narrative forms and critical practices that shape our varying conceptions of the contemporary. And it is an argument for how those forms and practices are attached to the cumulative histories of genre. In short, this book confronts the drift of the contemporary—its unsettled meaning and uncertain place in history—by turning to the historical drag of genre. What changes in a genre over time, and what stays the same? This question, I argue, perfectly captures the problem of how we decide what counts as contemporary. Surveying how older genres adapt to the new historical conditions of global capitalism, *Contemporary Drift* shows what it means to think of the contemporary not as a self-evident historical period but as a conceptual problem— and what it means to see contemporary genre fiction as a vital resource for resolving that problem.

While there is now a rapidly growing body of scholarly work devoted to explaining the conditions of our contemporary moment, what distinguishes *Contemporary Drift* is its claim that the project of historicizing the contemporary is inextricable from the dilemmas posed by the concept itself. What exactly are those dilemmas? To answer that question, I begin with four theses on the concept of the contemporary: four negatively phrased propositions that demonstrate how the contemporary defies some of our basic assumptions about what the term means and how it works.

1. *The contemporary is not a period.* Since at least the 1960s, it has been common practice to refer to the period of the late twentieth and early twenty-first centuries as *contemporary*. As a staple of book titles, conferences, and course offerings, the word now functions as easy scholarly shorthand for the ongoing history of the present moment. The pervasiveness of the term *contemporary*, however, belies its strangeness as a way of actually thinking about history. Though we talk about the contemporary as if it were the name of a clearly demarcated historical period, the boundaries of that period remain subject to disagreement and revision. Take what is now commonly referred to as the field of "contemporary literature." What time frame is the phrase supposed to cover? The open secret of the field is that no one really knows. *The Oxford Guide to Contemporary Writing* informs us that "'contemporary' means since about 1960."[2] In practice, however, the term is used variously to refer to post-1945, post-1960, post-1989, and post-2000 literature (with a number of alternative period breaks in between).[3] The contemporary is clearly an unreliable form of historical measure, a periodizing term that doesn't quite manage to periodize. With no agreed-on beginning and no ending in sight, the contemporary does not so much delimit history as drift across it. This historical drift makes the contemporary less a literary

or a historical period than a literary-historical *problem*, one that contemporary scholars haven't yet found a way to resolve.

2. *The contemporary is not contemporary.* Although the term *contemporary* evokes a sense of what is current, immediate, or up to date, it is not unique to the twenty-first century. Etymologically, *contemporary* first acquired a historical connotation (as a synonym for *modern* meaning "characteristic of the present period") at the end of the nineteenth century.[4] It did not become a fully institutionalized category until much later, with the mid-twentieth-century emergence of fields like contemporary literature and contemporary art. The first Institute of Contemporary Arts, for instance, was founded in London in 1946. It was followed in 1948 by the Institute of Contemporary Art in Boston (which that year controversially changed its name from the Institute of *Modern* Art), with several more museums of contemporary art opening—in São Paulo, Montreal, and Chicago—in the 1960s.[5] The 1950s and 1960s featured a similar burst of institutional energy around the idea of contemporary literature, as anthologies with names like *Essentials of Contemporary Literature* (1954) and *On Contemporary Literature* (1964) appeared alongside a new journal of record, *Wisconsin Studies in Contemporary Literature* (later renamed *Contemporary Literature*), which was founded in 1960. These institutional histories usefully remind us that the study of the contemporary has a history. In doing so, however, they also raise important questions about what counts as contemporary. After all, what was once "contemporary" about the art and literature of the 1950s is surely no longer contemporary to us.[6] The deictic, or indexical, force of the contemporary all but guarantees that its referent will shift over time. That drifting referent is further complicated by the drawn-out process of institutionalization itself, as it took several decades for the contemporary arts to become firmly entrenched as scholarly fields.[7] In a very real sense, then, the contemporary both is and isn't specific to our current moment. Seeming to index the time of our present as well as present disciplinary configurations, the term also invokes the history of its own institutional emergence and the even longer history of its historical meaning. In other words, it invokes all the contemporaries that aren't ours. Thus are we faced with the strange historical gravity of a concept that claims to ground us in the present even as it drifts backward into the past.

3. *The contemporary is not historical.* The emergence of the contemporary as a field of study challenged the basic methodological underpinnings

of literary and art history in ways that are still being reckoned with today. The art historian Richard Meyer remarks that as recently as the 1990s, "had someone proposed the practice of something called 'contemporary art history,' I could only have understood it as an oxymoron."[8] The contemporary has similarly been "a déclassé period among literary historians," as Gordon Hutner, editor of the journal *American Literary History*, reminds us.[9] What is déclassé or oxymoronic about the historical category of the contemporary is the difficulty of grasping as history something still moving through history. As a period that's not yet past, the contemporary doesn't afford us the usual privileges of hindsight and critical distance.[10] Without the benefit of critical distance, the contemporary is likely to register only as blank space or blind spot, unavailable to the rigors of historical analysis. In this way, the contemporary may simply seem too close to constitute a serious object of scholarly contemplation. The discomfort with studying the not-yet-historical conditions of the contemporary is especially pronounced in a discipline that has, over the last few decades, been shaped by the methodological resurgence of historicism. As Rita Felski observes, no recent critical movement has been able to "stop the current historicist tide" in literary studies,[11] a tide that at this point may not even be a tide so much as, in Amy Hungerford's words, "the water we all swim in."[12] Indeed, you would be hard-pressed to find a literary critic today who doesn't in some way believe that writing about literary texts means writing about their historical context. (I, for instance, certainly believe that.) But if historicism "now seems less a critical movement than a simple assumption about literary-critical work," what does it mean to make that assumption about the contemporary, a period in which historical perspective clearly doesn't function in the same way?[13] Put simply, can we historicize the present in the same way that we historicize the past? Whatever our answer to this question is, it requires us to seriously consider the possibility that modern historical thought—and along with it, current historicist methodology—reaches a certain limit when it comes to the ongoing, unfinished history of the contemporary.

4. *The contemporary is not mere presentness.* If the contemporary is not susceptible to traditional forms of historical analysis, one would at least expect it to be available to direct observation and immediate experience. Who can doubt that we experience every day what the historian Fernand Braudel calls "present life, in all its confusion"?[14] Indeed, one of the primary objections to the establishment of the contemporary as an academic field was

that it was already a self-evident part of students' daily lives and, for that reason, hardly warranted scholarly commentary.[15] As the preceding theses make clear, however, the contemporary is not so obvious or unmediated a category. This will not be news to current scholars of contemporary culture, who know full well that the field poses some unique problems. Today more books are published, more films are released, and more art is produced than ever before.[16] Without the benefit of hindsight, without the aid of an agreed-on periodization, and without the help of an established canon, it is a daunting if not impossible task to make sense of the constant proliferation of contemporary cultural objects. This is why, if the contemporary is merely synonymous with the ceaseless flow of present experience, it ceases to have much discernible meaning. To think of the contemporary as everything that surrounds us amounts to thinking of it as nothing at all.

Faced with these four negative statements, one may well be driven to conclude that the contemporary is simply unknowable. That is not the claim of this book. Yet the concept does challenge some of our standard assumptions about historical knowledge and interpretive method in ways that have not been adequately addressed. Given its fuzziness as a period, its drift through time, its diminishment of critical distance, and its incommensurability with everyday life, how does the idea of the contemporary come to have any meaning for us? One way to begin to answer this question is to consider the contemporary not so much an index of immediacy as a *strategy of mediation*: a means of negotiating between experience and retrospection, immersion and explanation, closeness and distance. Put simply, the contemporary is a critical concept. It must be imagined before it can be perceived; it is not just a moment that contains us but a moment that we must first conceive *as* a moment.[17] The contemporary compels us to think, above all, about the politics of how we think about the present. The contours and currents of our current moment—its temporal boundaries, its historical significance, its deeper social logics—are inseparable from the historically determined and politically motivated ways we choose to divide the present from the past. The political demands placed on us by our present depend on how we first decide what belongs to the present. They depend, in other words, on how we come to imagine what it means to be contemporary.

This act of imagining brings us to the threshold of fiction. The difficulties implied by the concept of the contemporary aren't merely the concern of contemporary critics. They are also, this book proposes, the increasingly urgent subject matter of late-twentieth- and early-twenty-first-century fiction. In *Contemporary Drift*, I show how the political, conceptual, and methodological questions posed by the contemporary are addressed by the popular narratives of our present moment. Accordingly, the practice of reading contemporary fiction undertaken in this book involves more than putting recent texts in context. It also requires us to consider how these texts generate their own formal and figural ways of explaining what counts as a context in the first place. How do aesthetic objects invent their own ways of thinking historically in response to the absence of historical distance? Framed by this question, *Contemporary Drift* is an attempt to understand what contemporary history looks like from the perspective of contemporary fiction. Through its attention to the historical, aesthetic, and conceptual dimensions of the contemporary, this book strives to be a work of both literary history and literary theory. More specifically, it could be said to be an experiment in how, in the context of the contemporary, the former comes to double as the latter: how any historical account of the contemporary moment must serve simultaneously as a theory of how that history is written.

In this book, the theory that best explains how we come to know our contemporary is a theory of genre. Genre, as I understand it in *Contemporary Drift*, describes how aesthetic forms move cumulatively through history.[18] The accretive history of genre is a measure of both change and continuity, diachrony and synchrony, pastness and presentness. Genres explain how aesthetic and cultural categories become recognizable as well as reproducible in a given moment, and they demonstrate how the conventions and expectations that make up those categories are sedimented over time.[19] Let's say that you are watching Kelly Reichardt's slow Western *Meek's Cutoff* or reading Michael Chabon's counterfactual detective novel *The Yiddish Policemen's Union*. Are you facing a cultural product that's new or old? Inventive or imitative? On one hand, we know a Western or a detective novel when we see one, which means we recognize the conventions that give the genre a history. On the other hand, we know there's something historically distinctive about these objects, which means we also recognize each genre as contemporary. Genres lead distinctly double lives, with one foot in the past and the other in the present; they contain the entire abridged history of an aesthetic form while also staking a claim to the form's contemporary relevance. If genres are one of the most basic units of literary history, they are also, I argue, a necessary starting point for coming to grips with the complex status of contemporary history. Genre shows us what differentiates the present from the past as well as what ties the two together.

Genre and the contemporary: two versions, this book proposes, of the same problem. That problem is how we determine what is contemporary and what is not. While the drift of the contemporary makes its place in history difficult to grasp, the drag of genre—the accretion or sedimentation of formal change over time—makes the process of becoming contemporary uniquely visible. This book's organizational decision to focus on genre fiction is also a methodological argument about what genre does: it gives us an alternative model for practicing historicism. Genre offers a singular view of contemporary history not by highlighting what's new in it and not by exposing what's old-fashioned about it but by showing how the very idea of the contemporary emerges out of a constant negotiation between the two. Because genres remain identifiable even as they change, they are ideally suited to tracking the tensions between novelty and continuity, presentness and persistence, that shape our notion of the contemporary. And because they refer to collectively recognizable and reusable templates, genres provide a powerful social tool for making sense of what is emergent and unfamiliar about our contemporary moment. The work of giving form to contemporary experience is intimately connected to what Lauren Berlant, in her theory of the historical present, calls the task of "assessing the way a thing that is happening finds its genre."[20] Here genre describes the incipient but shared conventions that make historical emergence visible and thinkable in the present. The idiom of genre thus allows us to put a finer point on precisely what the contemporary is: a set of shared conventions for categorizing our otherwise disorienting experiences of the present.

In the framework of *Contemporary Drift*, genre plays several roles. It provides a methodology—call it an alternative historicism—for analyzing the historical paradoxes of the contemporary. It describes the repeatable aesthetic and social patterns that help orient us amid the clamor of contemporary life. And last but not least, it constitutes a defining feature of contemporary culture itself. As a contribution not just to the theory of the contemporary but also to the history of *this* contemporary, *Contemporary Drift* contends that one of the distinguishing aspects of twenty-first-century culture is art's transformed relationship to genre. Whereas modernism is well known for its antipathy to genre, and postmodern culture is famously characterized by its pastiche of multiple genres at once ("the random can-nibalization of all the styles of the past, the play of random stylistic allu-sion"),[21] today contemporary literature is marked by noticeably different uses of genre. The "changing status of genre fiction," as Andrew Hoberek helps us define it, is currently playing out in two ways.[22] First, authors and filmmakers have become increasingly interested in working within the constraints of popular genres, as Colson Whitehead and Ben Marcus do with post-apocalyptic fiction (which I discuss in chapter 5), or China Miéville and Michael Chabon do with the detective novel (chapter 4), or Kelly Reichardt and Takashi Miike do with the Western (chapter 3). The resulting works of art are not superficial pastiches of dead styles but ear-nest attempts to contribute to the history of a given genre. Second, these "high-cultural" contributions to genre fiction have emerged alongside "a newer tendency to confer literary status on popular genres themselves."[23] The growing consensus that popular genres and their practitioners con-stitute meaningful objects of critical study in their own right is connected to the current resurgence of genre criticism as a method. Long considered a retrograde mode of literary criticism, genre has recently been revived and invigorated by a range of critics working within a variety of critical tradi-tions.[24] Taken together, these two trends—genre's recuperation by artists and by critics—map out a cultural moment in which genre now plays a powerful role in dictating both the concerns of art and the aims of its study.

Genre's current status as a mainstream cultural category motivates this book's turn to genre as a framework for interpreting the chaotic and incho-ate conditions of contemporary life. Drawing a connection between genre's cultural revitalization and its methodological and conceptual provocations, the following chapters offer five studies in how the drag of genre enables us to reimagine the drift of the contemporary. The five chapters of *Contempo-rary Drift* examine five familiar genres: the novel of manners, the noir film, the Western, the detective novel, and post-apocalyptic fiction. This selec-tion of genres is dictated first of all by a basic question, one as obvious as it is pivotal: Why are these genres still around? With this question in mind, each chapter uses the longer life span of a given genre as a backdrop to highlight how it has transformed in recent years and thereby acquired a newly contem-porary relevance. This approach allows me to make a claim about what is *contemporary* about each genre while also insisting that any such claim depends on first understanding what is *historical* about it. Taken together, the chapters of this book demonstrate how the evolution of generic form—from the altered depiction of bureaucratic disorientation in neo-noir films to the changing representation of working conditions in twenty-first-century post-apocalyptic fiction—allows us to narrate what counts as contemporary.

*Contemporary Drift* seeks to make larger claims about the conceptual, methodological, and historical consequences of thinking through genre. Such claims are best supported by studying how genre works across mediums rather than within a single one. In the effort to write a book not simply about some genres but about the *idea* of genre, I have included as many different kinds of genres as scholarly responsibility would allow. In order to accommodate both the need for generic diversity and the limits of my own intellectual training as a critic of narrative, I have chosen to restrict my analysis to novels and films. Among narrative mediums, film is the one most institutionally and commercially organized around the fine-grained divisions of genre (horror, thriller, rom-com); it is also where we find some of the best-known demonstrations of how popular genres—like film noir and the Western—transform into elite critical objects. On the other side of the media divide, the recent literary revival of genre fiction makes the novel an equally unavoidable site for considering the contemporary fate of genre. In light of the centrality of genre to these two mediums, a book about genre has little choice but to consider literature and film together. From this ostensibly discrepant pairing, other equally fruitful contrasts are suggested. The genres discussed in this book are meant to demonstrate the range of media forms, geographical itineraries, and historical trajectories—from novels to graphic novels to films; from the United States to England to Japan; and from a few decades of film noir to two centuries of the novel of manners—that genre allows us to talk about.

While the genres examined in *Contemporary Drift* may initially seem to be defined primarily by their differences from one another, they do share several important features. First, they all are popular genres. My earlier references to "genre fiction" (as it applies to both literature and film but doesn't extend, for instance, to poetry) mark this book's attention to the questions of cultural status raised by narrative genres whose mass production and manifest conventionality are widely thought to disable more pointed political and aesthetic commentary. Isn't *contemporary* just another word for *popular* anyway? Indeed, the notion of the popular or the mass evoked by these genres is one way to understand genre's connection to social life as

such: its capacity to categorize the features of artworks as well as the socio-
political conventions that organize and orient an emergent historical moment. My other motive in focusing on popular genres is to consider how
oscillations between low culture and high culture don't simply differentiate
genre fiction from artistic fiction but also internally organize genres themselves. For instance, what kind of cultural object is Colson Whitehead's
Proustian zombie novel *Zone One*? Why, we might wonder, would the win-
ner of the 2001 Pulitzer Prize for fiction (Chabon) immediately begin work
on a hard-boiled detective novel?[25] And what are we supposed to do with
Bret Easton Ellis's controversial *American Psycho*, which is either a distinguished descendant of Jane Austen and Edith Wharton or a crass instance of
pornography? Although we tend to place genre fiction firmly on one side
of the high culture/mass culture divide, these examples suggest that it just
as often works to bridge that divide. In doing so, genre fiction becomes a way
of mapping the shifting cultural terrain of the popular and the literary as
it is negotiated over time. Watching that terrain shift, as it does in each of
the following chapters, is ultimately a way to reassess the political and artistic claims still capable of being made on behalf of popular forms of literature
and film.[26]

Such questions of cultural and class status are inextricable from the question of gender. Tania Modleski's seminal work on women's popular culture taught critics to be attentive to the ways that much of feminized mass
culture is critically and culturally marginalized.[27] The cultural anxieties
attached to women's writing since the eighteenth century remain visible,
for instance, in the debates surrounding "chick lit." Dismissed as shallow
and frivolous (if not pernicious), chick lit, as Stephanie Harzewski explains
in her valuable history of the genre, "has been judged . . . a pink menace to
both established and debut women authors who perceive it as staging a
coup upon literary seriousness and undoing the canonical status" of women
writers from Austen to Sylvia Plath.[28] The perceived threat posed by chick
lit concerns its thematic depictions of consumerism as well as its commercial success. It is the popularity of this particular brand of women's writing, in other words—the genre's foregrounding of women's power in the
marketplace—that makes it a site of such intense cultural unease.

The connection between women's culture and commercialization is
similarly apparent in yet another chapter in the long history of gendered

marginalization, the changing status of television. Formerly derided as a purely commercial medium rooted in the feminized space of the home (think day-time soap operas), television has only recently become a fully "legitimated" medium open to aesthetic appreciation and scholarly analysis (think *The Wire*). As media historians Elena Levine and Michael Newman contend in their *Legitimating Television*, given the long-standing idea of television as a "feminized medium," the "cultural elevation" of television has taken place largely as a process of "masculinization." That process shifts the gendered markings of television—now epitomized by masculine shows as well as masculine technologies—while "leav[ing] in place the role of gender in classifying media."[29] Those same gender hierarchies also govern the clas-sification and reception of popular genres. Indeed, it will surprise exactly no one that the mass-market genres that have recently experienced an ele-vation in status are identifiably masculine ones: crime fiction, noir films, Westerns. These are, of course, also the genres studied in this book. This fact allows me to clarify both the book's aims and its shortcomings. *Con-temporary Drift* represents a study of what "legitimated" genres—that is, genres that have crossed the boundary separating low from high—are capable of telling us about the altered status of genre as a primary category of contemporary culture. As such, the book is also unavoidably a demon-stration of how the cultural legitimation of genre depends on genre's mas-culinization. Attempting to respond to this problem, my analyses of genre are in part attempts to challenge the conventionally masculine terms in which genres like detective fiction and Western films have too often been studied (by reframing them, respectively, in terms of temporality and the environment).[30] That said, the genres examined in this book must also be taken for what they inarguably are: symptoms of the conspicuous gender-ing of genre that continues to dictate—now no less than in the 1980s or the 1880s—how (and which) genres are allowed to be transformed from objects of popular entertainment to subjects of serious study.

In addition to being associated with both mass and masculine culture, the genres I discuss here are by and large linked to the United States, from the Hollywood origins of film noir and the Western to the American styles of naturalism (Edith Wharton, Frank Norris, Theodore Dreiser) and hard-boiled fiction (Raymond Chandler, Dashiell Hammett, Chester Himes). The context of the twentieth-century United States may thus seem to exert a kind of centripetal force on the textual examples studied in the following pages. Yet a key part of this book's interest in genre lies in the ways that genre constitutes its own kind of centrifugal counterforce, putting pressure on both the historical and the geographical constraints of context. Throughout *Contemporary Drift*, then, I will be less concerned with keeping these genres confined to one particular time and place than with showing how genres continually call such confines into question. The book features American writers read alongside British ones; films from Australia, Italy, Japan, and the United States studied side by side; and the analysis of narratives set everywhere from London to Mumbai to a fictionalized amalgam of old Europe and the new Middle East. The transnational pairings that motivate many of the chapters may seem to suspend national difference in favor of formal resonance. In doing so, however, they also remind us of the uniquely contemporary pressures being exerted on the category of the nation itself: the pressures of globalization. The geographical centrifuge that is genre is perhaps the quintessential cultural technology of an era of globalization, in which art (no less than other made objects) bears the increasingly visible imprint of the tension between local particularity and the global economy.[31] In this way, an internationally comparative view of genre offers a window onto the current conjuncture of globalized capitalism, even if such a view continues to be framed by U.S. economic hegemony. Exemplifying what it means to make art under conditions of globalization, genre maps out a world in which cultural transit takes precedence over temporal and spatial constraints.

The aim of the following chapters is to think movement and constraint together. To do so, each chapter offers a brief history of a given genre as well as a broader consideration of the geographic, historiographic, and taxonomic dilemmas raised by it. How do we explain the transatlantic movement of the novel of manners (chapter 1)? How do we contextualize an endlessly referenced and remade genre like film noir (chapter 2)? And how do we locate the ostensibly national and nationalist logic of a genre like the Western in light of its surprisingly global career (chapter 3)? Each of the book's chapters, in other words, makes certain strategic assumptions about the consistency, history, and location of a particular genre in order to show how genre works in turn to challenge those assumptions. Thus if a residually American and predominantly twentieth-century frame of reference seems at times to overdetermine the analysis of genre in this book, that is the result not of some unconscious presentism or U.S.-centrism but of a concerted attempt to establish (as a paradigmatic but not unique case) the national and historical borders from which each of these now globalized genres consistently escapes.

One final objection to this book's treatment of genre might be raised: Can a total view or decisive definition of any genre be achieved through only a few examples of it? Can genres, as abstract categories, ever be exemplified? Possibly not. But if the tension lodged in genre between instance and abstraction remains productive for my argument, that is because it parallels the tension between experience and concept that defines the problem of the contemporary. With this parallel in mind, *Contemporary Drift* approaches genre as an indispensable site for studying the relationship between examples and categories. Accordingly, my guiding assumption is not that the particular examples under discussion stand in for the entirety of a given genre. Rather, I consider each generic instance as an individual aesthetic object that both constitutes and transforms our idea of the larger genre to which it belongs. The history of any genre is, without question, doomed to be a partial one. You might call it a history of historical tendency: of the ways that aesthetic conventions trend simultaneously toward specificity and uniformity. To seek evidence of this double tendency in a handful of individual instances is not to mistake the part for the whole or the case for the category. It is simply to recognize the unavoidable truth that a category doesn't exist except through the instances that constitute it without being identical to it. If this is a lesson we learn from genre, it is one with serious implications for our understanding of the contemporary as well. In both cases, the lack of perfect congruity between instance and abstraction is the gap that calls forth the very practice of literary criticism.

In sum, this book offers a study in *how genres become contemporary*: how familiar aesthetic conventions mutate in response to changing historical conditions. Genre's blend of change and continuity, of drift and drag,[32] makes it a privileged site for exploring the process of becoming contemporary. Think of it as a controlled experiment in historical emergence. By holding certain features steady—the familiar landscape of the Western, the classic plot structure of the detective novel—genres first draw our attention to what changes; then they compel us to ask why. The five chapters of *Contemporary Drift* begin from five versions of this question. Why do recent novels of manners become obsessed with historical dates? Why do new versions of noir films lose the ability to contextualize their voice-overs? Why are today's Westerns set in the dead of winter instead of the dry heat of the desert? Why are twenty-first-century detective novels skeptical of open-endedness and ambiguity? And why do the latest post-apocalyptic narratives take an increasingly negative view of the work it takes to survive?

The answers to each of these questions require us to reckon with genre history, social history, and the methodological challenges posed by contemporary history. The intervention of *Contemporary Drift* is located at the intersection of these three histories. On one hand, the book aims to show how changes in these genres correspond to crucial features of contemporary capitalism: the global triumph of consumer society, the pervasion of geopolitical and environmental risk, and the precarious conditions of postindustrial work. On the other hand, *Contemporary Drift* argues that such generic changes generate their own distinctive ways of conceptualizing the contemporary itself. These two sides of the project are condensed in the keywords that title each chapter. These five key terms name both prominent aesthetic features and provisional historical frameworks. They designate the formal changes that distinguish the contemporary version of each genre, and they describe the unique historical forms through which these genres take the measure of their own contemporary moment. Reflecting both the aesthetic and the social dimensions of genre, these key terms convey not just an experience *in* the present but also a conception *of* it. In the contemporary novel of manners, the figure of the *decade* emerges as a way to respond to the alleged endlessness of capitalism at the turn of the twenty-first century. In film noir, the ostensibly nostalgic dynamics of *revival* challenge our commitment to historical specificity in the context of the postwar world system. In detective fiction, the temporality of *waiting* becomes a way to question the value of uncertainty in a society shaped by risk. In Westerns, unseasonable *weather* provides a framework for addressing the otherwise invisible process of climate change. And in the post-apocalyptic novel, the repetitive narration of *survival* offers a commentary on both the monotonies of work and the anxieties of unemployment. So what, finally, do we mean when we talk about the contemporary? The contemporary transformations of genre, I contend, allow us to answer this question in two intertwined and indispensable ways: first, through the aesthetic changes that index genre's adjustment to the emergent conditions of advanced capitalism; second, through the distinctive generic forms that offer their own unorthodox measures of contemporary history.


The contemporary is both a historical and a theoretical problem. For that reason, *Contemporary Drift* is both a historical and a theoretical book. The book's theoretical perspective is rooted in the preceding account of genre as an alternative methodology for historicizing the present, as well as in each chapter's argument about how a given genre gives us a particular way of formulating the idea of the contemporary as such. To claim that genre helps us understand the contemporary, however, is not meant to suggest that the concept of the contemporary doesn't have a history of its own. To provide a sense of that history, I want to explain briefly how the contemporary became both an established scholarly field and a broader cultural preoccupation. My intention is to show, first, how the very possibility of writing a book like *Contemporary Drift* is rooted in a series of gradual and often contested changes in the discipline of literary studies; second, how such an attempt to historicize the study of the contemporary is partly a story about the limits of historicism itself; and third, how the methodological limits associated with the contemporary reveal a set of deeper social and economic contradictions that, in the latter half of the twentieth century, began to alter our basic understanding of the present.

A history of the study of contemporary literature might begin as early as 1895, when a professor at Yale College named William Lyon Phelps proposed what he claimed to be "the first course in any university in the world wholly confined to contemporary fiction."[33] According to Phelps, the proposal created quite a stir; in newspapers across the country, he recalled, "my harmless little pedagogical scheme was discussed—often under enormous headlines—as a revolutionary idea."[34] Revolutionary enough, at any rate, to incense his colleagues at Yale, who said they would fire Phelps if he continued to teach the course.[35] (He complied.) The belief that contemporary literature was not a suitable topic for scholarship lasted for several decades after Phelps's pedagogical experiment. "Here is contemporary literature," John Crowe Ransom noted in 1937, "waiting for its criticism; where are the professors of literature?"[36] It was only after World War II, as classes in twentieth-century literature became both increasingly available and increasingly well enrolled, that contemporary literature professors made their presence felt. As Gerald Graff observes in *Professing Literature*, by midcentury "an institution that had once seen itself as the bulwark of tradition against vulgar and immoral contemporaneity was now the disseminator and explainer of the most recent trends."[37]

What explains this institutional trend toward the contemporary? For Graff, it was largely a product of the defeat of historical scholars at the hands of the New Critics, a defeat that signaled an emphatic turn away from historical context.[38] To explain it in this way is to see how contemporary literature became a scholarly field only at the moment when literary criticism ceased to see itself as a historical discipline. In short, the possibility of studying contemporary literature was dependent on the possibility of imagining literary criticism as something other than the study of history.[39] Yet the weakening of literary study's historical underpinnings leaves the field of contemporary literature in a difficult position. From the problem of judging which books will prove important to future critics to the even more basic challenge of determining the boundaries of the contemporary period, the absence of historical perspective really does make contemporary literature harder to make sense of than other literary periods.[40]

In this way, we may come to understand the field of contemporary literature—fixated on the critical distance that it is never quite able to achieve—as the most emblematic product, the purest expression, of a discipline that has for the past sixty years been torn between the formalist legacy of New Criticism and the cultural ambitions of historicism. Contemporary literature, in other words, is nothing less than the institutionalization of the tension between formalism and historicism that has shaped the postwar English department. The perennial question of whether contemporary literature is either good enough or distant enough to be a viable object of analysis is really a question of what kind of thing literary study is supposed to be studying: texts or contexts, literature or history. Contemporary literature can thus be thought of as something like the literature department's *bad conscience*: an expression of the vexed disciplinary relationship between literature and history by way of a literary period in which the status of history becomes a newly open question.

One way to understand how this bad conscience has manifested itself since the 1960s is to consider how the open question of contemporary history has played out not just in the codification of contemporary literature as a field of study but also in the parallel institutional consolidation of what we now call "continental" or "critical" theory. From the Frankfurt school to Michel Foucault, from the linguistic turn to the affective one, a half century's worth of literary theory has tended to see the history of the present as both an ultimate interpretive horizon and an unresolvable methodological obstacle. The history of "the history of the present" as a theoretical problem has been a history of attempts to understand why present-day history is so difficult to understand. Many of the twentieth century's sharpest critics of everyday life under capitalism—from Walter Benjamin to Max Horkheimer and Theodor Adorno to Henri Lefebvre—were acutely aware of the practical (or, as Lefebvre saw it, simply "editorial")[41] difficulties posed by the study of a present that wouldn't stand still.[42] In books like *Dialectic of Enlightenment* and the three volumes of *Critique of Everyday Life*—all of which wrestle with the problem of how to critique a present situation that is already in the process of changing—we see how Karl Marx's famous call for a ruthless critique of everything existing confronts the relentless temporality of the present in which those things exist.[43] As for Foucault, who did more than anyone to popularize the phrase "the history of the present," his emphasis was squarely on the *history* part. Foucauldian genealogy was a method for pushing the question of the present back into the past, where it could be better analyzed from a distance.[44] Finally, for those working in the wake of poststructuralism and of Jacques Derrida's famous critique of presence, the problem of the present has been less its constant movement or lack of distance than its dubious ontology, its resistance to being clearly demarcated or consciously thought. When the French philosopher Sylviane Agacinski asserts that the "reality of the present is . . . impossible to *frame*"[45] or when Lauren Berlant describes the present as something whose "shared contours one can only intuit," they both are referring to the same thing: what Berlant calls "the ordinary thoughtlessness of the present,"[46] or the presumed incompatibility between present experience and critical thought.

Substitute the term *present* for *contemporary*—as critics have begun doing only in the past decade[47]—and you still get the same problems. When, for instance, Paul Rabinow suggests that "the anthropology of the contemporary has seemed to me best done by doing it," or when the art historian Terry Smith defines contemporary art as "*art . . . created within the conditions of contemporaneity*," or when the philosopher Giorgio Agamben proposes that "what it means to be contemporary" is to "perceive . . . the darkness of the present," we see several times over how the contemporary has been enshrined as a figure of historical opacity, if not tautology.[48] To the extent that such accounts leave us in the dark, they make their point all the more clearly: to be contemporary, it would seem, is to confront one's basic inability to define the contemporary.

To trace the parallel emergence of the field of contemporary literature and the canon of self-reflexive critical theory is to discover a paradox at the heart of contemporary life: since the middle of the twentieth century, we have become at once more concerned with defining our current moment and more convinced of the difficulty of doing so.[49] One way to explain this intensified yet anxious preoccupation with the contemporary is to consider it in terms of what sociologists like Ulrich Beck and Anthony Giddens (and following them, literary critics like Mark McGurl) have encouraged us to think of as the shift from industrial modernity to "reflexive modernity," a transition that occurs once the processes of capitalist modernization have become so ubiquitous and entrenched that they spawn a range of public discourses devoted to endlessly assessing the consequences of such processes.[50] To view the second half of the twentieth century through the lens of what McGurl calls a "multivalent social dynamic of self-observation" (a dynamic that extends "from the self-observation of society as a whole in the social sciences, media, and the arts, to . . . corporations which pay more and more attention to their own management practices and organizational structures, down to the self-monitoring of individuals") is to see how a certain protocol of *historical* self-reflection—reflection on the idea of the contemporary itself—becomes a key component of both literary criticism and literary theory under conditions of reflexive modernity.[51]

The increasingly codified yet increasingly uncertain status of the contemporary remains poorly understood, however, if we fail to situate it in the specifically contemporary conditions of global capitalism. To track the evolution of advanced capitalism since the 1960s is to see a series of material changes to the measure and monetization of present time. These are changes to the most fundamental ways we conceive, consume, and experience the present. If today the present feels more difficult to pin down, that is because in ways both real and imagined it is more sped-up, elusive, and enveloping than ever before. From the "perpetual present" of postmodern culture to the "24/7" present of digital capitalism;[52] from the widespread extension of working hours to the unprecedented acceleration of cycles of production, circulation, and consumption;[53] from the nanosecond span of financial trading to the unfathomable life span of a warming planet:[54] these are just some of the ways that the development of a globalized, financialized, and flexible mode of capitalism can be seen to modify our basic sense of the present, turning it into something precarious yet perpetual, uncertain yet inescapable, at once crushingly constant and constantly disappearing. As it emerges in the Anglo-American academy in the second half of the twentieth century, the category of the contemporary is thus contemporaneous with a set of broader transformations in the substance of present experience. What those transformations tell us is that the contemporary is unthinkable outside the context of capital. The institutional consolidation of the contemporary as both a literary field and a theoretical question must be understood at a deeper level as a response to the fate of the present under the accelerated conditions of late capitalism.

In the twenty-first century, the contemporary comes to us as several things at once. It is a category of literary history. It is a problem for critical thought. And it is an index of the social transformations wrought by global capitalism. The aim of *Contemporary Drift* is to develop a theory of the contemporary that brings these three roles together. To do so, I use the formal developments of contemporary genres to assess the theoretical and political meanings of the contemporary. Each chapter highlights a certain methodological dilemma posed by the contemporary: how it challenges our conventional habits of interpreting, periodizing, or historicizing. And each chapter reads that dilemma not as a block to historical understanding but as a dialectical opening onto the deeper currents of contemporary history. While one objective of this book is to take seriously the critical challenge of the contemporary, its other objective is to begin defining what exactly the contemporary period is. If readers of this book are persuaded by its arguments, they will come away from it understanding what it means for these two objectives to be something more than mutually exclusive.

To further clarify the interrelation of these two aims, the book's chapters are arranged to move from the conceptual to the concrete, from the metahistorical to the historical. In the first three chapters, I consider the contemporary primarily as a methodological problem; in the last two chapters, I turn toward defining it as a historical period. Beginning with the issues of periodization (chapter 1), historicism (chapter 2), and temporality (chapter 3) that characterize the conceptual dimensions of the contemporary, I then move to the concrete contexts that I consider fundamental to understanding the history of our contemporary moment: the long-term crisis of climate change (chapter 4) and the immediate crisis of nonstop work (chapter 5). In building toward the dual historical frameworks of climate time and labor time, my intention is to give more specificity and substance to familiar but vague periodizing terms like *neoliberalism* and *post-postmodernism* by highlighting the ways that capitalism alters the very grounds of periodization, producing—at the diametrically opposed scales of the planetary and the workaday—the time frames that determine the true scope of "the contemporary."

It is genre that determines how those time frames become visible and thinkable to us. Although the problem of the contemporary clearly has a history, it is a problem whose solution requires us to think not just historically but also formally (through the conventions of genre) and theoretically (through the conceptual tools that generic form makes available); not just empirically but also imaginatively; in a word, aesthetically. At the core of this book is thus a sustained argument for seeing contemporary genres both as objects to be historicized and as resources for reimagining how historicism works within the too-close quarters of the present. The alternative historicism of genre shows us how the concept of the contemporary comes to life in our particular contemporary moment. As I demonstrate throughout this book, this is a moment shaped by a system of global capitalism whose effects—from the deep time of environmental crisis to the constant demands of postindustrial work—transform our most basic relation to the present.

The arbitrary measure of the decade, I argue in chapter 1, represents both the possibilities and the limits of the periodizing the present. Emerging from the classic fixation on period detail and social custom in the realist novel of manners, the decade becomes a central figure in contemporary novels of manners by Zadie Smith and Bret Easton Ellis, where it offers a provisional framework for organizing both writers' obsession with historically specific brand names and cultural references. Yet the superficiality of the decade as a form of periodization, I suggest, belies its own specificity to the post–Cold War period, a period shaped by anxieties about the "end of history" and the endlessness of capitalism. In response to these anxieties, the decade provides an ambivalent but necessary way of reasserting, through the fixed end points of the calendrical period marker, the inevitability of change. Moving from arbitrary dates to accusations of datedness, chapter 2 reconsiders what it means to view the contemporary as a revival, or a nostalgic repetition of the past. This view is especially common in regard to film noir, a genre that has haunted American culture since the 1940s. But how are we supposed to situate or contextualize a genre with such an active afterlife? Reading early noir films like *Double Indemnity* and *Sunset Boulevard* alongside later ones like *Sin City* and *The Good German*, I define the noir genre as a prolonged study in the problem of situating ourselves in the present. Ultimately, I argue, noir's revivals compel us to rethink the very idea of the "historical situation." In doing so, noir expands our sense of what it means to be contemporary, providing a longer view of the postwar social structures that continue to determine and disorient us. Chapter 3 turns from history to temporality, investigating what happens when contemporary time is felt to be a time of seemingly interminable waiting. This question is central to contemporary versions of the detective novel, which depict the temporality of waiting as both a symptom of and a hedge against a cultural logic of uncertainty. Seeking a new solution to the sense of indeterminacy that enthralls and confounds our contemporary moment, recent detective novels by Vikram Chandra, Michael Chabon, and China Miéville use the logic of the wait not to describe a state of delay or uncertainty but to imagine a brief, time-bound confrontation with uncertainty's others: certainty, knowledge, and belief. In the contemporary detective novel, waiting offers a complex but powerful response to the mysteries of a post–September 11 world that is felt to be endlessly at risk.

After the book's first three chapters highlight the conceptual and methodological challenges of the contemporary, the final chapters offer two more specific views, on two contrasting yet complementary scales, of the capitalist crises that define our contemporary moment. Chapter 4 demonstrates how the familiar desert landscapes of the Western have become a site for tracking the vicissitudes of the weather in an age of climate change. Tracing the meteorological history of the Western from John Ford, Robert Altman, and Sergio Corbucci to Andrew Dominik, Kelly Reichardt, and Takashi Miike, I show how the twenty-first-century Western has adapted to the unfamiliar weather patterns, altered seasons, and ecological devastation wrought by a warming planet. Against both the glacial movement of geological time and the primordial history associated with the Anthropocene, the implacable presentness of the Western's weather, I contend, provides a more contemporary timescale on which to measure the crisis of our changing climate. Through the global travels of the Western, we discover the basis for a truly global view of global warming. The last chapter turns from the long-term effects of climate change to the everyday logic of work, analyzing end-of-the-world fiction as a window onto the historical and political paradoxes of survival. I argue that the very notion of survival skills acquires new meaning in a neoliberal era in which life has become indistinguishable from work and stable work has become harder to find. Reading novels by Colson Whitehead, Ben Marcus, Cormac McCarthy, and Joshua Ferris, I show how the essential monotony of the post-apocalyptic genre has become a formal strategy for depicting the laborious yet precarious rhythms of postindustrial work. In the drama of post-apocalyptic survival, we see how the dim prospect of endless work runs up against the darker and distinctly contemporary possibility of no longer being able to get work at all.

If it is the absence of critical distance that condemns us to contemporary life, *Contemporary Drift* may be thought of, finally, as an experiment in too-close reading. Grappling with those texts that we are invariably too close to and whose historical context isn't yet fully clear to us, this book looks for the illuminating moments of formal change through which contemporary genres are able to give us some provisional historical perspective. Together, these five chapters show how recent works of genre fiction don't simply reflect contemporary events but reveal the conceptual strategies— the practices of measuring, framing, formulating, and periodizing—that generate our idea of the contemporary in the first place. The formal conventions highlighted by each genre and adopted as a guiding framework for each chapter represent the alternative measures of time and history that offer an immanent counterpoint to the opacities of historical closeness. These measures give us both the conceptual language and the imaginative distance to understand just what it means, today, to be contemporary. At the same time, as decidedly ambivalent and limited ways of historicizing, they remind us of our immersion in a present moment that we simply can't expect to comprehend in full. In the end, it may be *Contemporary Drift* itself that is fated to stand as irrefutable evidence of the contemporary dialectic between comprehension and closeness: on one hand, a survey of the literary forms and literary histories that bring our idea of the contemporary into being and, on the other, a document of what will surely turn out to be its author's sometimes shortsighted ideas about his own contemporary moment. Such are the risks and rewards of reading what's too close to us, the promise and peril of a critical history of the contemporary that can be based only on the mirage of critical distance. The pages that follow are, more than anything, an attempt to maintain that mirage—to read by the light of its flickering presence for as long as possible—in order to see how such an evanescent frame of reference might nevertheless leave us with an indelible image of our present.

# Chapter One

# DECADE

## Period Pieces

A day, a year once seemed useful gauges.

FERNAND BRAUDEL

He's helping define the decade, baby.

BRET EASTON ELLIS

## HOW TO NOT NOT PERIODIZE

*Time will tell. History will judge.* These chestnuts of conventional wisdom convey the simple and seemingly uncontroversial point that we cannot periodize our own present. To name the essence of our age, to define the contours of the current period, requires a kind of historical distance that is constitutively unavailable to those living in the midst of it. The difficulty of comprehending and historicizing the chaos of contemporary life is why, in Fredric Jameson's view, "the present is not yet a historical period: it ought not to be able to name itself and characterize its own originality."[1] Almost but not quite a period, the present casts into sharp relief what critics have variously labeled the "unfashionable," "unsophisticated," "paranoid," "imperfect," and "intolerable" practice of periodization.[2] Yet if the present marks the outer limit of what we consider periodizable, it also testifies to what Virginia Jackson calls our continued "fascination with and attachment to the subject" of periodization itself.[3] This ambivalent fascination means that periodization always reasserts itself, even in the case of a historical object like the contemporary that, strictly speaking, isn't yet historical. Despite the paradoxes of historical self-reflection, we can't quite give up on the possibility of periodizing the present. In this way, the contemporary period may be the quintessential example of Jameson's famous maxim in *A Singular*

*Modernity*: "We cannot not periodize."[4] As I argue in this chapter, Jameson's double-negative provides a particularly useful grammar for talking about contemporary history. While it may be impossible to definitively periodize the contemporary, it is also impossible not to try.

And try we have. No shortage of periodizing frameworks—from post-1989 to post-9/11, from the end of the American Century to the end of history—have been set forth to sum up the life of the late twentieth and early twenty-first centuries. But one term in particular offers an especially illuminating case study in the complicated relation between periodization and the present. That term is *postmodernism*, one of the most discussed, discredited, and unavoidable periodizing terms of the past half century. Only now, some fifty years after it first entered academic usage, is there something of a consensus about the usefulness (if not the exact meaning) of the term. Recent journal issues dedicated to defining "Postmodernism, Then" and to describing what comes "After Postmodernism" express a newfound confidence in the word's descriptive efficacy.[5] This development is hardly surprising: whatever postmodernism was, it is now a thing of the past and thus an object that can be brought into historical focus. Time, indeed, is now in a position to tell.

The maturation of postmodernism into an object of historicist inquiry should not let us forget the more complex relation to historicity that was built into the concept from the beginning. What made postmodernism unique was that, in Brian McHale's words, "postmodernism periodized itself."[6] From the start, it understood itself to be a period. But the project of self-periodizing turned out to be exceedingly difficult, weighed down by ambivalence and equivocation and wracked with worry over whether such a project was even possible. In many ways, it seemed not to be. In *The Origins of Postmodernity*, Perry Anderson reminds us that on the topic of postmodernism, "there was no consensus, only a set of oppositions . . . only disconnected interests and criss-crossing opinions."[7] This basic lack of "consensus" became the subtext of almost every theory of the postmodern. The essence of postmodernism as a periodizing framework was that it never seemed entirely adequate to the task of periodization. Of the countless books published on postmodernism, a surprising number begin with the embarrassed confession of this inadequacy. "It is almost standard practice for introductions to postmodernism to begin with the rather paradoxical assertion that postmodernism is impossible to introduce satisfactorily," notes one standard introduction.[8] "Postmodernism is an exasperating term," laments another.[9] A third book begins: "The concept of postmodernism . . . has come to suffer from semantic fuzziness. One cannot abstain from using the concept, but at the same time one does not know how to define it precisely."[10] Even the work that most famously bears its name harbors a surprisingly ambivalent attitude toward the word *postmodernism*. In the introduction to *Postmodernism, or the Cultural Logic of Late Capitalism*, Fredric Jameson justifies his choice of the term: "As for *postmodernism* itself, I have not tried to systematize a usage or to impose any conveniently thumbnail meaning, for the concept is not merely contested, it is also internally conflicted and contradictory. I will argue that, for good or ill, we cannot not use it."[11] This is less than a ringing endorsement. Even Jameson, it seems, recognized the double logic (or illogic) of the postmodern, seeing it as fuzzy and exasperating, "conflicted and contradictory," but nevertheless as a term he had no choice but to continue to use. It is as if in his attempt to periodize the present, Jameson chose not the word that would most accurately describe our historical moment but the one that would most distinctly capture the challenge of producing that historical description. To be sure, there is certainly something frustrating about all the dodges and disavowals that underwrite the discourse of postmodernism. Yet there may also be something familiar in them. We have seen this self-canceling formula before. Postmodernism, it turns out, is exactly what it looks like to not not periodize the present.

The problem of periodizing the present could thus be said to be a knot tied between two "nots." The paradox of not not periodizing remains audible, for instance, in the record-skip of what Jeffrey T. Nealon has more recently dubbed (in his book of the same name) *Post-Postmodernism*. Why did he choose this unwieldy word, which Nealon himself admits is "nonsensically redundant"?[12] Because this redundancy is part of the concept itself. Post-postmodernism, Nealon tells us, is "not necessarily something 'new'"; it is an attempt to "intensify, highlight, and redeploy" postmodernism, not to redefine or replace it. In other words, the author of *Post-Postmodernism* is hesitant to define the present as a completely novel period. The hesitation of the "post-post" (the announcement of a new that is "not necessarily" different from the old) essentially doubles down on the double negative, refusing to decide between novelty and continuity, rupture and repetition. The unavoidable sense of dissatisfaction that shadowed the periodizing discourse of postmodernism is further intensified by post-postmodern-ism, a term that Nealon claims he chose only "for lack of a better word."[13] The deeper lesson here, though, is that there are no better words for peri-odizing the present. We should never take an "epoch at its word," Marx wrote.[14] A term like *post-postmodernism* takes this caution to heart, con-firming in advance its future negation in the form of its own nagging sense of self-doubt. Post-postmodernism says: Do not take this period at its word. In this way, it continues to record the history of the present in the syntax of the double negative, turning periodization into an attempt at self-defi-nition that is indistinguishable from an act of disavowal.[15]

The limits (as well as limitations) revealed by these various attempts to periodize the present go a good way toward explaining what is so vexing about the term *contemporary*. As postmodernism has become both his-torical and historicizable, the problem of self-periodizing has not gone away; it has just been transferred onto the problem of the contemporary. In his introduction to the special issue "After Postmodernism," Andrew Hoberek demonstrates how increased certainty about what postmod-ernism was goes hand in hand with increased uncertainty about what contemporary literature is now: "If contemporary fiction is indeed post-postmodern, this does not exemplify some singular, dramatic, readily visible cultural transformation—the search for which in fact constitutes a post-modern preoccupation—but grows out of a range of uneven, tentative, local shifts."[16] Hoberek's insistence on the "uneven," the "tentative," and the "local" is an attempt to refuse the "singular, dramatic" work of periodiza-tion (here, too, "post-postmodern" appears as the name not for some major historical "transformation" but for the hesitation to characterize the present period in historically transformative terms). The problem of periodization thus becomes both bound up with and named by the contemporary. The contemporary is nearly, but not yet, a historical period. Perhaps our only choice is to put the contemporary in the double negative: to understand it as a *not not historical* period.

The argument of this chapter is that being *not not historical* takes a par-ticular form in contemporary writing: the form of the decade. As the cul-tural historian Steven Biel has argued, the decade is a "standard feature of popular historical understanding."[17] It is also a form of historical under-standing that may have a special relationship to the contemporary. Indeed, the truncated form of the decade seems to have become a preferred framework for imagining our present as a period.[18] Jameson, for one, sees something historically specific in the "caricature of historical thinking" that was emblematized in the late-century prominence of the decade, the widespread need "to return upon our present circumstances in order to think of them—as the nineties, say—and to draw the appropriate marketing and forecasting conclusions."[19] Ironically, it was Jameson himself who brought the study of the decade back to scholarly respectability with his influential 1984 essay "Periodizing the 60s." Even though "Periodizing the 60s" includes some of Jameson's earliest and most important ideas about periodization, it does not, oddly, say anything at all about its own choice of the periodizing category of the decade—an oversight that suggests just how "deeply ingrained in the historical consciousness of Americans" (in Biel's words) the decade is.[20] The ingrained importance of the decade is now nowhere more apparent than in academic studies of contemporary culture. Phillip Wegner's *Life Between Two Deaths: American Culture in the Long Nineties*; Samuel Cohen's *After the End of History: American Fiction in the 1990s*; Jay Prosser's edited volume *American Fiction of the 1990s*; Leigh Claire La Berge's *Scandals and Abstraction: Financial Fiction of the Long 1980s*; Adam Kelly's *American Fiction in Transition: Observer-Hero Narrative, the 1990s, and Postmodernism*; Jeremy Green's *Late Postmodernism* (whose title "refers," according to Green, "to the writing of the 1990s"); and Nealon's *Post-Postmodernism* (which begins with an attempt to "'periodize' the '80s") all examine recent literature and culture through the rubric of the decade.[21] This suggests that there is something about the form of the decade that makes it a particularly seductive way to respond to the question of the contemporary.

All these works of criticism share another notable feature: their decades never last just ten years. What Wegner calls the "long nineties" runs from 1989 to 2001; Nealon's 1980s stretch from the 1970s to the 2000s; and La Berge's history of financialization in the "Long 1980s" is one that begins "in the late 1970s" and "whose effects continue into the present."[22] In each of these cases, the arbitrariness of the decade as historical measure (why sets of ten?) becomes the alibi for its elasticity. Put simply, we use decades to talk about slices of time that aren't decades. Usually these intervals last for more than ten years; often they seem to last right up until the present moment. The decade thus mirrors the ambivalent state of being not not historical: the strange status of something that is almost but not exactly a period. If the decade offers a conveniently arbitrary way to frame or delimit the present, the flexibility of that frame reasserts the problems of temporal flux and historical unboundedness that make the present so difficult to periodize. The numerically predictable boundaries of the decade at once suppress and expose the mutable form of the present. This is how the decade—arbitrary, pliable, ironic—perfectly captures the contemporary's dialectical syntax of periodization.

Not confined to works of literary criticism, the problem of periodizing the contemporary also has its own literary history. The aesthetic struggle to frame the reality of social life as it flows through the present is the literary project known as realism. In *The Social Construction of American Realism*, Amy Kaplan explains how the realist novel attempts to "produce a social reality that can be recognized as 'the way things are,'" even though "the way things are" is never how they'll be for long. As Kaplan suggests, realism is a genre under constant threat by "the sense of the world changing under the realists' pens."[23] Realism does not so much contain the threat as expose it, demonstrating the tension between writing the present and watching it pass away. In this way, the genre of realism offers both a depiction of living history and a depiction of the difficulty of trying to depict history as it flows past us. In his seminal *Mimesis*, Erich Auerbach develops a similar account of the relation between the realist novel and the problem of the present. The key to understanding Honoré de Balzac's distinctive place in the history of modern realism, according to Auerbach, is that "he conceives the present as history."[24] Balzac's "*histoire du coeur humain* or *histoire sociale* is not a matter of 'history' in the usual sense— . . . is not, above all, a matter of the past but of the contemporary present, reaching back at most only a few years or a few decades." For Auerbach, realism's unusual notion of the historical present cuts two ways. While one of the "distinguishing characteristics of modern realism" is that "everyday occurrences are accurately and profoundly set in a definite period of contemporary history," the very idea of the contemporary as a "period" becomes troubled and possibly untenable. That's because in the realist novel, "the social base upon which [one] lives is not constant for a moment but is perpetually changing through convulsions of the most various kinds."[25] Here is the paradox that Auerbach discovers at the heart of the realist project: How does one depict the "period of contemporary history" as something that is also "not constant for a moment"? How can narrative realistically capture a contemporary that looks like a historical "period" but is still "perpetually changing"?

In fact, there is one historically specific yet highly time-sensitive form that the realist novel has traditionally used to capture both the historicity and the impermanence of a given present. That form is the system of social rules, customs, and fashions grouped under the rubric of *manners*. The novel of manners (perhaps the preeminent version of the nineteenth- and twentieth-century realist novel) turns a contemporary moment into a milieu of social class by reporting on the "customs of dress, tones of speech, and standards of conduct" that help police membership in that class.[26] In *Bad Form: Social Mistakes and the Nineteenth-Century Novel*, Kent Puckett describes how the nineteenth-century European novel of manners developed alongside the emergence of "etiquette as an increasingly autonomous social and, in fact, literary field." For Puckett, the novel of manners thus marked a "change in the way the codes of everyday life were imagined by and presented to the public," a change that "was coincident with the sharpening of other anxieties about the nature and sources of social authority" amid the political upheavals of nineteenth-century Europe.[27]

The issue of social authority was slightly different in turn-of-the-twentieth-century America, where, as Nancy Bentley argues in *The Ethnography of Manners*, the realist novel of manners aligned itself with the ethnographic discourse of anthropology as parallel ways of "mastering" a culture thought to be in decline. "Writing about manners," Bentley writes, "becomes the genesis of a modern liberal authority" founded on professional cultural mastery.[28] For practitioners like Henry James and Edith Wharton, "rewriting the novel of manners is an act of preservation directed against the threat of an exhausted tradition and a menacing modernity." Yet this is also an act that "renews the genre for the world it appears to resist," transforming the realist novel into a mode of ethnography that helps shore up "the authority of modern institutions—museums, social sciences, popular discourses of primitivism." Thus, Bentley argues, literary ethnographies of manners worked to "acculturate the American polity to a new society of consumption and corporate capitalism" by turning the customs of an older, aristocratic class system into an object of anthropological curiosity.[29] As the twentieth century wears on, however, a new question arises. In the new consumer society whose early emergence Bentley documents—a society of ever greater flux, mobility, and turnover—is it still possible to master the constantly changing conventions of culture at all? This is the question that Jerome Klinkowitz takes up in *The New American Novel of Manners*, which begins from the premise that "American culture" is no longer a viable "field for the novelist of manners, not because it was too rough and new but because it had fully eclipsed his ability to record it."[30] At a time when manners and conventions are changing so quickly that it is impossible to record them accurately, the contemporary novel of manners begins to look to Klinkowitz like a contradiction in terms.

How have contemporary novelists come to terms with the uniquely contemporary problem of cultural recording? My argument in this chapter is that since the end of the 1980s, novelists have responded to the historical instability of cultural and class conventions by anchoring the novel of manners in a particular discourse of historicity. That discourse is the decade. In recent realist novels of social class, we find the idea of "social milieu" reimagined as a matter of individual decades. In the *new* new novel of manners exemplified by Bret Easton Ellis and Zadie Smith, the work of documenting social conventions has become indistinguishable from the work of (in the words of Ellis's *Glamorama*) "helping define the decade, baby."[31] For Ellis and Smith, the decade is the answer to the question of how to capture, in literary form, the temporary norms and fleeting fashions of contemporary consumer culture. Endlessly cataloging the increasingly disposable and obsolescent objects of contemporary life (commodities, celebrities, clothing brands), Smith and Ellis turn to the logic of the decade—those familiarly reified notions of "the 1980s" and "the 1990s"—in order to imagine how the ephemeral objects and manners of their late capitalist present might add up to something as substantive and significant as a historical period.

Why, of all forms of historical thinking, the decade? If there is something artificial or superficial about the arbitrary period boundaries of the decade, that may make it an especially fitting concern for Smith and Ellis, both of whom are frequently accused of exemplifying a uniquely shallow and superficial literary sensibility. Ellis's "Brat Pack" novels have been criticized for being "obsessed with appearance," not "so much novels as advertisements," while Smith's books are "all shiny externality," fixated on "superficial . . . style, looks, dress."[32] In these terms, both Smith and Ellis could be regarded as signaling the total exhaustion of the social ambitions of literary realism, as the urgent need to map the social totality devolves

into the pointless attempt to catalog the ever expanding landscape of consumer goods. As Walter Benn Michaels and others have pointed out, however, Ellis's novels can best be understood as belonging to the long history
of the novel of manners. It is, Michaels suggests, an

interest in money and class . . . that establishes *American Psycho* as the novel of
manners (rather than mores) it declares itself (beginning with the epigraph from
Judith Martin) to be, with its notorious insistence on documenting the dinner, the
toys, and above all the clothes of its "yuppie scum" and with its establishment of
[Patrick] Bateman himself as the rightful heir of men like Edith Wharton's Larry
Lefferts.[33]

As documents of the "toys," "clothes," and class systems that define their
characters, the novels of both Ellis and Smith update the genre of the novel
of manners for an era of advanced capitalism, full-blown consumerism,
and celebrity culture. And as attempts to frame these superficial period details in the equally superficial periodizing framework of the decade, these
novels also document the peculiar sense of cultural history that emerges in
response to the contemporary desire to catalog and periodize the present.

Ultimately, we will find, the depiction of contemporary history—of "the
way we live now" (to invoke Trollope's famous phrase)—in the contemporary novel of manners is inseparable from the representational challenges
posed by a way of life that is changing even as we live it. Read together, the
novels of Smith and Ellis suggest a moment at which the novel of manners
has begun to recognize a crisis of its own historiography. Such recognition,
I contend in this chapter, corresponds to a larger crisis of historical thinking at the end of the twentieth century: the crisis of imagining historical
alternatives to the system of capitalism itself. The novel of manners seeks
to resolve these twin crises of cultural recording and historical thinking
by redescribing social milieus, systems of fashion, and the entire capitalist
world system as the expressions of particular decades. As a strategy for
grappling with the paradox implied by the phrase *the contemporary period*,
the decade not only expresses the difficulty of grasping a history in transition but also imagines constant historical motion to be what makes the
present a period—by ensuring that it soon comes to an end. By the end of
this chapter, meanwhile, no one will be surprised to discover that the decade
is a lousy way to count. As a way of exploring the pressures that periodization

continues to exert on the present, however, the use of the decade in the realist novel challenges us to reimagine what it might look like for contemporary culture to count as history, and to do so precisely at a historical moment when we are told that the very idea of history may no longer count for much.

## FASHION FORWARD

Details are superficial. They decorate fiction's surface. In Roland Barthes's famous account, the novel's "reality effects" have no meaning in themselves: "They say nothing but this: *we are the real.*"[34] Whether despite or because of the possibility of saying nothing, *American Psycho* has a virtually encyclopedic obsession with the details of period-appropriate dress:

Price is wearing a six-button wool and silk suit by Ermenegildo Zegna, a cotton shirt with French cuffs by Ike Behar, a Ralph Lauren silk tie and leather wing tips by Fratelli Rossetti. The suit I wear today is from Alan Flusser. It's an eighties drape suit, which is an updated version of the thirties style. The favored version has extended natural shoulders, a full chest and a bladed back. The soft-rolled lapels should be about four inches wide with the peak finishing three quarters of the way across the shoulders. Properly used on double-breasted suits, peaked lapels are considered more elegant than notched ones. . . . The tie is a dotted silk design by Valentino Couture. The shoes are crocodile loafers by A. Testoni.[35]

Such tedious details of high fashion may seem the apotheosis of Ellis's superficiality.[36] Nonetheless, style also has historical stakes. "To be *in style*," Puckett explains, "is to subordinate oneself to the rules of the moment, to risk the necessary obsolescence of the merely stylish or a damning ethical interestedness in the hope of achieving identity with a set of historically situated rules and conventions."[37] The "historically situated" conventions of style help conjure *American Psycho*'s historical moment. Ellis's excessively realistic gloss on the style of the times thus has a double edge. On one hand, the obsession with fashion seems to imply a remarkably shallow understanding of what history actually is. On the other hand, that shallow understanding makes a rather sophisticated historical point: that the flattening out of social and historical awareness is itself a historical product of the immense transfer of wealth taking place in the financialized era of the

1980s. What is authentically historical about the 1980s is, in fact, the decade's emergent ethos of superficiality. As Frances Ferguson suggests in her reading of Ellis's novel, in the "relentlessly superficial world" of *American Psycho*, "the clothes don't make the man; they show that nothing makes a modern man."[38] Better yet, the clothes show that at this particular moment in history, nothing matters but the clothes.

*Glamorama*, published seven years after *American Psycho*, develops a strikingly similar account of its present, except that the wealthy investment bankers are replaced by fame-obsessed fashion models and the designer brands supplanted by celebrity names:

"Check the Cs for dinner." . . .
  "Naomi Campbell, Helena Christensen, Cindy Crawford, Sheryl Crow, David Charvet, Courteney Cox, Harry Connick, Jr., Francesco Clemente, Nick Constantine, Zoe Cassavetes, Nicolas Cage, Thomas Calabro, Crisi Conway, Bob Collacello, Whitfield Crane, John Cusack, Dean Cain, Jim Courier, Roger Clemens, Russell Crowe, Tia Carrere and Helena Bonham Carter—but I'm not sure if she should be under B or C." (8–9)

The spirit of the age expressed in this passage resides not in the content of the names (most of which are doomed to obsolescence) but in their pathological repetition. This is the key to Ellis's narrative style: less narrating, more naming; less story, more sorting. It doesn't matter who Helena Bonham Carter is—it matters only where to file her; whether "she should be under B or C." *Glamorama* marks the moment when the celebrity name itself becomes the standard unit of measurement for historical time. Between the two novels, though, history's song stays the same. For Ellis, periodization is a seemingly endless process of reference and classification. In both *Glamorama* and *American Psycho*, the period is defined less by a specific set of names than by the relentless practice of naming. The difference is what kind of name counts as history at a given moment: the name you're wearing or the name you're sitting next to.

The distinction between these two moments, both novels repeatedly tell us, is a distinction measured in decades. *American Psycho* consistently describes its milieu in the language of the decade: "an eighties drape suit," "a more eighties sound" (134), "the late seventies/early eighties taste for New

Wave" (353), the looming "End of the 80s" (371). "But aren't the 1980s over?" asks a character in *Glamorama*. In their place, the latter novel gives us the shiny new decade of the 1990s: "The '90s are honest, straightforward. Let's reflect that" (59). Smith's *White Teeth*—an intergenerational saga of migration centered on two families in cosmopolitan London, the Joneses and the Iqbals—is even more explicitly organized around decades. Each section of the novel is set in a single decade: the first section takes place in the 1970s, the second in the 1980s, and the third and fourth in the 1990s.

As in Ellis's novels, Smith's description of each decade often relies on the sheer accumulation of period detail. Consider the clearly dated belongings of Millat Iqbal (rebellious, Westernized son of Samad), who has amassed "four years' worth of cool, pre- and post-Raggastani, every album, every poster, special-edition T-shirts, club flyers collected and preserved over two years, beautiful Air Max sneakers, copies 20–75 of *2000* AD magazine, signed photo of Chuck D, impossibly rare copy of Slick Rick's 'Hey Young World,' *The Catcher in the Rye*, his guitar, *The Godfather I* and *II*, *Mean Streets*, *Rumblefish*, *Dog Day Afternoon*, and *Shaft in Africa*."[39] Unlike Ellis's lists, these details are not synchronous; they don't all originate in the same moment. Their collection here, however, does capture something of the asynchrony of style, the way in which objects of the past may be recombined to forge a mode specific to the present. In *White Teeth*, that mode is encapsulated by Millat and his crew:

Millat's crew looked like trouble. And, at the time, a crew that looked like trouble in this particular way had a name, they were of a breed: *Raggastani*.

It was a new breed, just recently joining the ranks of the other street crews: Becks, B-boys, Indie kids, wide-boys, ravers, rudeboys, Acidheads, Sharons, Tracies, Kevs, Nation Brothers, Raggas, and Pakis; manifesting itself as a kind of cultural mongrel of the last three categories. Their ethos, their manifesto, if it could be called that, was equally a hybrid thing . . . kung fu and the works of Bruce Lee were also central to their philosophy; added to this was a smattering of Black Power (as embodied by the album *Fear of a Black Planet*, Public Enemy). . . . Naturally, there was a uniform. They each dripped gold and wore bandanas, either wrapped around their foreheads or tied at the joint of an arm or leg. The trousers were enormous, swamping things, the left leg always inexplicably rolled up to the knee; . . . and everything, everything, everything was *Nike*™. (192–93)

What Smith first calls the boys' "ethos" might be better glossed as the historical specificity of style: the rules that govern what to wear and how to wear it. The devil is in all those "inexplicable" details concerning where exactly one's bandana should be worn and which leg of one's baggy jeans is to be rolled up how high, conventions no less intricate than the recommended width of Patrick Bateman's suit lapels. The interest in these particular rules, brands (the trademark symbol is a nice touch), and cultural objects (Bruce Lee and Public Enemy) creates for Millat's crew something like a thin chronotope. Once again we are reminded that *style* is more than just another word for the vagaries of fashion. It is also a description of how social conventions are situated in history: how the conventions of dress come to possess a "particular . . . name" and a historically specific meaning at a particular time.

At that time, in 1980s multicultural London, the other name for what young Pakistani men look like, Smith tells us, is "trouble." The novel's lengthy description of what exactly trouble looks like is occasioned by Millat and his crew's being harassed by a subway security guard: "You boys not looking for any trouble, are you?" (192). The pivot from looking *for* trouble to looking *like* trouble announces the novel's deeper interest in the social logic of external appearance—the concatenation of style, stereotype, and historical situation. In Millat's case, the appearance that matters is not only the style of his clothes but also the color of the skin underneath them: "He knew that no one who looked like Millat, or spoke like Millat, or felt like Millat, was ever on the news unless they had recently been murdered" (194). The guard's question is clearly a form of racial profiling, the stereotypical association of social disruption with young brown-skinned men. In his snap judgment of Millat's various surfaces—the dissolute "uniform" of his "crew" alongside the troubling skin tone of his "breed"—the guard does what every child is taught not to do: he judges a book by its cover. Such a hoary cliché may seem inappropriate to the gravity of the situation, but the phrase is in fact quite relevant to this particular passage, as it is literally the judging of a book by its cover that sets the scene in motion. The book in question is *The Satanic Verses*, and the reason Millat and his crew are at the subway station in the first place is that they are traveling to Bradford in order to participate in the burning of Rushdie's novel that took place there on January 14, 1989 (the date is the title of this subsection of the novel). As if in ironic response to the guard's superficial act of profiling, Millat is looking not for trouble per se but for an equal opportunity to judge trouble—as he himself has just been judged—purely on appearances. Stereotypical reason thus emerges as both the symptom and the perpetuation of a historical moment that is particularly obsessed with the outward appearance of others. What you look like is what matters: the apparent superficiality of Smith's description of Raggastani style is really an echo of the racist logic of postimperial Britain as it responds to decolonization in the second half of the twentieth century.[40] In *White Teeth*, history plays out right there on the surface because it is surfaces themselves—from skin color to book covers—that catalyze the historical events of the time.

*American Psycho, Glamorama,* and *White Teeth* all investigate the ways that superficial details come to stand for entire decades. They do so, you might have noticed from the preceding quotations, by employing a particular rhetorical form: the list. The list appears to be the definitive literary style of the decade. Lists ground the paradox of the decade in parataxis; they crystallize the contemporary's inability to make the connections that would make it into a period. As Ruth Jennison argues in *The Zukofsky Era: Modernity, Margins, and the Avant-Garde*, the poetic strategy of parataxis "delivers a jolt to readers beguiled by the naturalness of their historical present."[41] Surrounded by the innumerable names, faces, and features of the present, the paratactic form of the list—"John Cusack, Dean Cain, Jim Courier, Roger Clemens, Russell Crowe, Tia Carrere"; "Becks, B-boys, Indie kids, wide-boys, ravers, rudeboys"—similarly de-naturalizes the present. Offering accumulation without totalization, the list enumerates the historical fragments of the present while withholding the comforts of the narrative that ought to make them cohere. In the form of the list, the elusive style of contemporary history is captured by the "jolt" of paratactic style itself.

To the lists that litter these three novels, let's add one more:

the poetry of John Ashbery, for instance, but also the much simpler talk poetry that came out of the reaction against complex, ironic, academic modernist poetry in the '60s; the reaction against modern architecture and in particular against the monumental buildings of the International Style, the pop buildings and decorated sheds celebrated by Robert Venturi in his manifesto, *Learning from Las Vegas*; Andy Warhol and Pop art, but also the more recent Photorealism; in music, the moment of John Cage but also the later synthesis of classical and "popular" styles found in composers like Philip Glass and Terry Riley, and also punk and new-wave rock with such groups as the Clash, the Talking Heads and the Gang of Four; in film, everything that comes out of Godard—contemporary vanguard film and video—but also a whole new style of commercial or fiction films, which has its equivalent in contemporary novels as well, where the works of William Burroughs, Thomas Pynchon and Ishmael Reed on the one hand, and the French new novel on the other, are also to be numbered among the varieties of what can be called postmodernism.[42]

This is the famous opening paragraph of Jameson's original essay on post-modernism, and it makes an even starker case for the relation between parataxis and periodization. If the concept of postmodernism was what it looked like to periodize (or, more precisely, to not not periodize) the present of the 1970s and 1980s, this paragraph shows how such an attempt relied not on the coherence of a single periodizing narrative but on the paratactic form of the list.[43] In Jameson's propensity for lists, we see that the attempt to theorize the period of the present depends on a rhetorical mode that leaves the work of periodization unfinished. Through the accumulation of period details and references that aren't explicitly connected, the list simultaneously invokes and inhibits the totalizing view of the period. It puts on display the raw material of the historical moment but does nothing to explain or interpret that material. The list—unable to name itself or to characterize the nature of the connections it has had to elide—catalogs everything we know about the present, in a form that reminds us of everything we do not know about it yet.

The list is not a narrative, though it is full of details. It is not meaningfully sequential, though it unfolds over time. It is not a period, though it is indispensable to periodization. The double edge of the list as literary form perfectly captures the double life of the contemporary, which both adopts and repels periodization, caught as it is between the flow of the present and the freeze-frame of history. The list gathers the materials necessary for periodization but fails to explain the relations among them. It provides a frame that is also an unframing, an accumulation that doubles as a disarticulation, a totality that is far from total. Finally, the list conjures the fleeting temporality of the commodity in an age of planned obsolescence. How can we hope to understand our historical moment when we don't know which products of that moment will be around long enough to become historically meaningful? Caught in the changing winds of fashion as well as the more inscrutable historical weather of the contemporary, the list makes it possible to weave the temporary details of commodity culture into the partially periodizing tapestry of the decade.

## MUSICAL INTERLUDE

The decade depicts our paradoxical desire to be at once inside and outside the present. In *American Psycho*, we catch a glimpse of this impossible perspective in the interruptive form of an interlude. The novel's immersion in everyday life in the 1980s is confirmed by banal, day planner–like section titles such as "Lunch with Bethany," "Office," "Thursday," "Video Store Then D'Agostino's." The banality of Patrick Bateman's errands only intensifies the contrast with his extreme acts of violence. Nevertheless, both the errands and the violence occur on the same plane of narrative time. The relentless progression of menial acts in the present is interrupted more than a hundred pages into the novel, however, by a section entitled "Genesis." Composed in the enthusiastic voice of the music journalist, the section makes the case that Phil Collins's band Genesis is in fact "the best, most exciting band to come out of England in the 1980s" (136). In doing so, it works to align the band's artistic trajectory with the idea of the decade as such. What Patrick's meditations on pop music make possible is a whole new way of thinking about history.

The interlude on Genesis expresses an interest in historical change unavailable to the rest of the novel. The developmental narrative encoded in the discography gives Patrick a vantage from which to see the 1980s as a self-contained period:

I've been a big Genesis fan ever since the release of their 1980 album, *Duke*. Before that I didn't really understand any of their work . . . all the albums before *Duke* seemed too artsy, too intellectual. It was *Duke* (Atlantic; 1980), where Phil Collins' presence became more apparent, and the music got more modern, the drum machine more prevalent and the lyrics started getting less mystical and more specific (maybe because of Peter Gabriel's departure), and complex, ambiguous studies of loss became, instead, smashing first-rate pop songs that I gratefully embraced. (133)

This is, first and foremost, a story of epochal break and historical change, of how Patrick became "a big Genesis fan" after the band eschewed its earlier style and evolved into a major pop group during the 1980s. In a purely narratological sense, the day-to-day immersion of the preceding sections of the novel is replaced here by a broader historical awareness, one concerned with how a band, a musical style, or an entire popular culture changes over time. What kinds of changes are these? It is no coincidence that Patrick's "embrace" of the band begins precisely in 1980. What Patrick is describing here is not just the trajectory of Genesis's career but also the larger transformations of U.S. culture in the 1980s, changes that the band allegorizes. Nineteen eighty, Patrick confidently announces, is when things got "more modern." This means the explosion of consumer technology ("the drum machine [became] more prevalent"), the rise of celebrity culture ("Phil Collins' presence became more apparent"), the collapse of the avant-garde ("too artsy, too intellectual"), the blurring of art and commodity, and a deeper cultural turn from sentimental intellectualism ("complex, ambiguous studies of loss") to the amoral pursuit of wealth ("smashing first-rate pop songs"). Patrick's explanation of how he came to "understand" Genesis is thus really a story of how he came to understand his own historical present. It is also a story of how such understanding depends on the particular form of the decade.

Two more musical interludes appear in the novel under the titles "Whitney Houston" and "Huey Lewis and the News," and these, along with "Genesis," are the only times in *American Psycho* when Patrick discusses the 1980s as a single period.[44] Genesis's "In Too Deep" is "the most moving pop song of the 1980s" (136); Houston's "How Will I Know" is "my vote for best dance song of the 1980s" (253); and Huey Lewis and the News's "Heart and Soul" is "the tune that firmly and forever established them as the premier rock band in the country for the 1980s" (355). What is notable about these moments of historical judgment is that they appear in interludes that are explicitly discontinuous from the rest of the narrative. Despite the novel's seemingly unwavering chronological movement, its obsession with what Patrick is doing, when, and where ("Video Store *Then* D'Agostino's"), the interludes make no reference to the events of the narrative or their own situations of enunciation. They seem to take place entirely outside narrative time.

Patrick's "I" persists through the interludes, but his narrative voice is altered, offering an emotionally inflected perspective (thoughtful criticism, enthusiastic affirmation) that is at odds with the disinterested neutrality of the narrative's tireless, robotic mechanisms of cultural recording. When Patrick describes Whitney Houston's debut album *Whitney Houston* as "one of the warmest, most complex and altogether satisfying rhythm and blues records of the decade" and declares that "Whitney herself has a voice that defies belief" (253), his register, both interpretive and affective, seems a far cry from the dry reportage of the narrative at large, which is dominated by Patrick's breathlessly monotonous descriptions of his male companions' wardrobes ("Armstrong is wearing a four-button double-breasted chalk-striped spread-collar cotton shirt by Christian Dior and a large paisley-patterned silk tie by Givenchy Gentleman" [137]). But Patrick's increasing resemblance to a feeling, thinking human being must be seen as the effect of a deeper formal shift that has endowed him with a capacity for authentically historiographical observation—the ability to assess the 1980s as a completed decade—only by excising him from his story. The historical life of the decade that Patrick is finally able to narrate is not, in the last instance, his own.

In their immeasurable distance from the rest of the plot, *American Psycho*'s musical interludes continue to insist on the unbridgeable gap between periodization and the present. While depicting Patrick's murderous descent into madness as a symptom of the moral blankness of consumer society, *American Psycho* repeatedly encounters, in the interruptive form of the interlude, the narrative gap between Patrick's lived vices and his larger view of the decade. The two irreconcilable narrative levels—plot and interludes—suggest that the demystifying power of history's critical distance remains, for the present, as unrealizable a fantasy as the moral redemption of Patrick himself. Patrick can get distance on his historical moment only in sections that are similarly distanced from the plot itself. In the novel's musical interludes, periodization turns out to be a dream from which the realities of the narrative, violent and banal alike, cannot help but awaken us.

## THE DATING GAME

The fantasy of historical distance comes to an end in both *Glamorama* and *White Teeth*. In these novels, historical distance is undone by a contradiction between the general category of the decade and the specificity of dates. Of course, there is always something a little weird about dates. As Joshua

Clover reminds us in his book *1989*, "dates are not always to be trusted." Clover's own exemplary investigation into the untrustworthy date of 1989 begins with the strange case of "La Marseillaise," which is sung to commemorate a date on which it did not exist. Famously associated with the storming of the Bastille in 1789, the song, Clover observes, "was not composed until 1792":

The song, that is to say, both does and doesn't belong to 1789. It summons affect, image, and event that seem located in that year without actually being from that year. This is saying something more than the truism that songs escape their original contexts and intentions, that messages shift. It puts on display the process by which process vanishes.[45]

The process that "vanishes" here is that of history itself, and the scene of the crime of its disappearance is the individual year. The misplaced song, which "both does and doesn't belong" to this particular year, mediates between dated specificity and historical process. Yet the song does not simply expose the unreliability of chronology (the "truism," as Clover has it, that history is more than dates). It also reveals the different, conflicting timescales that underwrite the process of dating itself. In the overdetermined interaction between song and year, we confront the tension that defines the broader context of the contemporary: the contradiction that explains what it means—to return to the refrain of this chapter—to be not not historical.

Pop songs pervade *Glamorama* and *White Teeth*. At first glance, these songs seem to sum up the feeling or express the vibe of a particular historical moment. But what they really do is call into question *which* moment the novels are actually talking about. In *Glamorama*, the full-length albums that so dazzled Patrick Bateman have been broken down into individually commodified singles, the better to be experienced as background music: "A couple walks out of the Crunch fitness center, carrying Prada gym bags, appearing vaguely energized, Pulp's 'Disco 2000' blaring out of the gym behind them as they pass a line of BMWs" (269); "Everything But the Girl's 'Missing' plays over everything, occasionally interrupted by feel-good house music, along with doses of Beck's 'Where It's At'" (275); "As the Chemical Brothers' 'Setting Sun' blasts out on cue we're back in Notting Hill at some industrial billionaire's warehouse" (287). Pop music makes up the sonic fabric of Victor's daily life; taken together, the songs are merely a soundtrack, "blast[ing] out on cue" from no discernible location. This sonic backdrop doubles as historical background, as these songs signify to the reader as exemplary artifacts of the 1990s. *Glamorama* is as meticulous in its musical knowledge as *American Psycho* is, similarly referencing songs, albums, and record labels. There is just one difference: in *Glamorama*, there are no years. Albums are not situated in history. Instead, historical time is replaced by running times, the durations of individual of songs: """Magic Touch," 'Aztec shouts out. I answer without trying. 'Plimsouls, *Everywhere at Once*, 3:19, Geffen.' '"Walking Down Madison,"' he tosses out. "'Kirsty MacColl, *Electric Landlady*, 6:34, Virgin'" (103). The attenuated durations of pop music haunt Victor's failure to act meaningfully in history. In the novel's climactic scene, Victor is unable to foil a terrorist plot because he has mistaken a song's trivial statistics for meaningful information. A printout reading "*Wings / Band on the Run / 1985 / 511*" is not, he discovers, coded flight information: "It's a song called '1985.' . . . It's on the *Band on the Run* album. . . . It's not a flight number. . . . It's how long the song is. . . . That song is five minutes and eleven seconds long" (499). In *Glamorama*, even history isn't history. The mention of a year ("1985") is only another song title, while the possibility of stopping the terrorist plot runs aground on the meaningless minutes and seconds that measure nothing more lasting than a song. Having effaced the historical context of its musical references, *Glamorama* turns pop music into a parody of context itself.

There is another reason that *Glamorama* fails to explicitly date any of its musical references. It is because the dates of all these songs don't actually line up. In the novel, Cindy Crawford is still the host of MTV's "House of Style," a job she left in 1995, while songs like Beck's "Where It's At" and the Chemical Brothers' "Setting Sun" play on in the background—both singles that were released in 1996. The novel's historical references do not necessarily interact in a historical way. While Beck and the Chemical Brothers may usefully stand in for a certain essence of 1990s culture, they nevertheless fail to align with the setting of the narrative. Focused on explaining the totality of the decade, *Glamorama* ends up referring to songs that, from the narrower perspective of the narrative's immediate present, did not yet exist.

This discrepancy, which might otherwise seem pedantic, if not plainly accidental, is in fact an unavoidable aspect of the logic of the decade; it's not a bug but a feature. As I discussed earlier, decades rarely obey their own implicit time frames. As Biel recounts in his history of the decade in popular culture, "*Newsweek*, in a slightly tongue-in-cheek attempt to get a jump on the competition, boldly proclaimed on 4 January 1988 that 'The 80s Are Over.'"[46] *Newsweek*'s proleptic proclamation is not so different from *Glamorama*'s, whose own attempt to "define the decade, baby" appeared in print in 1998, before the decade in question had ended. Here, again, we are forced to contemplate the uneasy fit between present time and the period of the decade. *Glamorama* shows what it means to be torn between the imagined totality of a decade that hasn't ended and the concrete particularity of a present that it can't pinpoint. If the novel succeeds in seeing itself through the totalizing lens of the decade, it does so by removing more specific dates from its universe of floating pop signifiers, a decision that undermines the coherence of the narrative's own present. Indeed, it is hard to say exactly when the novel is supposed to be set. Victor's love interest Jamie provides the only clue in the entire novel to when the story is taking place: "It was maybe ten-thirty or eleven and . . . in December 1990 . . . four years ago? . . . five?" (351, ellipses in original). So which is it: 1994? 1995? Asking when precisely *Glamorama* is set misses the more fundamental point of the passage, which is that Jamie herself does not currently know what year it is.

In a novel whose surfeit of celebrity names and pop cultural references seems to imply a basic fidelity to the tenets of realism, none of the characters knows that most inescapable detail of modern life: the date. In *Glamorama*, there is no discrete or datable present, only the loose framework of the decade. Having rejected *American Psycho*'s tenuous fantasy of critical distance, *Glamorama* collapses immediate experience and historical reflection into a single, contradictory narrative vantage, one that erases the present itself. Warned that "significance is rewarded in retrospect," Victor replies, "I think this *is* the retrospect, baby" (527). This is the novel's whole point and its whole problem. How can the contemporary be its own retrospect? An answer is supplied by the decade, which turns the present into a period by sacrificing the specificity of its dates, thus allowing it to exist in two times at once. In the paradoxical "retrospect" of *Glamorama*, everyday life in 1995 vanishes in the attempt to imagine, from within it, the decade of the 1990s as a unifying historical whole.

*White Teeth* has its own trouble sorting out dates, trouble likewise set to music. In the passage I quoted earlier about Raggastani style, Smith describes the "hybrid" aesthetic of Millat's crew as they attempt to board a train to Bradford on January 14, 1989: "Their ethos, their manifesto, if it could be called that, was equally a hybrid thing . . . kung fu and the works of Bruce Lee were also central to their philosophy; added to this was a smattering of Black Power (as embodied by the album *Fear of a Black Planet*, Public Enemy)." Here, as in *Glamorama*, we come upon a familiar tune playing at an unfamiliar time. Whatever it was that constituted the Raggastani ethos at the beginning of 1989, it is unlikely to have involved *Fear of a Black Planet*, an album that was not released until the middle of 1990. Once again, the detail does not fit the date.

Unlike *Glamorama*, however, which goes to great lengths to avoid mention of dates, *White Teeth* is cluttered with them (the dated subsection that includes the Raggastani passage, for instance, falls between two other dated subsections, all three of which are set in a section with two more dates as subtitles). The excess of dates in Smith's novel produces a strangely complicated account of history. "Dates are occult names," Marshall Brown remarks, "no more and no less." [47] The dates that fill *White Teeth* are names of just this sort, the spells we use to pin down a present from which we otherwise feel occulted.

Dates are in the very first sentence of *White Teeth*, and they are even the words we read before those opening words. The novel's table of contents lists four sections, each subtitle of which is a character's name followed by a pair of years: "ARCHIE 1974, 1945"; "SAMAD 1984, 1857"; "IRIE 1990, 1907"; "MAGID AND MILLAT 1992, 1999." In the novel's frequently mentioned philosophy of history ("What is past is prologue" [epigraph]; "the end is simply the beginning" [448]; "this is a rerun" [135]; "past tense, future imperfect" [379]), these pairs of years appear to convey the conventional historicist wisdom that the state of the present depends on the events of the past (or in one case, the future—a speculative foray I'll turn to in the next section). To understand Archie's life in 1974, the table of contents seems to say, you must take stock of his experience of the war in 1945; to fully grasp Irie's predicament in 1990, you would have to begin with the birth of her grandmother in 1907. The problem with this reading, however, is that it fails to notice that not all these years last a year. The year in *White Teeth* is not a uniform time span. Within each pair of years, we in fact find two different ways of denoting history. The second year in each set—1945, 1857, 1907, and 1999—refers to a specific event that took place *in* that year:

Archie's and Samad's first meeting with Dr. Sick at the end of World War II; Samad's ancestor Mangal Pandey's participation in the Indian mutiny of 1857; the birth of Clara's mother, Hortense, during the 1907 Jamaican earthquake; and the genetically predetermined death of Marcus's Future-Mouse, scheduled to occur on the last day of 1999. These four years name datable events, precise points in history. The other four do not. None of these years is attached to a narrative that takes place in the span of a single year. Instead, their function is to stand in metonymically for the present time frame in which each section unfolds. It does not take long to discover this discrepancy. As we see in the novel's very first line, the opening scene of the "ARCHIE 1974" section does not occur in 1974; it occurs "on January 1, 1975" (3). The same goes for "SAMAD 1984," whose narrative begins in 1984 but ends five years later, in 1989. Time and again, the time contained in the four year-marked sections of *White Teeth* lasts longer than a year.

In Smith's seemingly imprecise use of dates, we confront what Michael North calls "the duality of the year as a frame of reference." As North explains, "A year can be used as a date, as if it were punctual and precise, or as a period containing a great many other dates."[48] The doubleness of the year exemplifies what James Chandler, in *England in 1819*, refers to as "the problematic of the date."[49] In Chandler's landmark reading of Claude Lévi-Strauss, he suggests that our sense of history does not reside in a linear sequence of dated events but in an ascending scale of *kinds* or *classes* of dates (days, years, centuries, millennia, and so forth). Lévi-Strauss's transformative insight into "the historian's code," according to Chandler, is his suggestion that the concept of the historical period can function on all these scales. From the smallest to the largest, any dated unit of history can be a historical period. "To press the question of historical scale as Lévi-Strauss does," writes Chandler, "is to begin to see that events datable to *any* date on *any* order of magnitude must be both . . . narrated in sequence and arrayed as a set."[50] Every class of dates belongs to a larger period (as with the individual years that make up a decade or a century), and at the same time every class constitutes a period in its own right.

How much history can a single year contain? Chandler assumes a basic correspondence between the amount of time being measured and the kind of date being used. For him, a year can be a period, but it still lasts about a year. North, in contrast, points out that in popular use, "a year still contains a considerable amount of time, and certain years, especially years like 2000, may stand for whole centuries or even millennia, as the years 1800 and 1900 do for Friedrich A. Kittler."[51] *White Teeth* bears out North's suggestion. What happens in the section entitled "1984" does not stay in 1984; it does, however, stay within the 1980s. It's the same with the other sections: although the narrative present is not confined to an individual year, it is always contained in a single decade. If Smith uses the annualized date as both a point and a period, the kind of period she has in mind is always a decade. While the decade may be an unspoken part of the novel's form, it is an explicit part of the novel's rhetoric. Decades are a way of organizing the chaotic world of geopolitics: "The television . . . spewed out all the shit of the eighties—Irish bombs, English riots, transatlantic stalemates" (180). They are a way of accounting for the passing fads of culture: "Lycra corseting—the much-lauded nineties answer to whalebone" (222). And they are a way of both personalizing and personifying the inexplicable happenings of history: Alsana sees "everyone weeping for themselves and their children, for what the terrible eighties were doing to them both" (182), while Samad is "distressed and full of the humiliations of the decade" (207). In all these ways, the framework of the decade becomes a central feature of *White Teeth*'s historical imagination, an irreducible part of how the characters manage to understand their own place history.

The contemporary comprises dates but is not datable. This paradox takes shape in the category of the decade. Indeed, what is most significant about the dates that look like years but act like decades in *White Teeth* is that they are used only in reference to the present. The decade allows *White Teeth* to date its present by calling into question the present's dated specificity. The sincere but absurd work of precisely dating the present would make for a curious intellectual history of its own, one that might carry us from Virginia Woolf (for whom human character changed "on or about December 1910")[52] to Charles Jencks (who famously insisted, with the demolition of the Pruit-Igoe housing complex, that "modern architecture died in St. Louis, Missouri[,] on July 15, 1972 at 3:32 P.M.")[53] to Philip Wegner (who tells us that what we call "the 1990s" is really "the span between November 9, 1989, 10:30 P.M. CET . . . and September 11, 2001, 9:02:54 A.M. EST").[54] For Wegner, the start and end of the 1990s can be tracked to the hour, minute, and second. Then there's Zadie Smith. Here is how the fall of the Berlin Wall, and the new historical present the event supposedly introduces, is narrated in *White Teeth*:

*November 10, 1989*

A wall was coming down. It was something to do with history. It was *an historical occasion.* No one really knew quite who had put it up or who was tearing it down or whether this was good, bad, or something else; no one knew how tall it was, how long it was, or why people had died trying to cross it, or whether they would stop dying in the future, but it was educational all the same; as good an excuse for a get-together as any. It was a Thursday night, Alsana and Clara had cooked, and everybody was watching history on TV. (197, italics in original)

The first thing to say about this passage is that in 1989, there was no such day as "Thursday November 10." Smith has given us the wrong date. In the last year of the 1980s, November 10 was a Friday, not a Thursday; the "Thursday night" Smith has in mind is likely November 9, which is the actual date that the Berlin Wall fell. Perhaps Smith has simply made a mistake. Or perhaps it is the characters themselves who are confused about what day it is. After all, such confusion is exactly what the passage is about. The event "was something to do with history," though "no one really knew" what that something was. The recognition that there is something "*historical*" about this "*occasion*" is possible despite the absence of any knowledge of the wall itself (about "who had put it up or who was tearing it down or whether this was good, bad, or something else"). In this way, the passage is less about dating the end of the Cold War than it is about how dates themselves are tidy placeholders for the messy, haphazard, often inadvertent emergence of historical self-awareness. What Archie's and Samad's families are watching, in short, is the transition from one decade to another, the shift from the "terrible eighties" to the not yet "known"—and as yet un-datable—1990s. The novel's own adventure in misdating reminds us that our sense of history is not so much inaugurated *on* a date as *by* a date. The pinpoint accuracy of Wegner's clock readings can be the reward only of retrospection. A date comes to stand for an epochal shift only after the fact. Conversely, on the day in question, things are bound to feel a bit more uncertain—as uncertain, perhaps, as we feel trying to figure out on which day this "*historical*" scene is supposed to take place. This is what the most vigilant tracking of minutes and seconds cannot measure: the slow, error-riddled process by which the contemporary comes to recognize itself as "something to do with history" before it knows what exactly that something will turn out to be.

There is thus a sense in which "November 10, 1989" is no less accurate a starting point for the 1990s than "November 9, 1989, 10:30 P.M. CET." That is the sense in which neither date belongs to the decade it purports to introduce. Although Wegner may offer a more technologically precise gloss on the day the Berlin Wall fell, both he and Smith share an implicit understanding of the decade as a fundamentally imprecise or perpetually misnamed measure of history. In Smith's account, no more than Wegner's, the decade is a historical form that remains essentially unfaithful to its dates. This is what makes it such a powerful way of depicting the contemporary. It's not that ten years is a good estimate for how long a present tends to last; it's that the present, just like the decade, can't be reduced to a particular set of dates.

## THE SENSE OF UNENDING

"How interesting are the arguments about how to choose beginnings and ends?" Amy Hungerford wonders in her essay "On the Period Formerly Known as the Contemporary."[55] Her answer: not very. So why bother trying to periodize the present at all? One could well ask the same question of the novels just analyzed, whose paractic lists and unreliable dates don't inspire much confidence in the possibility of historical categorization. As a measure of history in the making, the decade novel seems destined to come up short. Yet an unperiodized present may also risk being an unending one. This is the deeper anxiety that courses through the novels I've been discussing. It's an anxiety that significantly reframes the shortcomings of periodization that these novels so prominently display. How, we have to ask, might our anxieties about these flawed forms of periodization begin to look different in the context of worrying about the endlessness of the present itself?

The specter of eternity haunts both of Ellis's novels. The final scene of *American Psycho* is set in Harry's Bar, where Patrick is contemplating "how life presents itself in a bar or in a club in New York, maybe *anywhere*, at the end of the century" (399, italics in original). The question of "how life presents itself" at this particular historical moment, not just here in Harry's

Bar but "*anywhere*," is followed by Patrick's realization of how hard it is to imagine an end to or an escape from his historically delimited form of life. Looking around Harry's, Patrick's gaze alights on a building placard whose ominous warning, written in blood-red letters, constitutes the novel's last words: "This is not an exit." Life in the decade of *American Psycho* is defined by the difficulty of conceiving any possible exit from it. The final words of *American Psycho* mirror the opening words of *Glamorama*, whose introductory epigraph (attributed to Krishna) reads, "There was no time when you nor I nor these kings did not exist." The ultimate sign of Patrick's times—the sign that tells him there is no exit from the times— marks here the foreboding entrance into Victor's times. Beneath the present that is meticulously cataloged in *Glamorama* is the belief that there is "no time" other than that present, no moment when life "did not exist" in its current form. In both novels, the trouble with contemporary life is that it feels like it lasts forever.

Perhaps the most striking vision of endlessness to be found in *American Psycho* and *Glamorama* is the fact that it's hard to tell where one novel ends and the other begins. Reading the two novels side by side, one may well begin to wonder: Has anything really changed here at all? The allegedly epochal differences that claim to separate the two novels seem to be erased by the books' thematic continuity. With slight tweaks to accommodate period detail, these novels tell a single story in a single way, the story of an unprecedentedly surface-obsessed culture interrupted by inexplicable bursts of violence, narrated with unrelenting monotony and clinical detachment: "Sex is mathematics. Individuality no longer an issue. . . . Intellect is not a cure. Justice is dead. . . . Surface, surface, surface was all that anyone found meaning in" (375). These lines, taken from *American Psycho*, would be no less at home in *Glamorama*. The brand names and celebrity faces may change, but the cultural logic of being obsessed with brands and celebrities remains the same. Even the allegorical calculus of the novels is kept constant. *American Psycho* shows how easily "mergers and acquisitions" can become "murders and executions" (206), while *Glamorama* suggests how professional modeling might serve as a model for mass violence:

How did he recruit people? . . . It was only models . . . and famous models. . . . He wasn't interested in anyone else. . . . He would use the fact that as a model all you do all day is stand around and do what other people tell you to do. . . . He preyed on that . . . and we listened . . . and it was an analogy that made sense . . . in the end . . . when he asked . . . things of us . . . and it wasn't hard to recruit people . . . everyone wanted to be around us . . . everyone wanted to be movie stars . . . and in the end, basically, everyone was a sociopath. (352, ellipses in original)

There is little difference, in other words, between a serial killer with political pretensions and a terrorist without any. Ellis's two satires of cultural decay are essentially interchangeable. In both, the exit-less world of late capitalism appears as a world in which *everyone is a sociopath*, in which every job implies a kind of violence, and in which all novels end up saying the same thing.

In the 1990s, when both novels were published, Ellis was not alone in worrying about the unending or eternal present. He was joined, most famously, by Francis Fukuyama, who notoriously declared the 1990s to be "the end of history," an end that promised an end to ends and thus a new time of endlessness. Fukuyama's argument needs little rehearsing today. For him, the end of history meant the end of ideological contradiction and of competition between opposing worldviews. The "unabashed victory of economic and political liberalism" signaled by the collapse of the Soviet Union represented "the end point of mankind's ideological evolution and the universalization of Western liberal democracy as the final form of human government." At the end of the twentieth century, following the defeats of fascism and Communism, liberal capitalism seemed to Fukuyama "the ideal that will govern the material world *in the long run*."[56] Such a run looked to be long indeed. This, for Fukuyama, was not an entirely salutary fact. At the end of his well-known *National Interest* essay, in a paragraph that has drawn considerably less critical attention, Fukuyama concluded on a more melancholic note:

The end of history will be a very sad time. The struggle for recognition, the willingness to risk one's life for a purely abstract goal, the worldwide ideological struggle that called forth daring, courage, imagination, and idealism, will be replaced by economic calculation, the endless solving of technical problems, environmental concerns, and the satisfaction of sophisticated consumer demands. In the posthistorical period there will be neither art nor philosophy, just the perpetual caretaking of the museum of human history. . . . Perhaps this very prospect of centuries of boredom at the end of history will serve to get history started once again.[57]

What stands to make the end of the history such a "sad time"? It is the sheer *endlessness* of the time: "endless solving," "perpetual caretaking," "centuries of boredom." The "victory" of liberal capitalism is in part a pyrrhic one. The end of ideological struggle—there are now "no large causes for which to fight"—condemns us to endless technocratic boredom. Even violent struggle itself, when it reappears, will be shorn of significance. As Fukuyama sees it, people "will struggle for the sake of struggle. They will struggle, in other words, out of a certain boredom."[58] The unheroic hero of Fukuyama's posthistorical drama is "the last man," a character whose acquiescence to this attenuated world makes him "something less than a full human being, indeed, an object of contempt, a 'last man' with neither striving nor aspiration." The sad boredom of the end of history is realized in the figure of the last man, whose life is shaped not by belief or principle but by the ceaseless temporality of consumer desire: "It is no accident that people in democratic societies are preoccupied with material gain and live in an economic world devoted to the satisfaction of the myriad small needs of the body."[59]

The numbing boredom of capitalist plenty; the sad possibility of the end of new possibilities ("this is not an exit"); the danger of a return to senseless "struggle" or violence simply for its own sake: all these features of Fukuyama's posthistorical present also perfectly describe Ellis's two decade novels, driven as they are by the rhythm of relentless, banal repetition—the same brand and celebrity names until the end of time—sporadically punctured by extreme and pointless acts of violence (violence done, one could no doubt say, "out of a certain boredom").[60] There is, nevertheless, one distinctive difference between Ellis's and Fukuyama's otherwise remarkably similar accounts of the terrible endlessness of late capitalist life: Ellis insists on dividing that endlessness into decades. What difference does a decade make? What does it mean to frame the anxieties of the end of history and the endlessness of the present within the clearly marked end points of the decade? While both novels describe the disturbing eternity of the capitalist present, the perennial present is interrupted and rendered ironic by the fact that each novel locates that sense of endlessness *in a different decade.*

In *American Psycho* and *Glamorama*, the decade makes it possible to write historical change back into a historical moment that otherwise appears to lack an exit. This makes change a matter of structure or form rather than human agency or personal character. The inexorable logic of the decade suggests that times will change whether or not we have the will to change them. The structural difference embedded in a decade—its implicit relation, in Lévi-Strauss's terms, to the entire class of surrounding decades—offers one way to defuse the threat of the eternal present. While the epigraph to *Glamorama* claims that "there was no time when" the present "did not exist," the opening pages of the novel suggest that this is not entirely true. There is, in fact, a name for the period of time before the novel's expansive present existed: the 1980s. The 1980s stand for everything that doesn't seem to fit the present moment: "Aren't the 1980s over? Don't you think opening a club like this is a throwback to an era most people want to forget?" (160); "It's just that this is all so . . . so . . . '89?" (12, ellipses in original). If the present of the 1990s is, by definition, incompatible with the prior decade—an era that now seems definitively "over"— then the inescapability or endlessness of the present in *Glamorama* also represents a very determinate end: the end of what *American Psycho* considered *its* own seemingly "exit"-less present.

The decade thus provides an artificial but nevertheless useful tool for carving out the possibility of historical change in a "posthistorical" age. Such arbitrary carvings may still seem effectively empty, frustratingly superficial. But they also explain the very real appeal of the decade as a literary form for writers newly faced in the 1990s with the prospect of endless capitalism. In an epoch haunted by a particularly insidious sense of endlessness, one tied to the ostensible triumph of global capitalism, the decade requires us to believe once again in ends. Echoing Ellis's concern with the transition from one decade to the next, Smith, too, is perhaps less interested in decades themselves than in the ends of decades, as announced by one of the novel's signature refrains: "'HAPPY FUCKING NEW YEAR!'" (217). This line, "bellowed" to celebrate the end of 1989, also marks the end of the entire section of *White Teeth* that is set in the 1980s. Smith's repeated reliance on New Year's Eve to telegraph historical turning points—"December 31, 1999, that historic night when Abdul-Mickey finally opened his doors to women" (448)—reveals how, in *White Teeth*, the conventions of dating make it possible (if only nominally) to locate change in history. To measure history in decades is to decide in advance when things—a section of a novel, if not a period of history—are scheduled to change. To yell "Happy fucking New Year" is to imagine that "the humiliations of the decade" can be overcome by something as simple as a flip of the calendar and a glass of cheap champagne.

Of course, this form of historical imagination has its limits. These become apparent at the end of *White Teeth*. After freewheeling across a post-colonial *longue durée* stretching from the 1850s to the 1990s, Smith's novel stops abruptly on the last day of 1999. Although it offers a few brief hints about the futures it won't be narrating ("a court case so impossible the judge gave in"; "a snapshot seven years hence of Irie, Joshua, and Hortense"; "December 31, 1999, that historic night" [448]), *White Teeth* is ultimately not willing to push its narrative beyond the present of the 1990s. Why not? It is likely that Smith—along with almost everyone else living in the last year of the century—saw the end of the decade as the moment of a potentially catastrophic event: the worldwide computer crisis of Y2K. In light of the expectation that computer systems would crash from one end of the globe to the other, the first day of the 2000s would have appeared to be literally unimaginable. No one knew what would happen; but of course, nothing did happen. The crisis of Y2K never materialized, and so the arrival of "the year 2000 itself came to seem almost anticlimactic."[61] The same anticlimax is embedded in Smith's decision to structure her novel around the unrepresentable arrival of a future that would turn out to make no difference to—because it was in fact no different from—the present. At the very end of *White Teeth*, the end of the decade foretells an epochal event (the radical break named Y2K) that never actually occurs. The change that Smith finds unimaginable during the 1990s is, by the time we arrive in the year 2000, no longer even noticeable.

This episode seems to show us everything that is wrong with thinking through decades, as the artificial, essentially meaningless end of the decade becomes synonymous with one of the most anticlimactic non-events of recent memory. Yet Smith isn't wrong to imagine that there is some historically transformative event on the horizon, some moment past which it would be foolish to assume that the present could continue to be narrated in the same way. It's just that once again, she's slightly off with the date. The 1990s did not come to an end on the first day of the year 2000. They may have ended, though, not very long after—"on or about September 11, 2001," as Sam Cohen wryly words it in *After the End of History*. "The events of that day," he writes, "were taken by countless cultural commentators to constitute . . . the end of an era." And not just an era, but a decade: "Responses to the events of September 11 took the form of postmortems on the recent past, most often on the 1990s."[62] In this way, the end of the era was also its beginning; September 11 retroactively produced the very idea of the 1990s as a coherent period. But what does any of this have to do with *White Teeth*? Am I actually suggesting that Smith's novel predicted a world-changing event it could not possibly have foreseen? I am not—though that has not stopped a number of critics from using September 11 as the occasion to impute exactly this kind of historical prescience to pre-2001 authors like Smith and Ellis.[63] As one critic remarks, *Glamorama*'s "graphic depictions of spectacular terror bombings foreshadowed, of course, the events of September 11, 2001."[64] In a reading like this, September 11 does not simply mark the end of the 1990s; it also recasts the prior decade as having anticipated—through eerie foreshadowing—its own end. From one perspective, this sort of uncanny anticipation seems highly implausible.[65] From another perspective, however—the one I've been exploring throughout this chapter—the 1990s can indeed be understood to foreshadow their own end, for this is exactly what the limited, liminal form of the decade is designed to do. In its tragically brief ten-year life span, the decade expresses the eternally impermanent conditions of the contemporary. It recognizes from the start that what makes the present a historical period is the fact that it must come to an end.

September 11, in that case, is just one of several possible names and dates for the inevitable end that the decade of the 1990s both did and did not foresee. Consider, for instance, what many scholars of post–September 11 culture themselves failed to foresee: the occurrence of yet another catastrophic event, the economic meltdown of 2008, that rewrote the history of the present once more, this time transforming the 2000s from the decade of homeland security into the decade of subprime lending and financial crisis. The lesson here is simple: it is unwise to periodize contemporary history before it has ended. What wisdom can be imparted by a decade, then? Decades do not predict historical breaks. But they do make us worry about when and how we'll know a new era when we see one. In this way, the decade becomes an imprecise yet strangely effective way to structure the expectation of historical change. The arbitrary boundaries of the decade, which do as much to tie periods together as to keep them apart, are nothing but an attempt to keep pace with historical movement: to account, you could say, for contemporary drift. The point, then, is not that the decade fails to predict change; the point is that the decade compels us to expect it. In the gap between arbitrary dates and actual history—between Y2K and September 11; between the fantasy of history's end and the reality of capitalism's continued catastrophe—the decade supplies an image of transition at a standstill, a picture of the seemingly endless calm before a storm of unforeseeable change. The storm will come; it always does. The decade compels us to account for that eventuality. It gives a name, and a form, to the inexorability of change. In an era of endlessness, the decade records the doomed chronologies that make the contemporary both contemporary and temporary—that make it now, for now.

# Chapter Two

# REVIVAL

## Situating Noir

The voice, separated from its body, evokes the voice of the dead.

MLADEN DOLAR

my own voice was the voice of the dead

STEPHEN GREENBLATT

### CONTEXT IS EVERYTHING

Like the decades discussed in the previous chapter, genres, too, have a strange relationship to dates. On one hand, every repeated or revived genre is likely to strike us as an essentially dated object. On the other hand, a genre's very power to repeat and recur challenges our ability to accurately date it. Both these problems—of dating and of datedness—haunt the genre of film noir. When was noir's moment? To what time, properly speaking, does noir belong? The task of situating noir is surprisingly disorienting; in our attempts to track the genre through time, we are just as likely to lose our way. That's because film noir has the strange distinction of being both one of our most historically rooted genres—a product of the postwar social upheavals of the 1940s and 1950s—and one of our most historically mobile.[1] Despite having been forged in the heat of American life in the middle of the last century, noir has consistently leaped out of that particular pan and into other historical fires, becoming a fixture in the popular culture of the late twentieth and early twenty-first centuries. The genre thus trades the specificity of its midcentury present for a more sustained, uncanny cultural presence. How, in that case, are we supposed to situate film noir? How do we account for its revivals? And how, this chapter asks, might the genre's persistent presence—its out-of-place place—in our own present bespeak a distinctive relationship between noir films and the contemporary's form?

Nothing could be less contemporary than a revival. Revived styles and recycled forms lack a critical relation to their present. In the case of film genres, critics have tended to see the problem of aesthetic revival either as a sign of the "nostalgia mode" of postmodern culture or as evidence of the commercial motivations of corporate studios.[2] These twin approaches to the problem of noir's reappearance provide useful insight into contemporary Hollywood's preference for remakes, sequels, and other means of harvesting the past for profit. Yet they do not fully explain the dynamics of genre itself. It is, after all, in the nature of genre to repeat. In Bliss Cua Lim's words, genre "is a formal, social, and industrial contract to repeat and return." Genres are thus "always temporally diverse . . . keying us to persistence, return, reinvention, and movement rather than stasis."[3] In noir, perhaps more than any other genre, repetition is the normal state of things. Start with this oft-repeated origin story: film noir came into being through repetition. It was invented in retrospect when a handful of American films from the early 1940s were screened in Paris following World War II, enabling French critics to view them as evidence of a consistent tone or style in American filmmaking.[4] This was a style they dubbed *film noir*. In the United States, several more decades passed before noir was fully understood as a genre. As James Naremore explains in *More Than Night: Film Noir in Its Contexts*, "In effect, film noir did not become a true Hollywood genre until the Vietnam years. . . . Whether classic noir ever existed, by 1974 a great many people believed in it . . . and it formed a rich discursive category that the entertainment industry could expand and adapt in countless ways."[5] For Naremore, what made noir a genre in the U.S. context was not the making of classic midcentury noir films but the *re*making of those films by Hollywood in the 1970s and 1980s. Once again, the time line of noir ends up twisting back on itself. Across these various accounts of film noir's displaced origins, from 1940s France to 1970s Hollywood, the one consistent thing we can say about noir is that it is a genre with a uniquely vexed connection to its immediate present.

The difficulty of situating oneself in the present is not just a feature of the genre's history. It is also a central concern of the films themselves. Built on the shaky foundation of false accusations, frame-ups, mistaken identities, double crosses, chance encounters, and other baroque contortions of plot, film noir is defined by the experience of confusion. Critics describe the "frustrating confusion"[6] felt by noir characters, the inevitable sense of disorientation that comes from getting caught up in plots and systems "beyond their comprehension."[7] As the philosopher Robert Pippin observes in *Fatalism in American Film Noir*, these are films in which "events come at characters much too fast and too confusingly to allow . . . reflection."[8] Such confusion is both the characters' and the viewer's. Noir plots themselves, Pippin notes, are notoriously "hard to follow; often even baffling, and we are as much at sea about what is happening as the male lead."[9] Disorientation, in short, is noir's degree zero. For characters and viewers alike, the essential experience of noir is being in too deep, in over your head, immersed in a predicament that is both out of your hands and beyond your grasp.

Film noir thus depicts, from its history as a genre to the workings of its plots, the challenge of making sense of one's contemporary. For the noir protagonist, this challenge often appears insurmountable. At a different narrative level, however, noir films do deploy a cinematic technique meant to resolve the problem of knowing the present. This technique is perhaps noir's most recognizable formal feature: the voice-over.[10] The premise of the voice-over is the promise of retrospection, of a later moment at which the current one will eventually make sense. This is what critical distance is supposed to sound like. Narrating from some point after the events of the plot, the noir voice-over offers an enlightened perspective capable of looking backward in order to see the bigger picture, which wasn't visible from right up close. That is certainly the impression given by Walter Neff, who, in that most exemplary of noir films, *Double Indemnity* (Billy Wilder, 1944), describes the purpose of his voice-over just so: "I just wanted to set you straight about something you couldn't see because it was smack up against your nose." The choice is clear: either the confusion of immediate experience or the clarity that comes from looking back on it. Speaking as most noir narrators do from the end point of the story, Neff suggests that he can untangle the confusing events of the plot only because he has the distance to reflect on them. Correcting misperceptions and setting the story "straight" become possible now that events are no longer "smack up against" Neff's nose but a good deal farther away. The voice-over, Neff boasts in voice-over, is able to give us the facts precisely because it comes after the fact.

There is just one problem with the idea that the voice-over enshrines the explanatory power of retrospective narration. Noir voice-overs don't explain very much. If they did, wouldn't viewers like Pippin find the plots less confusing? The voice-over clearly doesn't prevent us from being "at sea" in the plot; indeed, it seems to be what sets us adrift in the first place. Part of the reason for this is that noir voice-overs spend a surprising amount of time simply recounting the experience of being confused. This is a consistent theme in the voice-over narration of *Double Indemnity*: "How could I have known"; "The time for thinking had all run out"; "I tried to make sense out of it and got nowhere." At moments like these, the voice-over tells us what it's like not to know. Other times, the voice-over tells us things we already know: it simply repeats verbally what we're seeing on the screen. If one face of the noir voice-over is confusion, the other is redundancy. In *The Lady from Shanghai* (Orson Welles, 1947), the climactic revelation delivered via voice-over—"I was right, she was the murderer!"—comes after the diegesis has already made clear who the murderer was. In *Double Indemnity*, such moments of redundancy are at once more banal and more striking. "I stopped at a drive-in for a bottle of beer," says Neff's voice-over as we see him at a drive-in drinking a beer (figure 2.1). "I didn't want to go back to the office, so I dropped by a bowling alley," says Neff's voice-over as we watch him bowl. "She was even laughing," says Neff's voice-over, and there he is in the car with Lola Dietrichson, who, we confirm, is indeed laughing. What is going on here? Why is the voice-over telling us what we

FIGURE 2.1. Redundant *Indemnity*: "I stopped at a drive-in for a bottle of beer."

can see full well with our own eyes, what we don't actually need to hear? Oscillating between confusion and redundancy, the empty speech of the voice-over makes at least one thing clear: the meaning of the voice-over is not located in what it says.[11] The voice's words are not what we need to be listening to.

That leaves the physical fact of speaking, a fact inseparable from the question of where the speaker is speaking from. Voice-over is an exemplary instance of what the sound theorist Michel Chion calls *acousmatic* sound, "a situation wherein one hears the sound without seeing its cause."[12] The acousmatic voice is simply a voice you can't see. It's also a voice that lays bare our need to know the physical sources of the sounds we hear. To hear an acousmatic voice is immediately to wonder where the voice is coming from; "the listener is led all the more intently to ask, 'What's that?' (i.e., 'What is causing this sound?')."[13] Rather than allowing us to forget a sound's source, the *acousmêtre* only intensifies our desire to see it. The voice-over can't help but call attention to its missing source or absent cause, making us attuned less to what we're hearing than to what we're not seeing. As Chion explains, "The acousmatic situation . . . entails that the idea of the cause seizes us and haunts us."[14] To listen to voice-over is to be haunted by the often unanswerable question of where the voice that's talking to us is talking to us from.

Many, if not most, voice-overs are both acousmatic and nondiegetic. Because they aren't located in the diegesis of the films, they have no source for us to discover.[15] But this is not how the voice-over tends to work in film noir. In noir, the voice-over is almost always established as a diegetic presence, reinserted into narrative time and space. Thus in *Double Indemnity*, we see exactly where Neff is speaking from (in his office dictating his confession to Keyes), just as we see Al Roberts in *Detour* (Edgar G. Ulmer, 1945) narrating, lost and broken, from a truck stop; Frank Chambers in *The Postman Always Rings Twice* (Tay Garnett, 1946) telling his story from prison; Jeff Bailey in *Out of the Past* (Jacques Tourneur, 1947) confessing his traumatic past to his girlfriend; and Frank Bigelow in *D.O.A.* (Rudolph Maté, 1949) reporting the story of his own murder to the police. The noir voice-over has a fundamentally deictic function. It points to the here-and-now of the speaking subject; it describes—and circumscribes—his current situation. The noir voice demonstrates how an individual is situated in social space by depicting the institutional forces that have compelled him to speak in the first place. Indeed, what the noir voice-over most often narrates is how the subject has become entangled in the system or institution that now requires him to explain himself. Placing the speaker in the space of the prison, the police station, or the office, or in sites of routine, overlooked labor (gas stations, truck stops), the voice-over reveals the contours of the social and economic systems—the law, the corporation, the labor contract—in which the noir hero is caught up. If Walter Neff, for instance, is "little more than a cog in a bureaucracy" (as Naremore describes him),[16] we know this because his voice-over registers both his desire and his failure to escape his life's bureaucratic confines: confines that appear first as the walls of his office and last (in the film's famous lost ending) as the walls of the gas chamber.[17] In its obsession with the inescapable systems of work and justice, noir establishes itself as a profoundly institutional genre. What we hear in the noir voice-over is not just the voice of an individual but also the sound of the larger system that speaks through him.

Registering the call of the acousmatic voice—Where is that sound coming from?—the noir voice-over points us to its underlying source, which turns out to be its overarching social situation. The noir voice communicates the complex relation between a speaker and a context, the concrete entanglements of the individual and the systemic. We can put a somewhat finer point on these entanglements. What noir most urgently speaks to us about, this chapter argues, are the complexities of *being situated*.

"To speculate about situatedness," David Simpson suggests in his book *Situatedness*, "is to think about everything that is around one, synchronically."[18] *Situating*, of course, is also the watchword of literary studies in its regnant historicist phase. Always situate: this is the unspoken but long-standing motto by which literary critics do their work, vigilant in their efforts to place cultural objects in historical contexts. With so much situating going on in literary criticism, you might not guess that the philosophical concept of the situation doesn't actually imply historical specificity. It implies just the opposite: the irreducible uncertainty and abstraction that underlie our basic notion of context. For one thing, a situation is not a naturally occurring thing; it is a critical construct. As Ian Baucom observes in *Specters of the Atlantic*, "situations" are "artificial forms of time" rather than "natural entities [to be] discovered."[19] For another, a situation is not an immutable structure; it is a temporary framework. As Simpson explains, situatedness "has to do with being in the world, in place and time, in a way that is at once unignorable but also a bit provisional."[20] Lauren Berlant, in *Cruel Optimism*, makes a similar point: "A situation is a genre of living that one knows one's in but that one has to find out about."[21] Philosophically, the heuristic of the situation has long been used to mark out this provisional or not-yet-known territory, framing historical moments as they arise out of the complex choreography, the constantly shifting interrelation, of individual and totality.[22] Thus for Simpson, situatedness is "the designation of an antinomy or aporia." That antinomy concerns the fundamental tension "between the doggedly empirical . . . and the general or social historical," or between the ostensible empiricism of personal experience and the abstract generality of the historical moment to which individual experience invisibly yet undeniably belongs.[23] Accordingly, the central question posed by the situation is not how to define the local but how to move from the local to the general. It concerns how to turn historical experience into theoretical knowledge. As Fredric Jameson reminds us, "A crucial component of my *particular* situation as a unique individual is always the *general* category to which I am also condemned."[24] Because it negotiates the contradictory processes of specification and abstraction, the situation is less a milieu or a background than a principle of relation. To situate is not only to identify a context. It is also to ask how we theorize what counts as context in the first place.

The question of the situation—of how we form a temporary relation to the totality of our moment—is also a question about how we locate ourselves in the contemporary. This is why Chris Nealon considers the "hermeneutics of situation" essential to "historicizing the present."[25] For Nealon, the history of the present is inseparable from the present's status as a situation, a generalizable context we are currently in the process of generating. Indeed, situatedness speaks to our role in theorizing the context of the contemporary in a surprisingly literal way: by emphasizing the conceptual centrality of speech itself. Simpson, for his part, is acutely aware of the speech acts that underlie situatedness. As the subtitle of his book indicates, the work of situating is the work of "saying where we're coming from."[26] If that's so, then voice-over narration offers the perfect site for investigating what it means to be situated. Cinema's acousmatic voices transform the assuredness of the self-situating statement ("this is where I'm coming from") into a structural question: Where is that voice coming from? This irrepressible query, called up by every voice-over, becomes in film noir the proliferating drama of situating and being situated, the Russian-doll set of settings that slowly unveils a voice located in a body located in a physical place located in a social system. If the acousmatic voice always asks to be situated, noir deploys the voice-over in order to ask how we make sense of our contemporary situation. How, the genre asks, can we speak *about* our present moment when we're also speaking *from* it?

The aporia of the situation—which both establishes and unsettles our capacity to frame historical moments (our own most of all)—is what we find at the heart of film noir. We find it in the films' flustered protagonists, working desperately to understand the contours of the convoluted plots they're caught up in. We find it in noir's redundant voice-overs, which replace the content of the voice with its visual context. And we find it in the history of the genre as a whole, whose contemporary revivals challenge our ability to properly contextualize it. My argument in this chapter is that the genre of film noir can be defined by its sustained attention to the problem of situating; that this attention manifests itself in the form of the voice-over; and that noir's account of situatedness compels us to reconsider what it means to historically situate the genre itself. "Historicism's fundamental task," Baucom claims, is "dual: to place objects within their situations and to invent situations and periods of time in which to place objects."[27] By tracking how film noir both depicts the theoretical invention of situations and complicates our own attempts to situate it, we may come to see noir as a cultural form whose seemingly perennial relevance lies in its historically specific commitment to rethinking the stakes of historicism.

How do we sort out what belongs to a moment and what escapes it? How do we determine which moment noir itself belongs to? In the remainder of this chapter, I look at the classic (1940s and 1950s) phase of film noir alongside noir's contemporary (1990s and 2000s) revival in order to show how these ostensibly separate instances of the genre voice a shared interest in the slippery nature of historical situations. From the dawn of the media age in the first half of the twentieth century to the mediations of genre pastiche in the second half, the noir voice responds to its changing historical circumstances by questioning the changing assumptions about historical specificity. In both the earliest and the most recent noir films, the voice-over serves simultaneously as a physical index and a floating signifier. It oscillates between marking a particular place and marking the dispersions of temporal displacement. Despite those dispersions, however, the voices of noir may still have something to say about the particular circumstances of social life in the late twentieth and early twenty-first centuries. The problem of situating oneself in the present, this chapter claims, speaks to two larger and intertwined conditions of the long postwar period: first, the rise of an increasingly complex and unimaginably large world system; second, the institutionalization of a thought-form, historicism, that—as if in response to the immeasurable scope of that system—begins writing history on smaller and smaller scales.

Starting in the 1980s, new historicism became the dominant framework for literary and cultural studies, and since then, no critical movement has succeeded in dislodging the disciplinary centrality of historicism. As Rita Felski explains, historicism is a method that "sees contextualization as the quintessential virtue," and part of the reason for historicism's continued dominance is that no sane critic "could feasibly take issue with the idea of context as such."[28] However, context ceases to be a theoretical problem— that is, it ceases to seem like an "idea" at all—only when it is sufficiently shrunk down to size. That's why, Eric Hayot insists, historicism "promotes historical microscopism."[29] In *Why Literary Periods Mattered*, Ted Underwood testifies to this microscopism at first hand: "The first thing I was told in graduate school, in 1991, was to reframe questions about periods and movements as questions about spans of time no longer than five years."[30] The story of literary historicism in the late twentieth century is largely a story about how the notion of historical context becomes small enough to seem self-evident. As our basic understanding of context has shrunk, it has become increasingly difficult to historicize groupings of cultural objects that are spread out over longer periods of time—groupings like genres and genres like noir. In the context of shrinking contexts, film noir requires us to think bigger. It also teaches us how to do so. Read across a sixty-odd-year span, noir situates our obsession with situating within a long post-1945 present whose representative dilemma has been the problem of how to locate ourselves within increasingly bureaucratic institutions and an impossibly vast world economic system. Providing a longer view of the social and economic systems that continue to determine and disorient us, the wayward history of film noir—no less than our own wayward attempts to historicize it—reimagines the scope of the contemporary by rethinking the meaning of context.

## GRAMOPHONE, FILM NOIR, TYPEWRITER

The noir voice-over conjures a context. It bespeaks a situation. Yet from the genre's beginnings, the voice has proved to be a surprisingly unreliable index of what it means to be situated in a particular time and place. The unstable relation between the noir voice and its physical context has a clear source: the development of recording technologies in the early half of the twentieth century. "Media determine our situation," Friedrich Kittler suggests.[31] The classic cycle of noir films, however, amends this to say: Media determine what we think a "situation" actually is. Through a voice that can be recorded and replayed, repeated and resituated across space and time, early noir films grapple with the basic difficulty of situating ourselves, or keeping things in context.

How do we know that the voice we're hearing in a film belongs to the world it describes? This worry is clearly audible in *Double Indemnity*, which goes to great and sometimes contradictory lengths to counter the displacements of the recorded voice. The confession that Neff is narrating to us in voice-over comes two ways. First, we see Neff speaking in the immediacy of his office, and then we see him talking into a Dictaphone, recording his story for Keyes to listen to at a later date. This nexus of seeing, speaking, and recording gives the voice-over a reason for being (so *that's* why Neff is talking to himself in an empty room!), yet it also renders that reason contingent, inessential. Sure, we see Neff speaking, but we could just as well be listening to a recording. The contingency of the recorded voice seems to trouble *Double Indemnity* enough that it ends up trying to erase the specter of recording's displacement. In the last scene of the film, the camera pivots from Neff's face to a shot of the doorway behind him, where we see Keyes in the flesh, no longer the absent addressee of a recording but a physically present listener (figure 2.2). At the most obvious level, Keyes's presence seals Neff's fate: he has been caught and will not, as he had hoped, "escape to Mexico." But Keyes's appearance also poses a conundrum. If he has in fact been "standing there" in the doorway listening to the confession the whole time, then what is the point of the recording? Joan Copjec, one of the great readers of noir, suggests that *Double Indemnity* "deliberately severs this [voice-over] speech from its addressee in order to return us repeatedly to the image of a solitary Neff, seated in an empty office at night, speaking into a dictaphone."[32] But Neff turns out not to be solitary, and

FIGURE 2.2. Metaphysics of presence: the superfluous Dictaphone in *Double Indemnity*.

this makes the Dictaphone strangely superfluous. Keyes need never listen to the recording, since he's been there all along, luxuriating in the presence of Neff's voice. While the recording is fated to drift through time—severing speech from both speaker and listener—*Double Indemnity* doubles down on the immediate presence of the speaking voice. Concluding with the face-to-face reunion of Keyes and Neff, it is as if the film has forgotten its explanation for having Neff speak out loud in the first place. The film is thus caught between the confines of Neff's context ("cog" that he is in the machines of bureaucracy, law, and consumer capitalism) and the recording technology that puts a hitch in that context. The voice-over, meant to situate Neff and his confession in the concrete space of the Pacific All Risk Insurance Company, can be explained only by reference to the technological medium that produces a version of Neff who is not fully confined to his situation after all.

A similarly superfluous recording appears in the final sequence of what is generally considered the last of the classic noir films, *Touch of Evil* (Orson Welles, 1958). To finally snare the corrupt police captain Hank Quinlan, Mike Vargas must record his confession. To do this, Vargas plants a bug on Quinlan's partner Pete Menzies, who meets with Quinlan and tries to get him to confess. But to make sure the conversation is actually recorded by the transmitter, Vargas must himself be physically present. The result is almost vaudevillian, as Vargas, managing to remain just out of Quinlan's sight, sneaks around buildings, under a bridge, and through water in order to get close enough to the conversation to be able to record it (figure 2.3). That means getting close enough to hear it, which means—as Quinlan hears Vargas splashing around under the bridge and begins to speak to him— that the recording is now irrelevant. The plot to make a recording, to separate the voice from its immediate situation, becomes the very plot device that allows the film to bring its two main characters to the same place. Just like *Double Indemnity, Touch of Evil* uses recorded speech not to mark the inconsequence of face-to-face encounters but as the very means to generate them.

Both films insist on the immediacy of the voice and the irreducibility of its physical context. But their insistence is dependent on technologies of recording that must be disavowed and whose disavowal renders the situations of the films' speakers deeply contradictory. Neff's Dictaphone is the reason he's speaking from his office; Vargas's transmitter is what puts him in the same physical space as Quinlan; and each recording is meant to be used as evidence in the legal cases that will decide the criminals' fate. In each case, though, recording technology abruptly disappears from the scene,

FIGURE 2.3. Under the bridge: the physical proximity of recording in *Touch of Evil.*

leaving behind a physically present voice that no longer has a clear reason for speaking aloud. (Moreover, both Neff and Quinlan die at the ends of their respective films, meaning that the recordings no longer have much legal use either.) On one hand, the situation of the noir speaker is clearly determined by the technologies that prompt him to speak. On the other hand, because a recorded voice need not be physically present, the situation produced by recording technology is a fundamentally unstable one, an instability that must be forgotten in order to situate the speaker in a reliable, concrete context. The recording machine—Neff's Dictaphone, Vargas's transmitter—is nothing less than noir's deus ex machina; it arrives solely to bring the voice into being, and then it promptly disappears. Noir's abiding commitment to its speaker's context forces it to rely on, even as it disavows, a technology that calls the very idea of context into question.

The fault line at the heart of noir film is the attempt to situate a speaker through technologies that suggest there is no longer so simple a thing as an immediate situation. How do we know where we are or where we are speaking from if our recorded voice can speak anytime, from anywhere? The question is not a purely hypothetical one. It is also the basic mechanism of suspense in another classic midcentury noir, *Laura* (Otto Preminger, 1944). *Laura* brings the contextual paradox of the recorded voice to the fore, using technologies of transcription and recording to represent the possibility of being present in two places at once. The film begins with Waldo Lydecker's voice-over narration speaking over a scene in which Detective MacPherson roams through Lydecker's apartment, from which Lydecker himself appears to be absent. Eventually, MacPherson bursts into the bathroom, where we discover that Lydecker is home after all, sitting in the bathtub with a typewriter in his lap, typing the very words we have just heard his disembodied voice speak (figure 2.4). *Laura* thus begins with a clever inversion: while the voice-over leads us to assume that the owner of the voice is absent—an assumption that appears to be confirmed by MacPherson's snooping—both Lydecker and his typewriter (the transcribing technology that would have allowed the severing of words from their source) turn out to have been there with us in the apartment all along.

This inversion of the disembodied voice functions as a prelude to the more elaborate trick that *Laura* plays at its end. Warned that Lydecker is coming to kill her, Laura locks herself in her apartment and turns on the radio—only to hear Lydecker's voice speaking to her through his weekly

FIGURE 2.4. Voice-over as typewriter in *Laura*.

radio address. She is not alarmed, and why should she be? After all, the technology of the radio explains how we can hear a voice whose speaker is not himself in the room with us. The technology of recording, by contrast, does exactly the opposite; it enables the person who has previously recorded his weekly radio program to be speaking over the radio and at the same time standing right beside us. Such is the situation Laura is startled to discover. Listening to his voice on the radio, Laura looks up to see Lydecker standing there in the flesh, just as a second voice cuts in on the radio to say, "You have heard the voice of Waldo Lydecker by electrical transcription." Turning the ostensibly live transmission into an "electrical transcription," recording is not what severs Lydecker from his voice but what allows the two to merge back together, back in the room with Laura, waiting to kill her.

The contradictions of recording and displacement echo in *Laura*'s unlocatable last words, which have their own odd echo. In the film's final sequence, Lydecker is shot by Detective MacPherson and his fellow policemen. As he slumps to the floor, Lydecker gasps, "Good-bye, Laura." The camera then pans to a broken clock and lingers there for a few moments longer than is comfortable, until we hear Lydecker's voice one last time:

"Good-bye, my love." The sound of this second good-bye poses some problems. "From where do these words come?" asks Copjec.

Not from Lydecker, clearly, as he lies dead on the floor. The final living words issued from the diegetic space of Laura's apartment and from the visibly wounded body of Lydecker, but these words emerge from elsewhere. The difference between the two spaces is audible in the lack of room tone in the second "good-bye." This suggests that the final line was, like Lydecker's radio address, recorded in a sound studio, not on the film set and thus not from the diegetic space the film creates. In narrative terms, we would locate the place of their enunciation on the other side of death, somewhere beyond the grave.[33]

Of course, Copjec clarifies, "*Laura* is no horror film." How, then, are we to situate or make sense of these last words? The problem here is one of recording, and of the different "tones" that different recordings produce. The paradox of the speaking dead is replaced by the plane of the "electrically transcribed" voice, which emanates not from the beyond of the afterlife or from the inside of a coffin but from a decidedly smaller and less gothic box: the mechanical apparatus of the radio. Though we are not necessarily hearing a voice from "beyond the grave," we are still—through the dislocations of recording and radio—hearing a voice-over that is radically discontinuous with the film's diegesis. This discontinuity defines the nature of the voice in *Laura*. Resisting its apparent kinship with the supernatural, *Laura* instead registers the shock of the voice's technological abstraction. The point of Lydecker's final words is to have the final word on the impossibility of situating the voice-over, which up to now has kept reappearing in the apartment every time we assumed it was elsewhere. This reappearance is less a reassurance that the voice can be physically located than a simple reminder that the noir voice is never where we think it is. *Laura*'s last lines reveal the fundamental dislocation of Lydecker's voice, a dislocation whose source and symbol alike are his intimate relation to radio and recording. Neither absent nor present, neither immediate nor deferred, the voice in *Laura* has a strangely contradictory role: it surveys a particular historical moment—the radio age—while also showing how emergent technologies make it harder to tell what belongs to a given moment and what, to our horror, might escape it.

FIGURE 2.5. *Sunset Boulevard*: a tale told by a corpse in a pool.

Copjec may be right that *Laura* is no horror film. But what about *Sunset Boulevard* (Billy Wilder, 1950), which is, as everyone knows, narrated by a dead man? The film opens with the voice-over narration of Joe Gillis, who promptly identifies himself as the body we see floating facedown in a swimming pool (figure 2.5). This would seem to be the moment at which noir stops pretending that the voice-over is coming from any particular place in the diegetic present and acknowledges the voice's affiliation with that most supernatural or content-less context, death itself.

A rarely noted fact about *Sunset Boulevard*, however, is that Wilder originally intended to give Gillis's ghostly narration a more definite location. As Ed Sikov explains in his biography of Wilder, *Sunset Boulevard* was set to be released with a different opening, which would have followed earlier noir films by beginning with a frame story situating the voice in a particular physical location. That location was to be the morgue, where Gillis's dead body would be seen regaling the other corpses with the story of his murder. The original script described the opening scene this way:

An attendant wheels the dead Gillis into the huge, bare, windowless room. Along the walls are twenty or so sheet-covered corpses lying in an orderly row of wheeled slabs with large numbers painted on the walls above each slab. . . . The attendant exits, switching off the light. For a moment the room is semi-dark, then as the music takes on a more astral phase, a curious glow emanates from the sheeted corpses.[34]

The "sheeted corpses" then begin to chat—"Don't be scared. There's a lot of us here. It's all right"—and it is in this context that Gillis's story, like Neff's address to Keyes, unfolds. This attempt to situate the narrating voice evoked so much laughter in preview screenings that it was cut from the film at the last minute. Sikov sets the scene: "They took it to Evanston, Illinois, just north of Chicago. The lights went down and the film began. The camera rolled down Sunset Boulevard and into the morgue, the corpses started talking, and the audience erupted into peals of laughter."[35] The ostensible lesson of the anecdote is that the audience found the prospect of a dead narrator laughable. But isn't that exactly what *Sunset Boulevard* still has? What is most puzzling about the film's ill-fated framing device, then, is not why the audience laughed—ha, talking corpses!—but why, after the final cut of a film that is *still narrated by a talking corpse*, they stopped laughing.

The answer can only be that without having to see Gillis's body, the audience is now free to forget that the speaker is supposed to be dead. The possibility of forgetting this singularly important detail is no unintended consequence. The morgue is an all-too-literal reminder of where Gillis is speaking from, and the suppression of this reminder is what the film is all about. The story of *Sunset Boulevard* is in fact a story about forgetting that Gillis is dead. From the start, Gillis acknowledges that his story will be co-opted and his fate erased. As he puts it in his opening monologue, "But before you hear it all distorted and blown out of proportion, before those Hollywood columnists get their hands on it, maybe you'd like to hear the facts, the whole truth." The media, Gillis predicts, will write the story they want, and when they do, the essential fact to be "distorted" will be the literal fact of his own demise. If you've seen *Sunset Boulevard*, you know this is exactly what happens. In the closing scenes of the film, after Norma has murdered Gillis and the police have arrived at her house, a cop tries to phone the coroner ("Coroner's office? I want to speak to the coroner. *Who's on this phone?*"), only to be interrupted by the gossip columnist Hedda Hopper ("I am. Now get off! This is more important."). What underwrites the shift from coroner to gossip columnist is the sensationalism of the press, which is more interested in the salacious details of Norma's life than in the cold, hard fact of Gillis's death. However, as the film makes clear, this exploitative sensationalism is simply an extension of the normal functioning of Hollywood itself. There is, *Sunset Boulevard* argues in its closing scenes, no difference between the press and the movies—a point that the film, produced by Paramount Pictures, makes unmistakable when a Paramount News van packed with camera equipment pulls up in front of Norma's house. The reimagining of journalists as filmmakers is completed in *Sunset Boulevard*'s very last scene, in which the police lure Norma downstairs by encouraging her misrecognition of the press cameras as movie cameras. As she descends the stairs, her butler Max (played, in another cinematically self-aware move, by the Austrian director Erich von Stroheim) steps in to play the role of director, and the significance of Norma's famous (and famously misquoted) line—"All right Mr. de Mille, I'm ready for my close-up"—is her accidental insight that a media circus is indistinguishable from a movie set. For Norma, this mistake has one obviously positive upshot. If the arrival of the media has transformed Norma's life into a movie, this is a movie in which Gillis's death can become a purely cinematic fiction, a special effect or especially well-acted scene (figure 2.6).

The importance of *Sunset Boulevard*'s misbegotten frame story, then, is that it, too, is "distorted" and suppressed. The real meaning of Gillis's

FIGURE 2.6. All the world's a movie: Norma's final scene, directed by her butler, Max, who is played by the director Erich von Stroheim.

location in the morgue is that the film pretends it is *not* his location, and this kind of pretending is what the movie is all about. Indeed, it is what *all* movies are about. What else is the apparatus of cinema than a way of bringing the dead back to life? According to Mary Ann Doane, narrative cinema first emerged as a way to neutralize the shock of death: "The direct presentation of death to the spectator as pure event, as shock, was displaced in mainstream cinema by its narrativization. Technology and narrative form an alliance in modernity to ameliorate the corrosiveness of the relation between time and subjectivity."[36] With respect to this history, *Sunset Boulevard* both exposes the illusions of Hollywood movies and indulges them. These illusions, as J. Hoberman recognizes, have to do with cinema's capacity to simultaneously represent and repress death: "Even as it works to dispel the notion that motion pictures are made in heaven. . . . *Sunset Boulevard* evokes their uncanny aura—satirizing as it attests to the power of motion pictures to reanimate the past and restore the dead to life."[37] *Sunset Boulevard* critiques cinema's capacity for trivializing and misrepresenting the shock of death by calling attention to its own misrepresentation of Gillis's fate.

The "dream" afforded by cinema is what Norma "had clung to so desperately" and what, by the film's end, has "enfolded her." It is this same dream that, in both the film's story and its production history, allows *Sunset Boulevard* to pretend not to be a film narrated by a dead man. The laughable location of *Sunset Boulevard*'s voice-over is replaced in the end, as Norma says in the film's final lines, by "just us and the cameras—and those wonderful people out there in the dark." In the dark of the theater, what makes us wonderful is that we are willing to forget the thing whose literal truth we found too funny to believe, which is that the person telling us the story is also the person whose death the story depicts. Ultimately, the matter of life and death in *Sunset Boulevard* remains rooted in the paradoxical situation of the voice. In fact, Norma's downfall as a movie star is itself tied to a technological transformation concerning the voice: the invention of film sound. To be complicit in forgetting Gillis's death is to accept a world in which media—as both the apparatus of the film camera and the vocation of the gossip columnist—make it impossible to situate ourselves. Thus even though Gillis's voice cannot be traced to any particular time and place (at least not without prompting peals of laughter), it can be traced to the historical conditions of its dislocation. As in *Laura*, the media in *Sunset Boulevard* are at once the mark of a specific history and the means by which historical specificity—location and situation—is stretched to its breaking point. The dead narrator of *Sunset Boulevard* cannot be taken literally because he confronts us with a situation in which the voice has been displaced and dispersed, has been caught up in both the technology and the ideology of cinema, and has thereby been replaced by the provisional, mutable nature of situatedness itself.

In *Film Noir and the Spaces of Modernity*, Edward Dimendberg tells us that transformations in the nature of urban space and urban planning after 1939 led film noir to turn to media technologies of "simultaneity" as a means to "represent social life in an increasingly decentralized America knitted together by highways, radio, and television."[38] Besides representing social connection, these technologies also posed questions about sound and voice. The sound theorist Mladen Dolar claims that this was a uniquely acousmatic moment in media history, a time when voices were broadly severed from their sources: "Radio, gramophone, tape-recorder, telephone: with the advent of the new media the acousmatic property of the voice became universal, and hence trivial . . . we cannot see the source of the voices there, all we see is some technical appliance from which voices emanate, and in a *quid pro quo* the gadget then takes the place of the invisible source itself."[39] Classic film noir certainly testifies to the ubiquity of such "gadgets" (think of Mike Hammer's impressive telephone answering system in *Kiss Me Deadly* [Robert Aldrich, 1955]). In the cases I've discussed in this section, however, we see how these "trivial" technological artifacts produce a quite serious commentary on the paradoxes surrounding speech, speakers, and their situations. The media forms that underwrite noir express the emergent simultaneity of a technologically mediated society, a logic of simultaneity that disrupts not just (as Dimendberg argues) the social experience of city life but also the basic understanding of what it means to be present in a specific time and place. While sound technology situates noir in the increasingly mediated world of midcentury America, it also interrupts the dream of situated specificity. Neff's unnecessarily recorded confession, Lydecker's unlocatable last words, Gillis's repressed death: the noir voice-over both indexes and dislocates the speaker's specific situation. The context of classic film noir could thus be said to be its struggle with the slipperiness of context. The noir voice-over does not necessarily tell us where it's coming from. What it tells us is that the voice's invocation of context is beset by contradiction and that these contradictions are the products of the recording technologies that reshaped the nature of voice in noir's historical moment. From *Double Indemnity* to *Sunset Boulevard*, film noir's fixation on the question of where its speakers are speaking from reflects the genre's awareness of its own double-edged historical situation. This is a moment shaped by sound technologies that make it harder to believe in the self-contained substance of moments.

## BACK FROM THE GRAVE

Like Joe Gillis, noir itself just won't die. Although critics often assume noir to be "neatly contained in a perfect decade (1945–1955)," the genre had an active afterlife in the latter half of the twentieth century.[40] This begins with the well-known neo-noirs of the 1970s and 1980s—*The Long Goodbye* (Robert Altman, 1973), *Chinatown* (Roman Polanski, 1974), *Night Moves* (Arthur Penn, 1975), *Body Heat* (Lawrence Kasdan, 1981), and *Blood Simple* (Joel Coen, 1984), along with less auspicious remakes of *The Postman Always Rings Twice* (Bob Rafelson, 1981) and *D.O.A.* (Annabel Jankel and Rocky Morton, 1988)—which express the pessimism and paranoia of the post-Vietnam and post-Watergate eras. Starting in the mid-1990s, noir's revival began to seem fully nostalgic and self-referential, in films like *Pulp Fiction* (Quentin Tarantino, 1994), *L.A. Confidential* (Curtis Hanson, 1997), *Following* (Christopher Nolan, 1999), *Brick* (Rian Johnson, 2005), *The Man Who Wasn't There* (Joel Coen, 2001), *Sin City* (Robert Rodriguez, 2005), and *The Good German* (Steven Soderbergh, 2006). The last three films on this list represent the apogee of a style we might call *retro-noir*: all three are set in the past, shot in black-and-white, and pervaded by voice-over narration (which had fallen out of favor in 1970s neo-noir). The retro styling of these films has seemed to critics especially lifeless. Hoberman dismisses *Sin City* for precisely this reason: for trying to bring a long-dead genre back to life. As he wrote upon the film's release, "More than just the narrative comes full circle—in a way it's the history of pulp. All the visual ideas that the savvy comic-book artists of the '40s swiped from *Citizen Kane* return as the zombie accoutrements of pure digitalia."[41] For Hoberman, "the history of pulp" is a closed circle, a dead end; the aims or designs of genre are now nothing more than designer "accoutrements." In its brazen theft of styles that were stolen to begin with, retro-noir doesn't so much breathe new life into film noir as drag a once-buried genre back up from the grave.

But Hoberman is more than metaphorically right, as it is more than just genre that comes back from the dead in these films. It is also the dead themselves. A history of the noir voice-over must come to terms with this striking development: the narrators of recent noir films frequently turn out to be dead. Contemporary noir is shaped quite literally by the problem of revival, by a cast of speaking dead who ultimately bespeak the revivals of genre. The pseudo-supernaturalism of *Laura* and *Sunset Boulevard* now returns with a vengeance. To witness this return is to see recent retro-noir films as more than mere imitations. It is to see them, instead, as extending noir's abiding concern with situatedness by commenting on the cultural history of historicism that shapes their particular historical situation. These films do not revive a dead style. They depict and embody the temporality of revival itself. In doing so, they offer a commentary on how genre reframes the contemporary. Having begun at midcentury as an account of the difficulty of situating oneself in the present, film noir is now no less at home in our present, updating older concerns about the displacements of media to address the newer forms of historical mediation currently rooted in the commodified logic of genre.

I should note that the spectacle of the speaking dead is not exactly a rare sight in contemporary cinema. The secret of cinema in a digital age, Garrett Stewart argues in *Framed Time*, is its "phantom temporality."[42] For him, the transition in the 1990s from filmstrip to digital pixel has led to the recent proliferation of "time-warp plots," the most warped of which involve phantoms who don't yet know that they're dead. As Stewart explains, "Heroes or heroines (*The Sixth Sense, Vanilla Sky, The Others*) hunt down the mystery of ghostliness, or other related anomalies of embodiment, only to find that they have exposed the secret of their own previous and until-now unrealized murders." In Hollywood's "digital fantastic," the sequentiality embedded in the physical medium of film is replaced by the reversibility of the pixel, a reversibility that scrambles the temporal sequence of life and death, such that the dead, unaware of the fate that has already befallen them, simply go on walking and talking.[43]

The talking, I would say, is the interesting part. Film noir has long been haunted by the link between speaking and dying. "Nothing has seemed more obvious in the criticism of *film noir*," Copjec points out, "than this association of death with speech."[44] Kaja Silverman seconds this point: "The embodied male voice is likely to speak 'over' the image track only because of drastic circumstances, when it is (or recently has been) *in extremis*."[45] Even the films themselves agree with this assessment, as the noir-ish comic-book film *Kick-Ass* (Matthew Vaughn, 2010) tells us in voice-over: "And if you're reassuring yourself I'm gonna make it through this, since I'm talking to you now: quit being such a smart-ass. Hell dude—you never seen *Sin City*? *Sunset Boulevard*?"[46] In the last decade's retro-noir, the "association of death with speech" is made fully literal. The speaker's circumstances have become extreme indeed. The physical drama of revival plays an especially pronounced role in *Sin City*, whose characters cannot seem to stay dead. In one scene, Marv is strapped into the electric chair; the switch is pulled, his body gyrates gruesomely, and he slumps down as if dead, only to open his mouth and mumble, "Is that all you got?" Later, another of our hard-boiled protagonists, Dwight, is driving out of Old Town to get rid of the dead body of Jackie Boy. Jackie Boy's corpse is propped up in the passenger seat, and after a beat, it lifts its head—which has recently been impaled by a gun muzzle—and begins, croakingly, to speak (figure 2.7). This grotesque revival is rendered as mere matter of fact; the scene is given to us straight, with no visual cues of hallucination or ghostly visitation.

FIGURE 2.7. The speaking dead in *Sin City*.

Nothing at all seems askew—except, of course, the groaning corpse that happens to be sitting in the passenger seat giving Dwight advice. Dwight comments on the strangeness of the scene through his voice-over: "Sure he's an asshole; sure he's dead; sure I'm just imagining that he's talking. None of that stops the bastard from being absolutely right." In *Sin City*, it is not death that has the last word but the dead themselves.

What does it mean for the dead to speak? Narrative theorists have long been attentive to what Brian Richardson calls the "unnatural voices" of impossible or paradoxical narrators, narrators who blur Gerard Genette's well-known distinction between homodiegetic and heterodiegetic narration (narrators who belong to their story versus narrators who stand outside it).[47] Richardson himself sees these impossible voices as a defining feature of experimental writing in the second half of the twentieth century. But the question of the dead speaker has an even more privileged place in the history of literary theory. In his lecture at the historic "Languages of Criticism and the Sciences of Man" conference at Johns Hopkins University in 1966—widely considered the introduction of French theory to the American academy—Roland Barthes made the stray remark that it is impossible for speakers to announce their own death. "I can't say 'I am dead,'" said Barthes. Jacques Derrida raised his hand to disagree. Isn't there, he asked, an "extraordinary story" by Edgar Allan Poe in which a speaker says exactly those words?[48] There is indeed. "The Facts in the Case of M. Valdemar" tells the story of a man who is hypnotized right before the moment of his death and held in a trance so as to narrate the process of dying. After Valdemar appears to die, "a strong vibratory motion was observable in the tongue." Then "M. Valdemar *spoke*—obviously in reply to the question I had propounded to him a few minutes before. I had asked him, it will be remembered, if he still slept. He now said: 'Yes;—no;—I have been sleeping—and now—now—*I am dead.*'"[49] This sounds like supernaturalism. But the problem is not one of belief, plausibility, or the fantastic. The issue is far more quotidian: it is a problem of present time—or, to be precise, of the present tense. *When* are these words spoken? This is the question that Valdemar himself struggles to answer. In response to being asked whether he is still sleeping, Valdemar replies, "Yes;—no." The sticking point here is that the time of speaking can't quite be made to correspond to the linguistic tense he's required to use. So he corrects it to the present perfect ("I *have been* sleeping") and contrasts it with the immediate moment: "and now."

Why, though, does he say the word twice: "now—now"? Because he recognizes the temporal gap between the now of being dead and the now of saying so. The repeated "now" is Valdemar's attempt to pinpoint the exact moment at which the present of speech and the present of death resound together. But that moment never comes. Saying "now" and saying "I am dead"—just like saying "I am dead" and actually *being* dead—are separated in time by the simple act of speaking. The problem of being dead in "The Facts in the Case of M. Valdemar" is thus the same as the problem of being dead in film noir. It is the problem of being situated: of not being able to pinpoint where one's speech is coming from. To speak the words "I am dead" is to imply presentness, to intone immediacy, and at the same time to bespeak the very temporal process—from the word "I" to the word "dead" and from life to death—that undermines every claim to be in the "now." To speak of the now is to be forced to watch the now pass away before one has even finished saying the word.

The pressure that Valdemar's revival puts on presence is obviously one of the reasons Derrida found the story so appealing. Concluding his response to Barthes, he explained,

When I look for the *present* of discursive time, I don't find it. I find that this present is taken not from the time of *énonciation* but from a movement of temporalization which poses the difference and consequently makes the present something more complicated, the product of an original synthesis which also means that the present cannot be produced except in the movement which retains and effaces it.[50]

The present of speaking—the situation of enunciation—is constantly displaced by the time it takes to speak. For Derrida, this is proof of speech's secret subordination to what he later called the "drift" of writing (a point Barthes came to agree with when he revised his analysis of Valdemar to address Derrida's question at the "Languages of Criticism" conference). But this is not exactly the point of Poe's story. After all, Valdemar's words are not writing; they do not float free. All the trouble in the story stems from the fact that these words have been uttered *by* someone, that they are, as the narrator puts it, both a "sound" and a "voice." It is not hard to read or write the words "I am dead"; it is speaking the words that is the problem. It is a problem of speech's present: the "now—" that is both implied and displaced by a speaking voice we can't quite situate.

Returning to our present, we can see that it is the difficulty of pinpointing present time that retro-noir's dead speakers testify to. In these films, we can no longer figure out where the voice-over is coming from. This represents a clear departure from a film like *The Postman Always Rings Twice* (1946), which Frank Chambers narrates from death row. This location represents the truth of Frank's narration: it is both the explanation for why he's narrating and the system from which the narrator himself cannot escape. Remaking *Postman*, *The Man Who Wasn't There* tells the same story with only minor changes of names and subplots.[51] There is still a voice-over, and it still emanates from death row. Ed narrates the film from prison, where he has been asked to write a confession for a popular "men's magazine." In the film's final sequence, we see Ed finish writing his confession and then proceed to walk from his cell to the electric chair—while, throughout the scene, he continues to narrate. He speaks right up to the moment when he is restrained in the chair, the switch is pulled, and the screen fades to white. Ed's voice-over, like Frank's, eventually catches up to the story it's telling; but unlike Frank's, Ed's voice ultimately overtakes its own diegetic frame. This means that Ed is able to narrate not just the events leading up to his execution but also the event of his death itself, which he ironically describes as a way to find "all those things they don't have words for here."

If he's still speaking after he has stopped writing and left his cell, where is he supposed to be speaking from? Where does Ed find the words to describe the very thing "they don't have words for here"? This is the question, I've been arguing, that structures the noir voice-over, and it is one that gets a cannily uncanny answer in retro-noir. To return to *Sin City*, we find that speaking corpses are not only part of the film's plot but also part of its narration. The film's climactic unveiling of the otherworldly site of the voice-over happens to be one of the only moments in Rodriguez's otherwise panel-by-panel remake of Frank Miller's graphic novels that departs from its source material. At the end of Miller's novel *That Yellow Bastard* (book 4 of the Sin City series), Hartigan, the hard-boiled cop who has twice saved Nancy from the villainous child-molester Junior, kills himself. The how and why of Hartigan's suicide are less important than the precise sequence of his good-bye. In the third-to-last panels of Miller's text, Hartigan stares directly out of the page and aims his gun at himself as he gives the good-bye speech that appears verbatim in the film: "An old man dies, a young woman lives. Fair trade. I love you, Nancy." On the next page, spread out across the two penultimate panels, we see only a black background and large white letters spelling out "BOOM." The last pages of the novel then show us Hartigan's body—not centered on the page but set all the way to the far edge of the right panel—lying in the snow, with words beneath him, written in yellow, that read "The End."[52] Hartigan says good-bye, then he shoots himself. The end of his life is the end of his words as well as the end of the novel.

Miller is quite clear about this sequentiality. The gunshot comes at the last possible moment, after everything that needs to be said (Hartigan's confessions of forbidden love and suicidal honor) has been said. The film version of *Sin City*, however, reverses this sequence, exposing the paradox at the heart of the voice-over. In the film, Hartigan's speech, rendered in voice-over, appears to end with the words "Fair trade." At that point, he shoots himself, and the film reverts to a kind of photonegative image (white silhouettes overlaid on a black background) that is completely animated: the draining of detail and shading along with the replacement of live actors with animated sketches all suggest a kind of climactic transition from life to death, if not from film to comic. But this is neither the end of the film nor the end of the voice-over. It is only after Hartigan's body has slumped down into the snow that the final sentence of his good-bye speech is voiced: "I love you, Nancy." Suddenly departing from the novel that it has otherwise aimed to perfectly reproduce, *Sin City* turns Hartigan's last words into a voice that continues to speak—paradoxically and paradigmatically—after the moment of its death.

My claim is that the talking corpses of *Sin City* represent both the defining feature of retro-noir and the element that unifies the genre across time. In the most recent revival of noir, both the voice-over and the genre as a whole are revealed for what they really are: ghostly echoes, deathly reanimations, intrusions into the living present of forms from the far side of the grave. The most important thing that appears in these films is revival itself—the literal manifestation of film noir's historically uncanny relation to context. If film noir has always been a place where the dead have a voice, then we cannot be surprised to find the genre itself continuing to speak from beyond the grave. How it does so is the process I am calling "revival." This process is captured by the paradoxical temporality of the voice-over. The revived genre of contemporary noir makes revival itself the necessary figure for describing the genre's displaced historical situation. Revival teaches us how to situate a genre that doesn't seem to belong to our living present yet keeps coming back to life.

*The Good German* takes the vexed temporality of the voice-over to its limit, bringing the paradox of the speaking dead to bear on the fragile coherence of linear narrative.[53] The film uses three separate voice-over narrators—Jake, Tully, and Lena—with each speaking only once, piping up out of nowhere and disappearing just as unexpectedly. Tully is also the corpse that sets the film's mystery in motion, meaning that his voice-over is linked to a time that comes after his death. Tully's dissonant narration points to the voice-over's more general disruption of narrative time in *The Good German*. This disruption comes to a head in the third and final voice-over, which is spoken by Lena, the misguidedly "good" German of the title. Her voice-over is directly concerned with Tully's death, as Lena tells us that she was the one who killed him. Yet the revelation is stated with surprising flippancy, as if we already knew it: "I *had* to kill Tully," she says. Her confession is disorienting; the emphasis on the necessity of Lena's act takes for granted that we already know it was Lena who did it. She speaks as if the narrative has already identified her as the culprit, when in fact it's done no such thing. Lena's voice-over is thus strangely dislocated. Assuming that the diegesis has told us something it hasn't, Lena reveals that she herself doesn't know exactly where in narrative time she's speaking. The speaking voice's irreducibility to narrative time is confirmed by an interesting plot point: Lena never confesses her crime to any other character, so while the viewer knows the solution to the mystery, no one in the film ever figures it out. Just as the voice-over cannot be situated in narrative time, the information it conveys cannot be incorporated into the mechanics of the plot. In *The Good German*, the voice-over no longer bears any relation to the time or space of the narrative. Rather, the film insists on the ironic discontinuity that governs the relation between narrative events and the disembodied, disoriented voice that speaks over them. The undead temporality of the noir genre finds its fullest expression in the unknowable temporal coordinates of *The Good German*'s voice-overs.

The fluidity of generic time is formally registered in the floating voice-overs of *The Good German*. The film begins and ends, though, with more concrete invocations of genre's uncanny temporality. In the film's climax, Lena and her missing husband meet up—where else?—in a movie theater, which, we are told, is "in the French sector" (figure 2.8). What does it mean for an American film to visualize a French movie theater in postwar Europe? It means that the film is thinking of nothing less than the historical origins of film noir. Here is Marc Vernet's version of noir's displaced origin story: "The notion of *film noir* . . . was meaningful only for French spectators cut off from the American cinema during the war years and discovering in Paris during the summer of 1946, under the impetus of the

FIGURE 2.8. Postwar cinema: the origins of noir in *The Good German*.

Blum-Byrnes accords, a few detective films that would form the core of the genre."[54] The dislocations of the voice-over in *The Good German* are, in the end, simply echoes of the deeper dislocation that engendered the genre in the first place. In Soderbergh's film, film itself (in the form of the French movie theater in occupied Berlin) becomes a metaphor for the very process of transnational cultural exchange that, in the wake of World War II, produced film noir.

And it's not just a metaphor. The history of noir is more literally contained in *The Good German* from its the opening shots. The film begins with a montage of images of bombed-out postwar Berlin. This opening has an obvious intertext: *The Third Man* (Carol Reed, 1949), which begins exactly the same way. But *The Good German*'s montage is not merely an allusion to 1940s-era film; it is also an actual incorporation of it. These images, along with several other background shots used in the film, were taken from stock footage shot by directors in Germany right after the war, which Soderbergh and his crew found stored in several film archives. Some of the historical footage used in the film was shot by none other than Billy Wilder, intended for use in Wilder's *A Foreign Affair* (1948). Literally borrowing from one of the founding figures of midcentury noir, *The Good German* recovers and revives the very history it seems at first to only imitate. In doing so, it reminds us that film has the capacity not only to bring the dead back to life (as in Wilder's *Sunset Boulevard*) but also to literally splice together the histories of the dead and the living. Both the opening montage of period-produced stock footage and the climactic reference to the French theater show how genre governs the mise-en-scène of *The Good German*. The genre of noir explains how Lena can be in several places at the same time (a German character in an American film sitting in a French movie theater), and it also explains how a film like this one, shot in both 1948 and 2006, can be said to belong, in more ways than one, to two historical moments.

Writing on the fate of genre under late capitalist conditions of total commodification, Nicholas Brown encourages us to think of genre not as the main ingredient of pastiche or "null historicism" but as the grounds for a more "positive historicism": the history, condensed in an art object, of a particular form or formal problem.[55] In *The Good German*, *Sin City*, and *The Man Who Wasn't There*, that form is the noir voice-over, and the problem it poses *within* the films redirects the question that would otherwise be asked *of* the films: How are we supposed to situate them? The simple answer is that we can situate these films within the genre of film noir, and the deeper significance of that answer is that the problem of situating has been an essential part of noir since Walter Neff first picked up his Dictaphone. Genre, in other words, is both the source of and the solution to the problem of noir's revival. The figuration of revival in these films provides the lens through which we can look back and discover that the whole history of the noir genre has been a history of the disorientation, displacement, and unreliable immediacy that inhere in the voice-over—as well as in the anxieties of situatedness that continue to haunt our long postwar present.

The voice-over serves as noir's record of its own generic dynamics, an inscription of the temporal problems that come with bringing a genre back to life. The unsituated lives of the speaking dead are the very thing that consolidates noir across several different moments. These are the spirits that constitute noir's generic spirit—not just because they provide an allegory for genre's ghostly returns, but also because they represent the actual form to which noir continually returns. While it is no doubt absurd to think of the dead as literally speaking to us, there is nothing supernatural about the fact that cultural forms really do come back to life. Nor is there anything metaphorical in saying that these revivals put pressure on the predictable historicist impulse to situate each instance of noir in its own narrowly defined context.

"The ideology of a normative historicism," Eric Hayot laments, "structures the fabric of the literary profession."[56] Amy Hungerford agrees and thinks we ought to just go with the flow. The "solid dominance of historicism," she suggests, "represents not a wave but a tide, or even just the water we all swim in."[57] But what, in that case, is likely to be washed away? In her study of aesthetic categories, Sianne Ngai puts her finger on the pulse, and the weak point, of literary historicism:

"But surely what 'interesting' meant to Schlegel in the 1790s is categorically different from what it meant to James a century later! . . . Surely the agitated style you refer to as 'zany' in *Rameau's Nephew*, *The Gay Science*, and *I Love Lucy* cannot be individual instances of the same style. Are you not projecting the late twentieth-century zaniness of Lucille Ball's comedy back onto the older artifacts, thus violating their historical/cultural particularity?"

Let me address the criticism of this imaginary interlocutor (not a straw man, because his questions are quite legitimate). The "historical/cultural particularity" that would automatically require a late eighteenth-century German literary critic and a late nineteenth-century American literary critic to be treated in isolation from each other often seems presupposed rather than justified (and often is invoked in a way that seems to feel no need to justify itself). . . . A stronger response from a *longue durée* perspective is that the[se] . . . contexts are not really all that different.[58]

How can contexts that are a century and a continent apart be "not really all that different"? When we understand them to be bridged by something that measures historical time on a different scale—something like a style, a category, or a genre. These containers require us to zoom out, to broaden our view, and to reconsider how we correlate form and history, or how we might, in Ngai's words, "historicize differently."[59] Within the historicist culture that continues to dominate both our period and our profession, it is no surprise that noir's revivals would seem to be such scandalous affairs. The revivals and reappearances of genre raise difficult questions about a notion of "historical/cultural particularity" that is otherwise assumed a priori, and they call for a justification that historical microscopists (to borrow Hayot's apt description) "feel no need" to offer. Yet when Ngai says that the contexts of Schlegel and James or Nietzsche and Lucille Ball "are not really all that different," she is not repudiating context or abandoning history. Quite the contrary: she is asking the very question—What is a context?—that stands to revitalize a historicist method that has mistakenly deemed such a question too self-evident to require answering.

In that spirit, what would it mean to insist that the film noir of the 1940s and the film noir of the 2000s are not, in the end, all that different?[60] Such an insistence might allow us to notice, among other things, that the long postwar now bookended by noir is a period that undergoes a decisive transformation in its very sense of "the now." The postwar history called noir is, I would argue, a record of the changing experience of the present in late-twentieth-century U.S. culture. With its strange brew of immediacy and mediation, presence and dislocation, noir speaks both to the dizzying pace of technological change in the past sixty years and to the ways those changes redound on the basic situation of the present. The contemporary context capable of knitting together classic noir and its revivals—and that, as I argued in the introduction, underwrites the very emergence of "the contemporary" as a disciplinary category—is a context of heightened attention to the present as well as intensified uncertainty about it; or, to put a finer point on it, it is a situation of both increased awareness of the scope of the capitalist system and diminished ability to situate ourselves within that system.[61] These are the challenges—the disorienting scale of capitalism, the increasing subsumption of individuals into institutions[62]—that the scholarly commitment to specificity is one strategy for dealing with. But the principle of specificity is also a compromise, a bracketing of the totalities that expand within and across historical moments. The diminishment of scope produces diminishing returns. As Ted Underwood cautions, "Taken to an extreme, historical specificity can make itself disappear."[63]

We find a different response to the antinomies of the contemporary situation, I've tried to suggest, in the strangely persistent form of noir films. The speaking dead are one especially fanciful version of this response. But in view of the peculiar style of narration that unexpectedly links *Laura* and *Sunset Boulevard* to *The Good German* and *Sin City*, we must acknowledge that it is really the genre of noir as a whole, stretching out over time, that provides the most resounding response to the problem of situating ourselves in the contemporary moment—the problem, that is, of determining what the contours of the contemporary actually are. It is genre that instructs us not to be more specific but to expand our sense of how a situation, an institution, or an entire socioeconomic system holds together across time, despite either our best efforts or our unexamined assumptions.

## FAMILIAR HAUNTS

On the topic of the talking dead, there is one last thing we need to talk about. "I began with the desire to speak to the dead." These are not lines from another noir film, or from any sort of film, but the well-known opening words of Stephen Greenblatt's *Shakespearean Negotiations*, which have long been emblematic of the historicist turn I've been tracking in this chapter.[64] "The ghost story, the story in which the dead speak," writes Walter Benn Michaels, "is the privileged form of the new historicism."[65] As any good new historicist (Michaels included) would hasten to point out, Greenblatt confessed his dalliance with the dead the same year that Toni Morrison won the Pulitzer Prize for her ghost story *Beloved* (1988)[66] and just a few years before Derrida gave a talk at the University of California at Riverside entitled "Specters of Marx" (1993). Together, these conjurings can be said to inaugurate what Ian Baucom calls "our ghost-crowded age."[67] Our age of ghosts is the outward appearance of an era in which historicism itself has become both an intellectual stance and a cultural attitude. Michaels, for instance, reads *Beloved* as "a historicist novel," while Alan Liu describes "postmodern historicism" as a "pervasive sociocultural condition."[68] But none of this explains why such an implausible supernatural metaphor would become the emblem of the historicist culture of the late twentieth century. Even Greenblatt himself acknowledges the absurdity of his statement: "I knew that the dead could not speak." So why describe them as if they could?

Despite the sense of spectrality that is commonly associated with new historicism, Greenblatt doesn't say anything here about ghosts (and for all its apparent tendentiousness, his well-known reference to literary critics as "middle-class shamans" trades largely in the boilerplate of publishing house ad copy: they bring the past to life!). His emphasis, instead, is on the *speaking* part. Greenblatt's attempt to speak with the dead is in fact an attempt to name the very problem this chapter has sought to trace: the problem of the historical situation—that is, of historical particularity—as it relates to disembodied speech. Put this way, we ought to read the speaking dead less in terms of *haunting* than in the more mundane sense of the noun *haunts*: the places or contexts from which the dead, however unbelievably, are imagined to speak. In these terms, Greenblatt's desire to speak with the dead is really a desire to think about what constitutes a context. Beyond the ghost story, beyond the anecdote, beyond any other of its privileged forms, new historicism highlights the critic's conjuring of context.

The critical production of context is new historicism's most inescapable legacy. Surveying contemporary literary studies, Hayot concludes that "almost everyone now thinks 'new historically.'" This means the widespread inculcation of "a strong unstated theory of *era* as the final goal and subtending force of the intimacies of literary criticism."[69] The theory of era that Hayot identifies is the same theory that underlies Greenblatt's desire to hear the dead speak. It is the theory that assumes the dead are situated in a larger culture or context and that what they have to say is a means of discovering the essence of the era from which they're saying it. The premise of the theory is the idea that everything within an era is connected. Here is the true task of the new historicist: to make connections. The organizing, if often unspoken, question of every great new historicist work is, as Liu phrases it, "What is the connection? . . . What, that is, is the formal principle of connection holding plurality in unity? . . . what is the motive linking historical and literary fact—kings and plays, for example, or pigs and authority—within the unified, cultural artifact?" For Liu, new historicism is not a simple act of contextualization but a self-conscious commentary on the founding dilemma of literary criticism: the dilemma of coordinating "historical context and literary text." Trying to connect two very different things, such acts of coordination often end up feeling slightly embarrassing. Indeed, what new historicism most reliably produces, according to Liu, is a sense of its own embarrassment at making the connections that constitute a culture: "When I compare Wordsworth's picturesque eye to Bentham's panoptic inspector or the New Critics to the Civil War, I am embarrassed. All new historicists embarrass themselves in this manner; all create a metaphysical conceit of text-*like*-context as cryptoformalist as a Donne poem interpreted by the New Criticism."[70]

The more common name for this "metaphysical conceit" is *context*, which is both the product of connections (the homology between Wordsworth and Bentham reveals their shared context) and the retroactive justification for them (Wordsworth's and Bentham's shared context allows us to draw a homology between them). To contextualize or situate, then, is to privilege connection over causation, to replace historical determination with the innuendo of adjacency—history by power of suggestion. Greenblatt's desire to speak with the dead attests to the fragile and sometimes embarrassing nature of context that contemporary historicism simultaneously produces and assumes. To Liu, these contexts look like "metaphysical conceits," though we could just as easily call them ghostly apparitions: the spectral threads of homology and adjacency that knit together an entire historical era. In this way, the trick of new historicism is neither that it makes the dead speak nor that it speaks for them, but that it makes context itself seem simultaneously as concrete as an anecdote and as abstract as an analogy, or perhaps as immaterial as a ghost.

The fact that few critics writing today actively identify themselves as new historicists does not mean that the problems of context, connection, and mediation are no longer problems; it just means that these problems are now more widely taken for granted. Such problems hide behind a compressed historical focus and an emboldened empiricism that complains—not without merit—that the dead cannot *really* speak, without asking what the problem of the speaking dead actually is. It is not a problem of supernaturalism or shamanism, I have argued, but of the complicated and compromised nature of something else that has been haunting our discipline for some time: the specter of the specific historical situation.

The ghostliness, or critical abstraction, of context: this, finally, is what the dead speak to us about. While the metaphor of the speaking dead helps illuminate the work that goes into conjuring and consolidating the specificity of the past, it is most useful as a figure for understanding the ghostly or elusive status of the contemporary itself. In the context of the contemporary, the speaking dead invoke not the spectral persistence of the past but the ever present contradiction between experience and knowledge: between being *in* a context and understanding it *as* a context. On one hand, the present is what lives and what we live in; on the other hand, it is something we must consider dead—past, finished, closed off—before we can begin to fully know it. What is significant about the speaking dead is not only that they speak but also that they are dead, which is what makes it possible for us to know something about them. "What is 'living,'" David Simpson writes, "cannot be completely deciphered." This means there is something necessarily paradoxical about the "commitment to historicizing" the living present: "to live within a historical condition, even when hoping to see outside it, is still to live in it."[71] Still living in it (speaking) yet hoping somehow to get outside it (dying): this is how the speaking dead speak to the liminal status of our contemporary situation. What we talk about when we talk about the contemporary is, above all, the notion that we must get outside it before we can talk about it. There is more to contemporary life, after all, than merely living it. The figure for this paradox—as it materializes in new historicism, in film noir, and in the very logic of genre— is the corpse that keeps talking, finally able, in that contradictory state, to say something about its own situation. My point is that it says something about our situation too. To be contemporary is not necessarily to give up the ghost of things past. It's more like giving up the notion that, when it comes to our own living history, we aren't already a little bit ghostly ourselves.

# Chapter Three

# WAITING

## Mysterious Circumstances

I didn't know what I was waiting for, but something told me to wait.

RAYMOND CHANDLER

What is the meaning of their waiting?

SIEGFRIED KRACAUER

## UNSOLVED MYSTERIES

Literary critics' enduring interest in the figure of the detective is no great mystery. "The detective," in Shoshana Felman's famous account, "is only a detective in his (her) function *as a reader*."[1] Professional readers in the humanities may be comforted to see their own practices reflected in the well-founded suspicions of the detective. Canny detectives, no less than critical readers, know there is often more to a case, or a text, than meets the eye. Recently, however, this analogy has started to seem like a problem. In their much discussed essay "Surface Reading," Stephen Best and Sharon Marcus complain that readers who act like "deeply suspicious detectives" tend to "look past the surface in order to root out what is underneath."[2] Insisting that we should read not for what's hidden but for what's on the surface, Best and Marcus renounce the sort of reader who keeps faith in the existence of buried, disguised, or concealed meanings—the sort of reader who acts like a detective. Whereas Felman's suspicious reader assumes that one can truly know a text's "secret," Best and Marcus's surface reader rejects the presumption of epistemological "mastery," the self-aggrandizing belief that we can really know what lies beneath the surfaces of things. Even as they repudiate the *knowingness* of the detective, however, Best and Marcus reaffirm the value of knowledge as such. Surface reading may be a critique of the "excavation of hidden truths," but it is also an attempt to reclaim the "taboo" values of "objectivity, validity, truth" and to produce "more accurate knowledge about texts."[3] In their embrace of both modesty and accuracy, naïveté and empirical knowledge, Best and Marcus seem to have more on their minds than just the suspect practice of suspicion. As an intervention in the history of literary criticism, "Surface Reading" reminds us that this is a history not simply of how we read but of what we can know. The authors of "Surface Reading" are interested in reading less deeply because they want to be able to know things more certainly.

From this perspective, it looks as if Best and Marcus's commitment to "objectivity, validity, truth" is a hedge less against the immodesties of suspicion than against the uncertainties of literary interpretation, a practice whose watchwords since the middle of the twentieth century have been *uncertainty, ambiguity,* and *indeterminacy.* In *Seven Modes of Uncertainty,* C. Namwali Serpell suggests that uncertainty began as an aesthetic principle of modernism, only to become, starting at midcentury, an ethical value for literary criticism.[4] New criticism, deconstruction, affect theory, the new ethics: many different twentieth- and twenty-first-century critical movements have taken uncertainty to be both an object and an aim of criticism. The study of literary uncertainty tends to reinforce the uncertainty of literary study. Contemporary critics expect their investigations to be inconclusive; such inconclusiveness is its own reward. Dorothy Hale sums up this position when she claims that literature enables "the overthrow of epistemology by experience, the troubling of certainty by an apprehension that comes through surprised feeling."[5] Yet the "troubling of certainty" is itself what seems to trouble Best and Marcus, just as it worries one of the inspirational figures behind their essay: Bruno Latour. "Do you see why I am worried?" Latour frets in "Why Has Critique Run Out of Steam?" (one of the most cited essays of the twenty-first century). "I myself have spent some time in the past trying to show ' "*the lack of scientific certainty*" ' inherent in the construction of facts. . . . But I did not exactly aim at fooling the public by obscuring the certainty of a closed argument—or did I?"[6] The struggle to wrest a realm of certainty from a realm of uncertainty motivates the turns to surface, sociology, statistical analysis, and description that today constitute a kind of New Empiricism of literary study.[7] These are blunt instruments, to be sure.[8] Yet there is no doubt that in an age when uncertainty has clearly become an ideological weapon (in climate change denial and antiscience skepticism)[9] no less than a lived condition (in the widespread circumstances of economic precarity), it is worth asking slightly more suspicious questions about the logic of uncertainty that has shaped literary texts and their study for the past sixty years. Such questions suggest a new use for that summarily dismissed figure of suspicion, the detective. If we really want to understand how the dynamics of certainty and uncertainty, the tensions of knowing and unknowing, have played out during the twentieth century, we do not necessarily need a whole new way of reading. We could simply start by rereading an old-fashioned genre—the detective novel.

From its inception, detective fiction has concerned itself with the question of what we can know about the world. The detective's "goal," as Ronald R. Thomas writes in *Detective Fiction and the Rise of Forensic Science*, "is to explain an event that seems inexplicable to everyone else." The special power of explanation is harnessed by turning to empirical, observable facts. Beginning in the nineteenth century and continuing through the twentieth, Thomas argues, the literary history of the detective novel "coincide[s] with periods of unprecedented inventiveness in developing practical forensic devices that extended the power of the human senses to render visible and measurable what had previously been undetectable."[10] Relying on the forensic logics of visibility and measurement, the detective produces reliable knowledge of the empirical world. In this way, the classic detective story promises what the critic Dennis Porter calls "an end that is always in some sense looked forward to as an end to contradiction and uncertainty."[11]

But the genre of detective fiction not only traces the rise of forensic reason and epistemological resolution; it also records their fall. The story of the detective novel in the twentieth century is largely a story about the steady intrusion of doubt and uncertainty into the detective's world. In *Gumshoe America*, Sean McCann suggests that the experience of doubt first takes the form of early-twentieth-century skepticism about the fantasy of civil society implicit in the nineteenth-century detective stories of Edgar Allan Poe and Sir Arthur Conan Doyle. For McCann, hard-boiled writers like Dashiell Hammett, Raymond Chandler, and Chester Himes document the "fall of New Deal liberalism" by voicing their suspicions about the stability of liberal consensus.[12] The political disappointment that shaped the hard-boiled style of the first half of the twentieth century became, in the second half of the century, a growing disillusionment with rational epistemology as such. As McCann and Michael Szalay observe in their intellectual history of the 1960s, this was a cultural moment in which "complaints against science and rationality became increasingly common, and invocations of the irrational and mysterious took on newfound authority."[13] The emergent cultural authority of the "irrational and mysterious" is nowhere clearer than in late-twentieth-century changes to the mystery genre itself. Whereas Doyle's Sherlock Holmes could isolate more than "fourteen [separate] characteristics" unique to a particular typewriter ("there is some little slurring over of the 'e,' and a slight defect in the tail of the 'r'") and thereby positively identify the criminal who used it, Thomas Pynchon's Oedipa Maas struggles in vain to interpret the overwhelming mass of evidence accumulating around her (scrawled post horns, W.A.S.T.E. receptacles, doctored stamps) and ends up unable to conclude anything at all.[14] In the history of detective fiction, the dream of Enlightenment reason runs aground on the drama of postmodern indeterminacy. The countertradition of indeterminate detective fiction that runs from Pynchon to Roberto Bolaño marks the point at which the nineteenth-century ur-genre of scientific authority morphs into its opposite, collapsing into the ambiguity of what Porter dubs *anti-detection*, in which "what is missing in the end is the satisfaction of desire that comes from 'knowledge.'"[15] Paul Auster, describing the amateur detective of his *City of Glass*, inscribes the motto of his era of anti-detection: "He had nothing, he knew nothing, he knew that he knew nothing."[16]

But what does it mean to know nothing—and to know that you know nothing—at the end of the twentieth century? It might mean that we are living in a world "driven increasingly by a dynamic of *nonknowledge*."[17] This is one critic's description of the epistemology that underlies what Ulrich Beck calls contemporary "risk society," a society in which we become increasingly aware of how little we know about the risks that surround us. In Beck's account, risk society represents a phase of "advanced modernity" defined by the "production, definition, and distribution of techno-scientifically produced risks."[18] The thing about risk, though, is that it is invisible, potential, speculative. A society defined by risk is a society defined by the unknown rather than the known. Risk society thus represents a world in which "unknown and unintended consequences come to be a dominant force in history and society." The unintended and the unknown are the conceptual pillars of a world in which "ultimately *no one can know about risks*" because risks cannot be seen, experienced, or empirically verified. In risk society, "everyday thought . . . [is] *removed from its moorings in the world of the visible*," and so the very possibility of empirical knowledge is dissolved.[19] Faced with so many invisible hazards, unpredictable threats, and unintended side effects, all we can know is how little we can know about the risks that proliferate throughout our present. This paradoxical knowledge of our own nonknowledge suggests a new way of making sense of the postmodern anti-detective novel. In the late twentieth century, the uncertainties of detective fiction reflect nothing less than the fundamental uncertainty—the hazardous, irreducible mystery—of a present that is constantly yet invisibly at risk.

Today it is no longer just techno-scientific risk (pollutants, toxins, pharmaceutical side effects) that hang like a cloud over the world. It is also a new kind of geopolitical risk. The idea of unforeseeable political violence is associated most famously with the events of September 11, which, despite having obvious historical and political causes, were widely described as "definitively unpredictable."[20] The discourse of unpredictability served to establish September 11 as a paradigmatic instance of the terrifying uncertainty under whose shadow we are condemned to live. The diffuse uncertainties of risk society come together in the metonym "9/11," an easily pronounced placeholder for the unending anticipation of some unpredictable catastrophe. What Brian Massumi calls the "climate of uncertainty" in the air after September 11 cultivated a politics of the unknowable, a form of governance (instantiated in the so-called Bush Doctrine of preemption and enacted in the endless war on terror) that was founded on the assumption that the United States could never adequately imagine, let alone foresee, the unknown threats it faced.[21] As Massumi explains, "The uncertainty of the potential next is never consumed in any given event. There is always a remainder of uncertainty, an unconsummated surplus of danger."[22] Preemption makes uncertainty the new rule of geopolitics. Such a rule is immune to disproof. The uncertainty of threat, whether from toxins or terrorists, is as unconfirmable as it is inexhaustible.[23]

Faced with the inexhaustible uncertainty of a world at risk, it may now be the aesthetic of uncertainty that has exhausted itself. As the world becomes more uncertain, uncertainty becomes a more dubious ideal. But what comes after uncertainty? To answer that question, this chapter examines three twenty-first-century detective novels—Michael Chabon's *The Yiddish Policemen's Union*, Vikram Chandra's *Sacred Games*, and China Miéville's *The City and the City*—that, in both their form and their politics, express a changed relationship to uncertainty. These novels seek a solution to the uncertainties that enthrall and confound our contemporary moment. They find it, I suggest, not in the usual place we find detective fiction's solutions—in the narrative's ending—but in the *wait* we undergo before we get there. The wait in these novels is both a symptom of and a hedge against a cultural logic of uncertainty. On one hand, waiting reflects what it's like to live in a state of endless anticipation and constant worry. On the other hand, waiting complicates the very nature of expectation, drawing our attention away from the unknown future and back toward the unfurling conditions of the present. Although waiting invariably springs from a state of uncertainty or delay, in Chabon's, Chandra's, and Miéville's novels, it also affords us a brief, time-bound confrontation with uncertainty's others: certainty, knowledge, belief. It does so by reminding us that knowing takes time. Responding to a geopolitical conjuncture that increasingly exploits and thrives on uncertainty, these new novels of the wait rethink the relation between the known and the unknown by showing us how knowledge plays out, dialectically, over time.

The standard assumption about detective fiction is that everything that matters happens at the end. The end is where we discover the solution that is the point of both the detective's work and the reader's. The blood of detective fiction's form (no less than the blood that launches its mystery) rushes right to its ending. The presumption of this narrative physiology leads Franco Moretti to conclude that detective fiction is itself only a means to end: "Detective fiction's ending is its end indeed: its solution in the true sense. The *fabula* narrated by the detective in his reconstruction of the facts brings us back to the beginning; that is, it abolishes narration. Between the beginning and the end of the narration—between the absence and the presence of the *fabula*—there is no 'voyage,' only a long *wait*."[24] By fulfilling the promise of resolution and reinstating the law and order of utter explicability, the detective story, in Moretti's view, cancels itself out. The solution to the mystery "abolishes" a story whose sole point was to transport us to the solution. So "what happens," Tzvetan Todorov asks, in the normal narrative of detection? "Not much. The characters of . . . the investigation do not act, they learn. Nothing can happen to them."[25] At the very last moment, the investigator learns, explains, names names (Moretti: "only the name of the murderer counts").[26] Before that, there is nothing to do but wait.

The wait, Moretti and Todorov imply, is simply a waste. That is why, once closed, neither the case nor the book has much need of being reopened. Moretti asks rhetorically, "Who, in fact, ever 're-reads' a detective story?"[27] Actually, plenty of people. Like the writer P. D. James: "I enjoy rereading my favourite mysteries although I know full well how the book will end."[28] And the critic Fredric Jameson: "Inveterate readers of Chandler will know that it is no longer for the solution to the mystery that they reread him."[29] Whereas Moretti assumes that the appearance of the solution is the only reason for reading a mystery, both James and Jameson suggest another possibility: What if the solution isn't what we're reading for?

While it's easy to imagine that the point of reading is to get to the end, the frequent disappointment of endings is enough to make even some of the great theorists of narrative endings reconsider. Take Peter Brooks, whose famous *Reading for the Plot* describes "the active quest of the reader for those shaping ends that . . . promise to bestow meaning and significance on the beginning and the middle," but who admits that the promise of the end is often left unfulfilled: "We know that any termination is artificial, and that the imposition of ending may lead to [our] resistance to the end."[30] Endings are an imposition, in both senses. We desire and abjure them in equal measure. No less an authority on endings than Frank Kermode warns that "to seek an answer is to be disappointed."[31]

With the inevitability of this disappointment in mind, we may begin to rethink the concluding satisfactions of the detective novel. In *Resisting Arrest*, Robert A. Rushing insists that scholars of detective fiction mistakenly "believe that the genre delivers satisfaction through the solution of the mystery when, in fact, *no one is satisfied by the solution*."[32] One reason for our dissatisfaction is the dispiriting realization that, as readers, we are not actually capable of solving the mystery ourselves.[33] The first "Rule for Writing Detective Stories" set forth in 1928 by S. S. Van Dine in his famous manifesto was "1. The reader must have equal opportunity with the detective for solving the mystery."[34] As Rushing points out, however, this rule "virtually never describes the compact between author and reader. On the contrary, even a cursory glance through detective fiction will show that the mystery's solution almost invariably involves subtle but important facts that were concealed from the reader, or depends on esoteric knowledge the reader is almost certain not to possess."[35]

Mysteries, we inevitably discover, are not solved by a shared commitment to logic but by some capricious, unforeseeable interpretive leap. Even Poe knew this. The inventor of the "tale of ratiocination" understood the inherent irrationality of the detective's display of rational prowess. As he announces in the opening sentence of "The Murders in the Rue Morgue" (widely considered the first detective story written in English), "The mental features discoursed of as the analytical are, in themselves, but little susceptible of analysis."[36] Here in the founding words of the genre, Poe admits that there is no way to explain the detective's special power to provide an explanation. From the inexplicability of Dupin's methods (which "have, in truth, the whole air of intuition")[37] to the loose ends that Chandler famously failed to tie up in *The Big Sleep*, there is always a frisson of uncertainty that lingers in detective fiction's endings.[38]

If that's the case, then it doesn't make sense to think of the detective genre as being defined by its solutions. The essence of the genre must lie elsewhere, not in the ending, but in the temporal distance *between* reading and ending—in the built-in delay that makes the reader wait.[39] To assume that the meaning of the detective story lies in its end (whether fulfilling, disappointing, or altogether absent) is to miss the crucial way that detection, structured by delay, situates meaning in time. The temporal form of waiting is the real secret of detective fiction. In the lag between reading and revelation, we confront not just the anticipation of narrative fulfillment but also the anguish of unfolding time. Although the detective story promises to tell us what we want to know, its true function is to remind us again and again that, as readers embedded in time, we do not know everything yet.

So what—to echo Kracauer's question in the epigraph to this chapter— does it really mean to wait? Of course, this question could be asked of every detective novel. It has begun to be asked by detective novels themselves, however, only in the past ten years, in the context, I've suggested, of a contemporary moment increasingly in thrall to the logics of uncertainty and anticipation. Expressing new uncertainties about the contemporary value of uncertainty, Chandra, Chabon, and Miéville deploy the detective genre in order to confront waiting as both a formal problematic and a thematic problem. For these authors, the detective's literal experience of waiting launches a deeper literary investigation into the epistemological and political consequences of the durations that inhere in detection. At the ends of *Sacred Games*, *The Yiddish Policemen's Union*, and *The City and the City*, each detective is left waiting, but not because a solution has been withheld. On the contrary, mysteries are solved, murderers named, conspiracies, if not thwarted, at least brought to light. If the detectives have all the answers, what are they waiting for? The reassertion of waiting in these novels registers a growing ambivalence about uncertainty itself. Having learned the lessons of postmodernism, these authors cannot fully commit to epistemological certainty. Having learned the lessons of the world around them, they also realize that they can no longer afford not to.

Waiting is what it looks like to accept and to question uncertainty at the same time.[40] To understand how this works, we can think of the detective's wait as a corollary to what Amy Hungerford, in *Postmodern Belief*, describes as the contemporary "belief in meaninglessness." For Hungerford, empty or content-less belief works to "bridge the gaps between conviction and relativism." In doing so, it provides a counterpoint to postmodern culture's "celebration of endless indeterminacy."[41] Reframing indeterminacy as duration, the detective novels I examine in this chapter bridge the same gap by reimagining waiting as a form of knowing. The long wait of the detective genre (embedded in every detective novel but made manifest only in the contemporary detective novel) discloses the temporal mediation of meaning: the ways that reading and knowing are subject to time. As we become aware of how time shapes knowledge, we may also learn something new about the nature of contemporary time—the ever changing circumstances of a present that, though it may be temporarily unknown, is not, in the end, unknowable.

## THE LONG WAIT

The wait that structures both *Sacred Games* and *The Yiddish Policemen's Union* begins when the personal becomes political. Detectives Sartaj Singh and Meyer Landsman repeatedly uncover the persistence of political and cultural tensions roiling beneath seemingly personal crimes, the specter of mass violence implied by the stink of a single corpse. The corpse that begins *Sacred Games* is that of Mumbai crime boss Ganesh Gaitonde, who has killed himself (along with his platonic love interest, Jojo) while hiding out in a bomb shelter. In his attempt to reconstruct what happened to

Ganesh, Sartaj discovers a more urgent and still active plot: Ganesh had been working for a powerful Hindu guru, and right before Ganesh died, he unwittingly helped Guru-ji smuggle a nuclear bomb into Mumbai. Guru-ji plans to detonate the weapon in the middle of the city and blame it on a fake Islamic fundamentalist group, the Hizbuddeen (Army of the Final Day), in order to incite a war between India and Pakistan. "Every golden age," Guru-ji tells Ganesh, "must be preceded by an apocalypse. It has always been so, and it will be so again. . . . Every great religious tradition predicts this burning, Ganesh. We all know it's coming."[42] The spiritual distinction between hero and villain—Sartaj is a Sikh who no longer believes in God, Ganesh is a recent convert to Hinduism and a devout disciple of Guru-ji—is in fact a disagreement over the present's relation to the future. Guru-ji's aim is to bring about the end of the world in order to replace the fallen present with a redeemed future, while Sartaj, striving to save the present from the future, must prevent the end from ever arriving.

The body that Landsman finds at the beginning of *The Yiddish Policemen's Union* belongs to Mendel Shpilman, the disowned son of the most powerful rabbi in Sitka, Alaska. This body, too, contains political and religious multitudes. The local investigation into Mendel's murder reveals a globe-trotting plot—organized by Sitka's Orthodox Jews and backed by the United States government—to bomb the Islamic shrine in Jerusalem (which, in Chabon's counterfactual globe, is part of Palestine), rebuild the Jewish Temple there, and "hasten the coming of Messiah."[43] As in *Sacred Games*, the prospect of religious violence hanging over *The Yiddish Policemen's Union* is tied directly to the frustration of prophecy's unfulfilled promise. Tired of the endless deferral of messianic redemption, Rabbi Shpilman, like Guru-ji, conspires to realize the dream of the distant future in the immediate present, to "basically *force* Messiah to come" (295, italics in original). The problem with the religious extremists who populate both books, then, is that they are unwilling to wait. "Theirs was not," Chabon's narrator remarks, "by definition an endeavor that attracted men with the talent for waiting" (339).

The mysteries of the particular dead bodies slowly fade into the background, replaced by more intractable political and religious conflicts. The inability to resolve the larger hostilities between Jews and Muslims, between Muslims and Hindus, and between India and Pakistan is one reason both detectives feel fairly hopeless about resolving their cases. Sartaj laments,

"In this Gaitonde affair, there would be no justice, no redemption. There was only a hope for some partial explanation of what had happened" (557). What's odd, though, is that there is in fact a full "explanation" of the "Gaitonde affair," and "justice" too. Guru-ji's plot is foiled; his men are apprehended; their nuclear weapon is confiscated. Landsman similarly expresses a hopelessness about his case—"So the killer of Mendel Shpilman, whoever it was, is walking around free. So, so what?" (397)—that is at odds with its apparent resolution. Just a few pages after Landsman's shrugging abdication, Mendel's killer remains neither anonymous ("whoever it was") nor free; Landsman's Uncle Hertz has confessed to the crime and is, we are assured, "already under arrest" (405). So why, when they are right on the verge of solving these mysteries, do Sartaj and Landsman accept the utter hopelessness of finding solutions?

These moments of hopelessness simultaneously point to and depart from the recent lineage of the detective genre, which has made the inconclusive or uncertain solution a familiar feature of the genre. The surprise in these novels is the discovery that there are facts yet to discover. Like Sartaj and Landsman, we are quite willing to accept that these mysteries are unknowable—and like them, we are wrong. Still, a sense of anticipation does linger beyond the closed case in these novels. Call it a shift from the unknowable or unpredictable to the *unresolvable*: from epistemology or prediction to politics as such. The feeling of waiting that haunts both detectives registers the unresolved political crises that structure the novels, the social tensions and religious conflicts that pose a constant threat. Here waiting is no longer waiting to know something. Rather, it is waiting to see how the detective's knowledge will turn out to make a difference—or not to— in the world at large.

Landsman is disappointed at the end of *The Yiddish Policemen's Union* because although he has unmasked the participants in the conspiracy, he has not prevented their plans from being carried out. At the end of the novel, the bombing of Qubbat As-Sakhrah still takes place. The final scene of Uncle Hertz's confession is set directly against the aftermath of the bombing; the epistemological order putatively restored by the naming of the murderer is juxtaposed to the political chaos of a world teetering on the brink of apocalyptic conflict: "All these people rioting on the television in Syria, Baghdad, Egypt? In London? Burning cars. Setting fire to embassies. . . . That's the kind of shit we have to look forward to now" (406). Solving the case has ultimately revealed how far Landsman is from being able to resolve the social instability that has exploded in the world around him.

In *Sacred Games*, Sartaj experiences a different kind of disappointment. Having successfully stopped the terrorist plot, all he can think about is the possibility of the next one. Prevention, after all, only forecloses closure. To stop one apocalyptic threat means having to wait for the next one. This much is made clear in the climactic scene of *Sacred Games*, in which Sartaj has tracked Guru-ji and his stolen nuclear weapon to a safe house in Mumbai. On the verge of apprehending the villains and averting apocalypse, Sartaj's partner Kamble is "rigid with excitement and anticipation" (875), while "inside the command post, there was an expectant silence . . . filled with waiting" (876). The anticipation leads to nothing. Despite both the expectations of the police force and the implicit promise of the text's omniscient narration, the successful raid on Guru-ji's hideout takes place entirely offscreen, beyond the purview of the narrative. Sartaj and Kamble are forced to wait in the command post "far away" from the action:

Nothing changed in the room, but then, from far away, came a series of pops, and then another, phap-phap-phap, phap-phap-phap-phap. And then a last little boom. A moment passed, and from the front of the room, a cheer grew and spread. Anjali Mathur came running through the clapping crowd. "We're safe," she said. "We're safe." (876)

The climactic confrontation between good and evil is reduced to a series of nonsense sounds, meaningless onomatopoeia. If the "series of pops" that began the detective's investigation promised an action-packed resolution, the "last little boom" registers the letdown that more often accompanies the end. At the end of the novel's labyrinthine plot, what we discover is the secret not of unknowability but of anticlimax. With respect to the global turmoil of which this particular case was only the smallest symptom, it is indeed true that "nothing changed." Sartaj considers the paradox of saving a world that will need to be saved again and again: "So, with those little banging sounds far away, apparently the world had been saved. Sartaj didn't feel any safer. Inside him, even now, there was that burning fuse, that ticking fear" (877). The gap between expectation and event reminds us once more of the peculiar nature of apocalyptic anxiety, which is fueled by something that hasn't happened—yet. The bottomless nature of this "ticking

fear" makes solving one particular case seem negligible, a purely temporary stopgap. Sartaj "trie[s] to feel satisfaction," but he can't (877). The feeling
of this failure—of the insignificant, impermanent nature of the solution—
is the feeling of waiting: "Sartaj stayed outside. He listened to the flapping
of the flag on the temple, and watched the water. He had the sense that
something was about to change. He was waiting. But he wasn't sure it ever
would" (880).

Both *Sacred Games* and *The Yiddish Policemen's Union* are haunted by
this letdown, the disappointment not of the unknown but of the futility of
knowing. As Chabon's narrator phrases it, "The exaltation of understanding, then understanding's bottomless regret" (400). The bottomless regret
triggered by understanding is the response to a world in which knowledge
is not enough to change things. At the end of these novels, neither detective is waiting for an answer; instead, the answer has left them waiting. The
efficacy of epistemological closure reaches its limit in the uncertain realm
of geopolitical catastrophe. The logic of the wait thus pivots on its axis. No
longer pointing toward an anticipated future, the wait redirects our attention to the complexity of a present in crisis. In this way, waiting becomes a
measure of knowledge's entanglement in time's unfolding. We know . . .
now what?

## BELIEVE IT OR NOT

Is waiting only an endless deferral, an absence of events, an erasure of
agency? Looking at the endings of these two novels, it might seem so. But
that may just be because Chandra and Chabon are engaged in questioning
the significance of detection's ends. More interested in waiting than in ending, both authors turn our attention to the logic of faith or belief that governs both the temporality of detection and the epistemology of a world at
risk. Risk, according to Beck, must "be *believed*" because it "cannot be experienced *as such*." In this way, belief becomes an expression of what it
means to live in the newly "*speculative* age" of risk society, a world whose
hazards can never be empirically perceived or confirmed.[44] Unconfirmed
belief is also the secret ingredient of detection's narrative form. While readers of detective fiction wait impatiently for the mystery to be solved, what
keeps them reading is the fact that they believe it will be. Between reading
and revelation, waiting represents a willingness to believe that the wait will

be worth it. In these two forms of belief—social and formal—we discover a more complicated or dialectical relationship between the speculative nature of risk and the structure of faith inscribed in the detective novel. Whereas risk indexes the disintegration of scientific knowledge, reading detective fiction allows us to keep faith with knowledge by recognizing it as a temporal problem, a matter of the time it takes to know.

The connection between waiting and belief was surprisingly central to the work of the Frankfurt school, for which it offered a way to respond to the depredations of urban modernity. For Siegfried Kracauer, waiting represents a much-needed solution to the crisis of faith in modern life, a way of assuaging the "metaphysical suffering" occasioned by the "lack of higher meaning in the world." Rejecting the responses of both the nihilistic skeptic and the "true believer," Kracauer concludes:

Perhaps the only remaining attitude is one of *waiting*. By committing oneself to waiting, one neither blocks one's path toward faith (like those who defiantly affirm the void) nor besieges this faith (like those whose yearning is so strong, it makes them lose all restraint). One waits, and one's waiting is a *hesitant openness*, albeit of a sort that is difficult to explain.[45]

The "openness" of waiting makes it a dialectical figure for grasping both the diminished possibility and the continued necessity of what Kracauer calls "communal belief." In a world where total belief is naive and total skepticism is disabling, the temporality of waiting represents a commitment to present time itself. "Waiting in the here and now," Kracauer writes, transforms faith from a foregone conclusion to a matter of time. It thereby reopens, however provisionally, the possibility of belief. Waiting "consists of tense activity and engaged self-preparation. It is a long path—or, better, a leap requiring a lengthy approach."[46] This anxious, engaged sense of anticipation—an attunement to the temporality of belief as "a lengthy approach" to knowing—provides an alternative predication for belief, a way to navigate between the opposing poles of rational skepticism and religious dogma that frame twentieth-century modernity. A similar sense of waiting as a dialectical form of faith is clearly at stake in Walter Benjamin's famously cryptic theory of messianic time. In the last of his "Theses on the Concept of History," Benjamin writes, "We know that the Jews were prohibited from investigating the future. . . . This does not imply, however, that for the Jews the future turned into homogeneous empty time. For every second of time was the strait gate through which the Messiah might enter."[47] In Benjamin's description of a messiah who "might enter" at any "second"—but who, so far, has not—we see once more that sense of "hesitant openness" described by Kracauer, a way of reframing messianic or revolutionary belief as a matter of being willing to wait. For both Kracauer and Benjamin, the "tense activity" of waiting represents a last resort for maintaining belief in a fallen world, a means of reasserting the laborious temporality of political commitment.

The same tense relation between waiting and religious belief plays a central role in Chabon's and Chandra's otherwise thoroughly secular novels. As one of Chabon's characters puts it, "It's Messiah. . . . What else can you do but wait?" (127). Both *The Yiddish Policemen's Union* and *Sacred Games* feature detectives—one atheist Sikh, one secular Jew—who are lapsed believers struggling with the continued allure of religious devotion. At the end of *Sacred Games*, Sartaj wonders "whether within himself there was some forgotten, subterranean strand of belief" (435). Landsman, too, ultimately finds something appealing about the peculiar temporality of Jewish faith—"the principle, thinks Landsman, that every Jew has a personal Messiah who never comes" (331). The fact that both novels feature religious fundamentalists cast as villains further highlights the detectives' flirtations with belief. For Sartaj and Landsman, the opposite of fanatical belief is not non-belief. It is a different mode of belief. While the two detectives battle against the inflexible content of religious extremism, they remain enchanted by the mere fact, the basic form, of belief. This is what Hungerford calls "belief in meaninglessness" or "belief without content," which she sees as a central feature of both religious and literary life since the 1960s. This form of belief may be, as Hungerford eventually concludes, questionable "in political or even moral terms." However, we can also see it as a necessary dialectical response to the uniquely contemporary tensions "between conviction and relativism, between doctrine and pluralism, between belief and meaninglessness."[48] These are the tensions, I've been arguing, that animate the contemporary detective novel. Caught between undecidability and dogma, these novels use the genre's standard temporal form to call forth the empty form of belief. Whereas Hungerford zeroes in on belief's emptiness, Chabon and Chandra remind us that belief is in fact always filled with something: time. Belief without content, in these novels, is the product of a wait without end.

The secret connection between waiting and belief limned in the detective novel turns in part on the nature of secrecy itself. Commenting on Frank Kermode's *Genesis of Secrecy*, Hungerford suggests that for Kermode, "secrecy is what makes literature literary." Here the secrecy of literature is connected to religious belief. Secrecy marks out a sort of "spiritual mystery at the heart of the literary enterprise."[49] D. A. Miller similarly describes "secrecy" as an essentially "spiritual exercise," a promise of knowledge that, because it may never be fulfilled, is really a matter of faith.[50] In this way, secrecy can be thought of as a formal counterweight to the wait. Simply put, the secret is what keeps us waiting. To see how waiting, belief, and secrecy are bound together in contemporary detective fiction, we need to look at how each of these novels revolves around a peculiar kind of secret—one that, unlike the novels' other mysteries, is never explained. These specters of the inexplicable are not celebrations of uncertainty or affirmations of the unknowable. Rather, the unspilled secrets of both novels stand in for the temporality of belief as it structures both the experience of waiting and the act of reading.

The secret at the center of *The Yiddish Policemen's Union* concerns Mendel Shpilman. Mendel is the Tzaddik Ha-Dor, the potential messiah of his generation. The potential is never realized, a basic condition of the novel's version of Jewish messianism: "Every generation loses the messiah it has failed to deserve" (197). Neither worldly nor holy, Mendel performs a series of small miracles but cracks under the expectations they carry, descending into drug addiction, which retroactively casts his miracles into doubt. As Rabbi Shpilman tells Landsman, "Miracles prove nothing except to those whose faith is bought very cheap" (141). If it is not proof of the divine, what exactly does the miracle do? If Mendel is not the Messiah—he dies a destitute junkie rather than a redeemer of the world—what do his miraculous acts mean? Mendel's inexplicable acts of healing, comfort, and foreknowledge show how the secret of faith lingers in time. At a key moment in Chabon's novel, Mendel demonstrates this to Alter Litvak, a secular, skeptical Jew whose cynical empiricism is brought to the brink of the otherworldly. Litvak, like many of the novel's nonbelievers, flirts with belief in the form of physical ritual. For decades, Litvak has carried around a *yahrzeit* candle to honor of the memory of his wife, but he has never chosen to light it. Upon meeting Litvak, Mendel betrays an intimate knowledge of this ritual, despite the fact that Litvak has never told a soul about it:

There was a click, and a scrape, and then Litvak leaned wonderingly forward and poked the end of the cigar into the flame of his own Zippo lighter. He felt the momentary shock of a miracle. Then he grinned and nodded his thanks, feeling a kind of giddy relief at the belated arrival of a logical explanation: He must have left the lighter back in Sitka, where Gold or Turtletoyb had found it and brought it along on the flight to Peril Strait. Shpilman had borrowed it and, with his junkie instincts, pocketed it after lighting a papiros. Yes, good. . . .

"Go, Reb Litvak. Light the candle. There's no prayer you say. There's nothing you have to do or feel. You just light it. Go on."

As logic drained from the world, never entirely to return, Shpilman reached into Litvak's jacket pocket and took out the glass and the wax and the wick. For this trick, Litvak could make himself no explanation. (354)

The lack of explanation (how does Mendel know about Litvak's private ritual?) is not cause for conversion. The passage depicts not the onset of Litvak's belief but the absolute limits of his nonbelief. The "shock" of the miracle causes cynical reason—the hallmark of both the nonbelieving Jew and the no-nonsense detective—to confront the limits of its perception, the lacuna of its power. There is no choice in the passage between a secular and a religious explanation or a materialist and a metaphysical one. Instead, the miracle is permanently suspended between the two, making the desire for "logical explanation" inseparable from the possibility of there being "no explanation" at all. Explanation's "belated arrival" can always be indefinitely deferred. But the real challenge here is posed to the reader: What sense can we make of a miracle thrust into the rational world of detective fiction? Litvak's search for explanation—for the "logic" that is "never entirely to return"—is also ours. Like him, we are not immediately transformed into believers by reading this passage. But we are subject to a similar crisis of belief (the belief that there is always a rational explanation) that is staged as an experience of time. To have faith in the possibility of eventually finding a logical explanation is to be willing to wait for as long as it takes for that explanation to reveal itself.

*Sacred Games* similarly leaves one aspect of its narrative form mysteriously inexplicable: the status of Ganesh's narration. Although Ganesh performs the duties of first-person narrator for more than half the novel, he has also, all the way back on page 46, managed to take his own life. The novel treats the event as the straightforward engine to a purely secular mystery: Why did Ganesh Gaitonde kill himself? When Sartaj complains that there can be only a "partial explanation" of "the Gaitonde affair," he is referring partly to the mysteries that subtend any suicide. The novel, however, is able to offer much more than a partial explanation, because it includes five hundred pages of Ganesh himself explaining it. The mystery of Ganesh's suicide is thus displaced onto a more fundamental and resolutely formal problem, which the novel neither answers nor even treats as a question: How in the secular world is Ganesh able to narrate in the first place?

Because none of the other characters is able to register the problem, *Sacred Games* leaves its readers alone to deal with the impossibility of believing the matter plainly before their eyes: the intrusion into the logical world of detection of a confessing corpse.[51] As the novel begins, Sartaj follows an anonymous tip to Kailashpada, where Ganesh has sealed himself in his nuclear shelter. While they are waiting for the bulldozers to arrive to break down the doors, Ganesh talks to Sartaj through the speaker system, beginning the lengthy story of how he became a gangster. When the police break down the doors, Ganesh shoots himself, and Sartaj, unsettled but more or less uncurious, goes home. The chapter ends with these lines: "But what did it matter, any of it? Gaitonde was dead. Sartaj turned over, thumped his pillows determinedly, arranged them, and lay down his head and slept" (50). If Gaitonde is simply "dead," then that should be the end of it. There is nothing to do but handle the tangible objects of the material world ("thump" and "arrange" the pillows) and go to sleep.

But with the first words of the very next chapter, the comforting dream of a decipherable, secular world is interrupted, ensuring that we will not sleep so soundly again: "So, Sardar-ji, are you listening still? Are you somewhere in this world with me? I can feel you. What happened next, and what happened next, you want to know. I was walking under the whirling sky riven by clouds . . ." (51). Ganesh begins with a strange reversal: it is not he, the haunting ghost, who is spectrally present in Sartaj's world, it is Sartaj who is "in this world with" Ganesh—the other world, we can only assume, of the dead or of spirits or of the divine. Why does Ganesh assume that

Sartaj is "with [him]" in this other world? Because Ganesh understands his reader. In Kailashpada, Ganesh had begun telling Sartaj the story of his life but did not have time to finish it, and he knows that Sartaj—who, recalling Felman's definition, is *only a detective in his function as a reader*—will naturally want to know how it ends. Reading is the durational desire for knowledge, the drive "to know," in Ganesh's knowing repetition, "what happened next, and what happened next." Yet the anticipatory stance of reading, Ganesh recognizes, is as much about deferral as it is about fulfillment, and so it carries Sartaj paradoxically into "this" other "world," a world of ghosts or gods that is defined by its inability to be rationally explained. Explanation is reduced to a chain of movements ("what happened next, and what happened next"), where answers are no longer end points but only momentary stops in a longer process of questioning. The desire "to know" is thus inseparable from the desire to read. Reading recasts explanation as a process embedded in time. In *Sacred Games*, our desire to explain the world runs up against the hard surface of the inexplicable or otherworldly. Yet the inexplicable does not constitute the impossibility of explanation or knowledge. Instead, it reveals to us, in perfectly circular fashion, the very origins of what we are reading: the formal secret of the novel's narration.

The "suspicious, unduped reader," Felman tells us, is the opposite of "the naïve believer"; "suspicion (the intelligence of reading)" is, from the first, opposed to "faith."[52] *Sacred Games* and *The Yiddish Policemen's Union* complicate these oppositions, figuring reading as the temporal logic that situates us between two poles: naïveté and knowing, faith and suspicion. To read like the detectives in these novels is to read for secrets that are suspended between the secular and the divine, the logical and the mystical, the banal and the revelatory. It is to wait for a thorough explanation or demystification that, like Landsman's messiah, "never comes"; and it is also to continue to believe, if only through form, in the imminent arrival of that explanation. The waiting involved in reading is thus neither a withdrawal from expectation nor a refusal of revelation. Set uncertainly between unknowing and knowing, the detective work of Sartaj and Landsman does not pretend to be able to explain everything. But it does explain something about the complicated case of their contemporary moment. Giving new meaning to the long wait, these contemporary detective novels put their faith in the temporality of detection. In doing so, they are able to illuminate those elements of the present (the possibility of the miracle, the specter of the divine) that, stubbornly remaining secret, keep us waiting in order to compel us to keep reading.

## UNCERTAINTY'S PRINCIPLES

The drama of belief that bubbles up in China Miéville's *The City and the City* concerns not God but country, the faith that underlies the idea of national belonging. Miéville's novel tells the tale of two cities, Besźel and Ul Qoma, that are, from a strictly geographical perspective, one city. They occupy the same space. Whether you are standing in one city or the other (the cities belong to different countries; speak different languages; use different currencies; have different social customs, manners of dress, and styles of architecture; and occupy different positions on the global economic ladder) is a matter of mentality as much as of legality. The citizens of each city are trained from childhood to scrupulously "unsee" the other city, ignoring no less than half the persons and places that populate their streets: "The streets were crowded with those elsewhere. I unsaw them, but it took time to pick past them all."[53] The imagined community (to borrow Benedict Anderson's famous phrase)[54] of each city is built on the imaginary act of unseeing. "No one can admit it doesn't work," one character finally admits. "So if you don't admit it, it does" (310). To unsee, in other words, is to believe—despite the physical evidence directly before your unseeing eyes—that you belong to one nation instead of the other.

In the absence of a physical boundary, the cities' separation is solely a matter of belief. For that reason, belief itself must be policed. Between Besźel and Ul Qoma, there exists a separate legal body whose role is to punish anyone who breaches the invisible border between the cities. The body is known as Breach, and "the only violation Breach punishes [is] the existential disrespect of Ul Qoma's and Besźel's boundaries" (64). Much like the cities' imaginary boundary, Breach is everywhere and nowhere, its absence feeding its omnipotence. "Don't you think we're watched by powers?" one character asks another. "'Sure. Sure. You asking me where they are?' It is a more or less meaningless question but one that no Besź nor Ul Qoman can banish" (45). To the extent that, as another character puts it, Breach is some "spooky shit" (46), it too is largely a matter of belief. But not solely belief: there is no question that Breach really does exist (it submits paperwork to the two city legislatures, for instance). Breach's invisible but implacable authority mirrors, even as it polices, the imaginary boundary between the cities. It confirms to the citizens that the boundary really is there, even if they can't visibly detect it.

Into the breach goes the Besźel police detective Tyador Borlú, who, as the novel opens, discovers in Besźel the body of an American woman, Mahalia Geary, who was supposed to have been living in Ul Qoma. The discovery launches a case that spans both cities, exposes an international conspiracy between Besź nationalists and American corporate interests, reveals the killer to be a Canadian archaeology professor named David Bowden, and ends with Borlú leaving Besźel (this will have been "the last case of Inspector Tyador Borlú of the Besźel Extreme Crime Squad") to become an agent of Breach. What is at stake in the shift from policing in Besźel to policing as Breach? On the last page of the novel, Borlú reflects on his new position: "We are all philosophers here where I am, and we debate among many other things the question of where it is that we live" (312). To describe the members of Breach as "philosophers" concerned with the philosophical or existential question of Breach is to clarify what Breach's role in this world really is: neither to confirm nor to demystify belief but to *alleviate uncertainty*. The problem that Breach embodies is the very problem that it exists to resolve. That problem is how to know where one stands, how to be sure of "where it is that we live." One can say that one lives in either Besźel or Ul Qoma only because Breach cannot. Breach's ambiguous legal and physical status simultaneously reflects and deflects the foundation of uncertainty on which life is built in the "overlapping cities" (311). To live in Besźel or Ul Qoma is to live, Miéville tells us, in a permanent state of "urban uncertainty" (43). The delicate art of seeing and unseeing, after all, is continually threatened by the possibility of ambiguity or confusion: "He was silhouetted against the skyline, of Besźel or Ul Qoma or both I could not tell" (49). This looming ambiguity is literalized in Breach, which is able to thrive as an invisible yet inescapable presence in both cities only because no one is sure which city it belongs to—which means that no one is willing to risk noticing them and inadvertently breaching. Agents of Breach speak both cities' languages and dress in a style that could belong to either place, and it is this deliberate ambiguity concerning where they belong that Breach exploits in order to establish its authority. "Are you in Besźel or Ul Qoma?" Borlú's Breach mentor, Ashil, asks him. "Neither. I'm in Breach," replies Borlú. As such, Ashil explains, "No one knows if they're seeing you or unseeing you" (254). It is because "no one knows" where Breach belongs that it is able to lurk undetected "in the interstice" (312) between the two cities. The uncertainty of Breach's legal and geographical standing (To whom do they answer? Where are they located?) becomes a way of managing the "urban uncertainty" of the cities. Breach's constitutive uncertainty is what allows the cities to be certain of their separateness.

For Miéville, the unlocatability of the law is, at bottom, a philosophical question ("we are all philosophers here"). It appears that he has two particular philosophers in mind: Carl Schmitt and Giorgio Agamben. Miéville has a doctorate in international relations and has written an academic book on international law, which includes an extended commentary on Schmitt.[55] *The City and the City* makes explicit reference to Schmitt's theory of sovereign decision (Breach: "You're beyond the law now; this is where decision lives" [246]), as well as to Agamben's widely known extension of that theory in his book *Homo Sacer* (as when Borlú describes Breach as a "community of bare, extra-city lives" [312]). Agamben defines "the paradox of sovereignty" as "the fact that the sovereign is, at the same time, inside and outside the juridical order."[56] The same paradox is, of course, the central premise of Miéville's novel, where it is Breach that represents "an alien power" (64), a form of sovereign authority that lies outside the jurisdictions of the two cities even as it establishes the laws that function within them.

My point in turning to Agamben here is not to apply an arbitrary but trendy theoretical framework to Miéville's novel; it is to call attention to the novel's own twenty-first-century cultural awareness. Both Schmitt and Agamben acquired new academic currency in the wake of September 11, when the paradoxes of U.S. and British sovereignty returned with a vengeance, in the form of suspended civil liberties, indefinite detention, restrictions on immigration, and the sense of a semipermanent state of emergency.[57] The new urgency that September 11 bestowed on the ideas in *Homo Sacer* (which was published in Italian in 1995 and translated into English in 1998) is one of the main reasons the book became a surprise academic best seller.[58] (The mid-2000s also saw the republication of several of Schmitt's major works.) Agamben himself seems to have recognized the retroactive significance of September 11 to his work, as his next book, *State of Exception* (published in Italy in 2003 and the United States in 2005) explicitly addressed the situation of post–Patriot Act sovereignty ("in the detainee at Guantanamo," we learn, "bare life reaches its maximum indeterminacy").[59] For Miéville, then, the prospect of writing a detective novel—literary genre of the law par excellence—in the first decade of the twenty-first century seems to have been unthinkable except as a meditation on the increasingly self-evident contradictions of international law in its new state of exception.

But Agamben's work on the state of exception and the paradoxes of sovereignty does more than supply a legal and political history. It also establishes a theoretical worldview. One of the most frequently used words in *Homo Sacer* is *indistinction*. Agamben speaks of "a zone of irreducible indistinction," of "a paradoxical threshold of indistinction," of "difficult zones of indistinction." The essential undecidability of the exception "comes more and more to the foreground as the fundamental political structure" of "our age."[60] At the same time, it comes to the fore as a structure of thought. "The thought of our time," Agamben insists, "finds itself confronted with the structure of the exception in every area":

Language's sovereign claim thus consists in the attempt to make sense coincide with denotation, to stabilize a zone of indistinction between the two in which language can maintain itself in relation to its *denotata* by abandoning them and withdrawing from them into a pure *langue* (the linguistic "state of exception"). This is what deconstruction does, positing undecidables that are infinitely in excess of every possibility of signification.[61]

Philosophers of the exception include not only Schmitt but also, referenced on a single page of *Homo Sacer*, Alain Badiou, Claude Lévi-Strauss, Émile Benveniste, and Jacques Derrida. As the common thread linking this set of thinkers, the exception comes to seem less like "the 'nomos' of the modern"[62] and more like the law of the postmodern—an essential feature of structuralist and poststructuralist theories of language that trade meaning and reference for the arbitrary, undecidable play of the signifier. The distinction of Agamben's obsessive focus on indistinction is that it corresponds to an entire postwar philosophical project committed to busting the myth of the determinate, the logical, and the legal through the ceaseless discovery of the uncertain and indeterminate "in every area," from the outward atrocities of Guantánamo Bay to the internal structure of language itself.[63] As a philosopher of the uncertainties of sovereignty, Agamben is also a prime example of how uncertainty itself became a key philosophical and political principle in the late twentieth century.

"It is on the basis of these uncertain and nameless terrains, these diffi-cult zones of indistinction," Agamben suggests, "that the ways and the forms of a new politics must be thought."[64] *The City and the City* literalizes such "uncertain terrains." But the real point of the novel is to probe the limits of those terrains—to register, at this moment in history, the increas-ingly intolerable fact of uncertainty as a lived condition. Nowhere is this clearer than in the novel's climactic scene, in which uncertainty itself is wielded by one of the novel's villains as a kind of terrorist weapon. After a frenetic showdown on a helipad with the corporate and political conspira-tors (Miéville has a taste for the occasional cinematic set piece), Borlú dis-covers that Bowden—the homicidal archaeologist—has escaped from his apartment and made his way to the customs checkpoint that controls the border between the cities. In the chaos of the moment, however, the police aren't sure whether he crossed, and so, to their horror, they do not know which city he currently resides in. Exploiting his extensive knowledge of both cities' clothing, customs, and mannerisms, Bowden is able to render his whereabouts thoroughly undecidable. As the Ul Qoman detective Qus-sim Dhatt tells Borlú, "The way he's moving . . . the clothes he's wearing . . . they *can't tell* whether he's in Ul Qoma or Besźel. [ . . . ] They don't even know if they can *see* him. But he's not breaching either. They just . . . can't tell" (292–93). "In that uncertain state," Borlú realizes, "no would stop Bowden. No one could" (293). Bowden is "urbanly undecidable" (297): "He walked with equipoise, possibly in either city. Schrödinger's pedestrian" (295). The uncertain, the undecidable, the Schrödingerian: What else is be-ing staged in these final pages but the logical end and the corroded legacy of the once-privileged forms of postmodern indeterminacy? Bowden is us-ing the world's uncertainty against it. Flouting the ambiguity that is both essential to and unthinkable for Ul Qoma and Besźel, he reveals uncer-tainty to be a state of suspended social animation. It literally stops the cities from functioning. This is exactly what Bowden wants. His undecidability is calculated to permanently defer the arrival of legal judgment against him.

Eventually, Borlú convinces Bowden to give himself up, and the scene ends, somewhat anticlimactically, with his apprehension by Breach. How exactly does this happen? Who was legally authorized to make the arrest?

Even Borlú isn't sure. In the final pages of the novel, he broaches the matter
with Ashil:

"But the thing is, he never breached." I had not voiced this anxiety to Ashil before.
He turned to look at me, massaged his injury. "Under what authority was he . . .
How can we have him?" [ . . . ] "I mean," I said, "I know Breach doesn't answer to
anyone, but it . . . you have to present reports. Of all your cases. To the Oversight
Committee." He raised an eyebrow at that. "I know, I know they've been discredited because of Buric, but their line's that that was the makeup of the members,
right, not the committee itself. The checks and balances between the cities and
Breach is still the same, right? They have a point, don't you think? So you'll have
to justify taking Bowden."

"No one cares about Bowden," he said at last. "Not Ul Qoma, not Besźel, not
Canada, not Orciny. But yes, we'll present a form to them. Maybe, after he dumped
Mahalia, he got back into Ul Qoma by Breach."

"He didn't dump her; it was Yorj—" I said.

"Maybe that's how he did it," Ashil continued. "We'll see. Maybe we'll push him
into Besźel and pull him back to Ul Qoma. If we say he breached, he breached." I
looked at him. (308–9)

"If we say he breached, he breached": you would be hard-pressed to find a
more textbook example of what Schmitt and Agamben call the sovereign
decision, the act of deciding who is subject to the law in a way that is itself
not subject to the law. Breach decides who breached by virtue of an absolute, nearly mystical authority.[65] As the ones who make it possible for there
to be laws in the two cities, they themselves do not answer to those laws.

What may be most notable, though, about this seemingly exceptional
moment in the novel—the moment when Breach breaks the rules to make
the rules—is how generic it is. It is the exception that detective novels have
always been willing to make. In an essay on Raymond Chandler and James
Ellroy, Lee Spinks proposes that "Agamben, Schmitt, and the state of
exception . . . offer the most productive theoretical context within which to
understand the development of a particular *literary* genre: the American
roman noir."[66] Across the history of the genre, the detective is always an
exception. For Spinks, a classic hard-boiled novel like *The Big Sleep* "insists
on the ambivalent position of the detective outside and inside the sphere of
law," while the work of a writer like Ellroy "describes a world in which the

exception now coincides absolutely with the rule" (in other words, a world where the police themselves are violent criminals).[67] One way or another, whether it's an outsider acting like the police or the police acting like criminals, the detective novel consistently finds the boundary between the legal and the illegal, the juridical and the extrajuridical, impossible to patrol. This does not cast the genre into crisis. Instead, it constitutes the genre's founding moment. The fictional detective exists to make certain decisions about how to overcome the uncertainties and indeterminacies that otherwise hinder the workings of the law.

*The City and the City* may look at first glance to be a commentary on the acts of imagination—the fictions and faiths—that structure the social order, but it ends up as something quite different: an allegory about overcoming uncertainty. Miéville wields the legal ambiguities of the detective genre as a way to combat the intolerable conditions of the uncertain and undecidable. Of course, this is itself a paradoxical solution: a recognition—not unlike Agamben's own—of the mutual entanglements of certainty and uncertainty, legal boundaries and zones of indistinction, authority and its self-contradictions. Acknowledging the paradox of its proposed solution to the problem of uncertainty, *The City and the City* offers several models of what it looks like to live *in between*, "in the interstice" or at the "crosshatch" of national belief and "urban uncertainty." One model is proposed by Borlú in the novel's final lines. Responding to the philosophical "debate" within Breach over "where it is that we live," Borlú offers his own answer: "On that issue I am a liberal. I live in the interstice yes, but I live in both the city and city" (312). Here the deconstructive neither/nor of undecidability is replaced by the "liberal" pluralist possibility of the both/and. In this view, Breach is no longer a paradoxical authority that lies between or beyond the two cities; it is the practical governing body that lives in both at once. Pitted against such a reasonable, liberal solution is the one offered by Bowden. For him, being "undecidably" in both cities at once is a way to shut down the basic civic and social functions of each one. "He's been *waiting* for someone to notice him," Borlú realizes, watching Bowden (293, italics in original). Of course, no one is willing to notice him (because no one wants to breach), which is fine with Bowden, who is content to wait forever. Suspended in a permanent state of undecidability, his wait—and its promise or threat of infinite deferral—implies the unfeasibility of the liberal both/and. He really does at this moment "live in both the city and the city" (as

Borlú later describes himself), and no one has any idea what to do about it. Perhaps not even the novel itself—for the way it solves this narrative puzzle (through the deus ex machina of Breach's unchecked authority: "Maybe we'll push him into Besźel and pull him back to Ul Qoma") suggests something undeniably sinister, if not expressly totalitarian, about the unregulated power of Breach. Invoked to resolve an impasse that according to the novel's own rules can't be resolved otherwise, Breach's decisive power over Bowden gives the lie to Borlú's dream of Breach's liberal neutrality.

So what does it really mean to live uncertainly, in between? Is it a site of liberal pluralism or of extralegal totalitarianism? Actually, there is a third option. The description of Bowden's endlessly deferred, deliberately counterproductive wait is not the only kind of waiting the novel affords. For a good chunk of the book's opening pages (it is impossible to say how many), *The City and the City* offers a different interpretation of the wait. Although the novel functions largely as an inversion of the postmodern anti-detective novel—seeing indeterminacy not as the inevitable end point but as the initial problem to be solved—there is one question it never explicitly answers. This is a question that, starting in the novel's opening chapter, no reader can avoid asking: not so much *whodunnit* as *what world is this?* What exactly is the imaginary relationship between these two cities? The secret of the novel's speculative setting turns out to be a rather astonishing literary feat of suggestion and innuendo, for at no point does Miéville ever tell us directly that the two cities are located in a single space. In contrast to the eureka moments that usually attend a detective's epiphany, there is no clear moment in the novel at which the reader becomes aware of shifting decisively from confusion to understanding.

The magic of the novel—its own leap of faith—is that we come to understand its impossible geography all the same. Forced to wait for an explanation that seems never to come yet turns out to have come and gone without our noticing, we can draw only one conclusion: understanding takes time. Miéville's unspoken explanation is not a withholding of knowledge. It is a case for knowledge's irreducible temporality. To read *The City and the City* is to confront waiting as a distinctly accretive form of knowledge, a measure of the slow accumulation of facts by which, without entirely realizing how or when, we come to know the world around us. Threaded through the novel's unfamiliar (and in a certain sense inexplicable) setting, waiting exposes the two subterranean structures of belief that are inseparable from reading: first, the suspended disbelief that allows us to accept the unfamiliarity of this speculative world; second, the affirmative belief that as long as we keep reading, we'll eventually figure out what exactly we're reading about. In *The City and the City*, the interminable wait of indeterminacy is countered by the wait for a full explanation of Miéville's intricately imagined narrative world. This wait does come to an end. It just so happens that we cannot say exactly when that end arrived and revealed to us, without our fully knowing it, a strange new world of comprehension.

## NOW OR NEVER

"The future is an illusion," Chandra writes in *Sacred Games*, "but the present is the most slippery illusion of all" (324). It is our slippery yet desperately needed knowledge of the present that this chapter has sought to investigate through the literature of detective work. It is no coincidence that the debates about reading with which the chapter began are similarly preoccupied with the problem of the present. Indeed, one of the starting assumptions of "Surface Reading"—which introduces a special issue of *Representations*, "The Way We Read Now"—is that the now we presently live in is, unlike past ones, quite easy to know: "So much for the way we read. What about 'now'? In the last decade or so, we have been drawn to modes of reading that attend to the surfaces of texts rather than plumb their depths. Perhaps this is because, at the end of the first decade of the twenty-first century, so much seems to be on the surface."[68] Here we see how the anxieties about certainty and empirical knowledge that inform the call for surface reading turn out to rest on a particular if slightly peculiar idea about the present: that with so much of contemporary history now "on the surface" for all to see, there is little that remains unknown about it. Surface reading presents itself as the methodological corollary of a contemporary—our own twenty-first-century present—that is unprecedentedly knowable.

Is this really our present? The coeditors of "The Way We Read Now" see the problem of the now somewhat differently. In the last line of their afterword, Emily Apter and Elaine Freedgood, in a tone at once conciliatory and celebratory, observe that any conversation about how we read is bound to be subsumed by the problem of when that "we" is situated: "In the meantime, *now* is *then*, and the ways we read and can read have already changed their method and modes, and they cannot, happily, be enumerated."[69] The play between "now" and "then" points simultaneously to the inexorability of change and the lag with which it is registered. By the time a dominant method has been recognized as dominant, it will already have been displaced. For Apter and Freedgood, the now is what "cannot . . . be enumerated" or accounted for. The ability to describe one's present implies that it has already become part of the past. Reading thus turns out to have an especially complicated relationship with the present: first, because the way we read is subject to change in, and to the change of, the present; and second, because the present appears to constitute the absolute limit of what we are able to read. Because "now" is constantly slipping back into "then," present time eludes our attempts to read or interpret it.

So how do we read the now? How do we interpret our constantly changing present? These are the questions that detective novels allow us to answer. They do so by making visible the elusive temporality of the present itself, or what Apter and Freedgood call "the meantime." In the time that stretches from mystery to explanation, detective fiction illuminates the meantime by means of the wait. Waiting represents a uniquely literary response to the tension between what we know and what we don't know about the contemporary. Against Best and Marcus's suggestion that the present is self-evidently knowable, and against Apter and Freedgood's implication that the now is endlessly elusive, the long wait of the twenty-first-century detective novel depicts a contemporary animated by the temporal dynamic, or dialectic, of *knowing* and *unknowing*. The contemporary is evenly split between what we are able to detect in it and what we have yet to know about it. This division at the heart of contemporary history can best be described as a wait.

The temporality of secrecy that structures the contemporary detective novel brings us face-to-face with the secret of the contemporary, the mystery of the now. In *Georgic Modernity and British Romanticism*, Kevis Goodman describes the present as "a version of the Heisenberg uncertainty principle: the difficulty of recording and recognizing history-on-the-move, or, to invoke grammar rather than physics, the difficulty of treating or recreating the historical process as a present participle . . . rather than as a past perfect."[70] This is not to say that the present is irreducibly uncertain. Rather, for Goodman, the present captures time in motion, history as process. These are the same aspects of the present revealed in the form of detective fiction.

Confronting the "uncertainty principle" of the contemporary, the detective novel translates uncertainty into temporality so as to transform unknowing into waiting. This is why the wait is not a form of disappointment or deferral but a description of our inchoate, unfolding contemporary. Waiting turns the *not* of the unknowable present into the *not yet* that makes the present the irrefutable evidence of our fall into time.

The day-to-day temporality of the wait is exactly what Sartaj Singh discovers on the final page of *Sacred Games*. Waiting may have previously felt like the failure of epochal change, but here it gives Sartaj a different way to measure present time. Having successfully averted nuclear annihilation and now on his way to another day of work, Sartaj is stuck in a traffic jam. The gridlock has been caused not by an accident or obstruction but by the simple act of waiting itself: "A party of Municipal men were working on a hole in the road. They weren't actually working, they were standing around the hole looking at it, and apparently waiting for something to happen" (945). The traffic jam is then an extension of the workers' wait: "Meanwhile, a vast funnel of traffic pressed up against the bottleneck. Sartaj was . . . hemmed in by a BEST bus and two autos, and there was nowhere for anyone to go, so they all waited companionably" (945–46). Traffic is perhaps our most iconic symbol of wasted time (time in which there is nothing to do but watch time pass). Here, however, that waste is transformed into a "companionabl[e]" wait. What makes this wait so social, so sociable, so unexpectedly "happy" (946)?

The experience of the traffic jam unmasks the wait as a basic condition of everyday life. In the very last lines of *Sacred Games*, the link between the time of the wait and the unit of the day is made explicit: "He patted his cheeks, and ran a forefinger and thumb along his mustache. He was sure it was magnificent. He was ready. He went in and began another day" (947). In contrast to the anxious expectation of terrorist threat, the anticipation or "ready"-ness here is a knowing stance toward the passing of time. Sartaj is "ready," perhaps for anything, but he is not ready for anything in particular. In this way, the end of *Sacred Games* reimagines the "end time" of both religious eschatology and the classic detective novel, turning the end of the narrative into the end of a day, which is always the beginning of "another day." The day, perhaps our most elemental unit for measuring the present,[71] installs us in a time that, neither repetitive nor teleological, must be understood as a wait: a temporal logic that both separates one day from the next and ties the days together. The wait is what makes the present continuous, and it is also what makes the present continue inexorably to pass.

Knowing takes time. This basic point—a necessary response to both the absolutism of dogma and the fetishism of uncertainty—is most powerfully confronted in the time it takes us to read.[72] This chapter has tried to explain how the time taken up by reading may also be a lesson in the nature of contemporary time. The novels of Chandra, Chabon, and Miéville teach us that the time we spend waiting is not time wasted but time regained and rendered visible, time understood as the constitutive element of an ever changing present. The present, of course, is the open secret that everyone is in on. It is the absent cause of social life, the empty signifier for what both determines and conjoins us. Ostensibly resistant to being read, seemingly invisible to those who live within it, the present is frequently described as a mysterious burden, a "deadening weight," as one critic calls it, "that usurps time."[73] The long wait of detective fiction, in contrast, allows us to take back usurped time. In the time of detection, we embark on Kracauer's "lengthy approach," the time that separates the unknowable from the knowable, the blinding from the blindingly obvious. As Benjamin remarks in *The Arcades Project*, waiting is not simply a matter of "pass[ing] the time" but a way to "invite it in": "He who waits takes in the time and renders it up in altered form—that of expectation."[74] Expectation "alter[s]" time precisely by slowing it down, stretching it out: by forcing us, finally, to take our time. In the time taken up by reading, the present transforms from an invisible burden into a form of unfolding, from a "weight" into a wait. The wait whispers to us the real secret of the contemporary: that its secrets cannot be kept secret forever.

*Chapter Four*

_____

# WEATHER

## Western Climes

Everyone notices the weather.

## TODAY'S FORECAST

"You call this hot?" This question—uttered early on in *High Noon* (Fred Zinneman, 1952)—could well be the motto of the classic Western. Westerns veritably swelter.[1] From Howard Hawks to John Ford to Sergio Leone, the midcentury Western is all parched deserts and parched men, big skies and burning suns. Those suns—which set in the west yet rarely set in the Western—draw our attention to a feature of the genre that is as obvious as it is easily overlooked: the weather. As Jane Tomkins writes in her famous book *West of Everything*, in the Western "a person is exposed, the sun beats down, and there is no place to hide."[2] Westerns expose us to the elements, to sun and rain and snow and drought. The Western is a thoroughly *weathered* genre, shaped by the unpredictable yet inescapable dynamics of the atmosphere. Of course, the Western may be considered weathered in another sense, too. What was perhaps the most important genre of American cinema sixty years ago is, today, almost irrelevant. Yet in that exemplary snippet of small talk uttered in *High Noon*, we can hear the echo of a different kind of contemporary relevance for the Western. "You call this hot": once the signature expression of the Western's generic climes, this line is currently nothing less than the signal question of global warming—the urgent slogan of a planet shaped by melting glaciers, rising sea levels, extreme storms, extended droughts, and temperatures that will continue to rise well beyond what the human species is content to call hot.

This chapter argues that the meaning of the contemporary Western resides in the ways it both inherits and alters the genre's sustained yet often unremarked attention to the weather. First, I show how the classic and revisionist Westerns of the mid-twentieth century exhibited an intense, if largely apolitical, interest in the weather. Second, I demonstrate how twenty-first-century Westerns adapt the genre's general atmospheric awareness to an era of publicly acknowledged atmospheric crisis. Overall, my aim is to show how the Western begins as a genre about *climate* and how it develops into a genre about *climate change*.

Climate change is an undeniable fact of contemporary history. But how contemporary is it? Even as climate change "saturate[s] our sense of the now," as Dipesh Chakrabarty suggests, it also raises difficult questions about what exactly counts as *now*.[3] The anthropogenic transformation of the climate began roughly three centuries ago, when the Industrial Revolution dramatically increased the concentration of greenhouse gases in the atmosphere. The consequences of this transformation, in turn, will last "hundreds of millennia" into the future, according to the climatologist David Archer.[4] Extending both backward and forward in time, climate change challenges our conventional sense of history, invoking a historical process that plays out not in the familiar life spans of human generations but in the long, slow march of geological time. One name for our dramatically extended climatic present is the *Anthropocene*. Coined in 2000 by the chemist Paul J. Crutzen and the biologist Eugene F. Stoermer, the name Anthropocene denotes the new geological epoch—following the Holocene (which began approximately 11,000 years ago), the Pleistocene (2.5 million years ago), and the Pliocene (5.3 million years ago)—in which human action begins to alter the planet's geological and atmospheric processes.[5] Even at the semantic level of the name itself (which roughly translates as "the new time of man"), the Anthropocene announces the fusion of two radically different timescales: the human and the geological. As an attempt to name the history of human-forced climate change, the Anthropocene reminds us that this is a history measured not in the usual human units of years and decades but in centuries and millennia. "The climate crisis," Chakrabarty contends, "produces problems that we ponder on very different and incompatible scales of time," from the history of the planet to the history of human life to the history of industrial capitalism.[6] Drawing together these seemingly incommensurate yet deeply entangled histories, the Anthropocene puts the human crisis of climate change in geological perspective. In doing so, it compels us to situate the current crises of things like rising sea levels and life-threatening droughts in a far larger time frame, from the hundreds of years of imperceptible atmospheric change that laid the ground for contemporary conditions to the hundreds of thousands of years over which the effects of that change will continue to be felt.

The extended timescale of climate change seems to stretch the notion of the contemporary to its breaking point. Set against the unimaginable unfurling of deep time, how can the apparent solidity of our present moment not—like a greenhouse gas—melt into air? No less militant a thinker of the historical present than Walter Benjamin was already sensitive to the relative insignificance of the present compared with the extended time line of the universe:

"In relation to the history of organic life on earth," writes a modern biologist, "the paltry fifty millennia of *homo sapiens* constitute something like two seconds at the close of a twenty-four day. On this scale, the history of civilized mankind would fill one-fifth of the last second of the last hour." The present, which, as a model of Messianic time, comprises the entire history of mankind in an enormous abridgment, coincides exactly with the stature which the history of mankind has in the universe.[7]

Benjamin reminds us that thinking geologically requires a radical rethinking of the present itself. In the geological and biological history of the earth, the present is a mere fraction of a second, practically nonexistent. Or as the climatologist Archer puts it, "In geologic time, a century is nothing, an eyeblink, so let's be geological and consider the last century and the next century to be 'the present.'"[8] Following Archer, Tim Morton insists that the whole point of talking about the Anthropocene is to make the present absent: "The Anthropocene is only potent because it magnifies a fundamental feature of reality for human inspection. This feature is the nonexistence of the present as such." For Morton, "Ecological awareness is without the present." This is because awareness of climate change implies a temporal scale at which any sense of *now*—along with the thinking subject who would sense it—disappears; at this scale, "there is no me, no human even, worth talking about."[9] The elongated time line of climate change has prompted a more general scalar shift among literary critics, who have become increasingly interested in notions of deep and geological time as ways to reframe, if not to reject, the illusory presence of the contemporary.[10] If the phenomenological present is something like a "swift-running stream,"[11] thinkers in the humanities could be said to have shifted their attention to the geological process that carved out the streambed in the first place, at a rate so slow and over a time span so long as to render the present, by comparison, only the barest trickle, the tiniest drop.

The sublime chasm of geological time, swallowing up any sense of the contemporary, is not the only way to frame the history of climate change, however. Not for nothing do Crutzen and Stoermer date the beginning of the Anthropocene to the dawn of industrial capitalism at the end of the eighteenth century: "This is the period when data retrieved from glacial ice cores show the beginning of a growth in the atmospheric concentrations of several 'greenhouse gases,' in particular $CO_2$ and $CH_4$. Such a starting date also coincides with James Watt's invention of the steam engine in 1784."[12] To periodize the Anthropocene in this way is to understand it as concomitant with what Andreas Malm has dubbed *fossil capitalism*. Fossil capitalism describes the moment when capitalism's desire for ceaseless expansion became dependent on fossil fuels. What draws capital to coal is the promise of abstraction. In the "geological compression of time and space" effected by fossil fuels, which offered a portable and storable form of energy, capitalism discovered a new way "to produce its own abstract spatio-temporality." Coal allowed capitalism to free itself from the constraints of concrete space and time (specifically, the constraints of locally sourced water power). In doing so, it laid the groundwork for an economic system that doesn't just melt things into air but also, through the burning of fossil fuels, directly "influence[s] the atmosphere."[13] This account of the Anthropocene—as, in Malm's words, "the geological epoch not of humanity, but of capital"[14]— suggests that the history of the climate crisis may have a more perceptible place in the history of our present after all. Less an Anthropocene than a "Capitalocene"[15]: this is one way to articulate a more dialectical relationship between what is unthinkable about climate change (the slowness of the change, the long-term deferral of its effects) and what is thinkable about it (its emergence within a capitalist system that remains intensely present to us). Even as it extends deep into the geological past and far into the atmospheric future, the climate crisis remains intimately tied to the ongoing history of modern capitalism.[16]

My point in underscoring the connection between the invisible history of climate change and the visible history of capitalism is to return to a question that I worry has been lost in the depths of geological time: On what more thinkable timescale do we in fact manage to grasp—as we clearly, if partially, do—the presence and presentness of climate change? There is one obvious place we confront the presence of the climate crisis: in the weather. What is more contemporary, more current, than the weather? Paradigm of the continuous present tense (think of the classic language textbook example: It is raining), weather marks out what is happening right now. From the daily weather report to the constantly updated smartphone app, the self-evident presence of the weather renders it deeply banal. As Benjamin laments in *The Arcades Project*, "Nothing is more characteristic than that this most intimate and mysterious affair, the working of the weather on humans, should have become the theme of their emptiest chatter." Benjamin, though, was also attuned to the temporal dimensions of the weather, to "the double meaning of the term *temps* in French": time and weather.[17] From the perspective of time, our incessant chatter about the weather may not be so empty after all. The social custom of chatting about the weather is best understood as a collective way of pinpointing the shared yet fleeting time of the now.[18] According to Frances Ferguson, this is how weather came to be "incorporated into conversation over the breakfast table and in the elevator, the most egalitarian topos in the social repertoire. It was a sociable theme precisely because the reports were time limited, variable, changing."[19] What makes the weather sociable is its invocation of a present that is at once socially particular and fundamentally transient. The weather's banal status as a "sociable theme" also makes it an indispensable social form for addressing the complexities of a present that is "time limited," "variable," and constantly "changing."

When it rains or snows, in short, we know what *now* means. And when it snows in June or fails to in January, we know, or think we know, that something about the now is different, off-kilter, altered. In the context of climate change, however, weather is a surprisingly vexed figure: an urgent warning sign (because there is no doubt that climate change is changing the weather) as well as an unreliable indicator (because no isolated weather event can be clearly connected to climate change). "The terms *weather* and *climate* are often used interchangeably," the geologists B. Lynn Ingram and Frances Malamud-Roam explain, "but there are important distinctions. Climate refers to the statistical description of weather over a given period of time and for a given region, including the weather extremes."[20] Climate represents a historical pattern, while current weather conditions (say, a distressingly warm winter) may be only an isolated instance or a statistical outlier. As the environmental historian Gillen D'Arcy Wood suggests, "One's experience of long-term changes in the weather takes place between the statistic and the anecdote."[21] Weather is anecdotal, and climate is statistical; there is no middle ground between the two. Because climate is a historical average, it can be neither confirmed nor refuted by any particular instance of odd weather. The Climate Central organization (a group of scientists and journalists) offers this example: "A 100° day in New York in July is hotter than average, but by itself it doesn't mean the climate is getting warmer. A string of 100° days in New York in July doesn't necessarily mean the climate is getting warmer."[22] The point here is that there is an empirical as well as a conceptual gap between isolated weather events and long-term climatic trends. Compared with the statistical tendency of a climate, weather is epiphenomenal, anecdotal, unrepresentative of what's really in the air. Thus beware the weather: it may not mean what you think.

The weather, immediate and ephemeral, seems ill suited as an access point to both the long-term average of climate and the slow-motion history of climate change. Yet if we want to confront the cold truth of a warming planet, changes in the weather may be all we have. As the earth's temperature continues to rise catastrophically by as much as 7°F (4°C) over the next century, the slow change in the global mercury is, Archer admits, "not really noticeable to most of us in our daily lives." What is noticeable, though, is "the frequency of extreme climate events such as strong storms, rainfall, and heat waves."[23] What is visible, in other words, is weather, which may have a more dialectical relationship to climate than we first thought. As Climate Central puts it: "Weather Is Not Climate. Climate Is Not Weather. Except They Kind of Are."[24] This imperfect equivalence rests on the fact that changing weather is nothing less than what climate change looks like. From this perspective, that "string of 100° days" may not be so epiphenomenal or unrepresentative after all—not when the first decade of the twenty-first century was the warmest ten-year period ever recorded. Here, then, weather begins to look less like a phenomenological distraction or a statistical mistake and more like an unavoidable way of mediating our relation to the abstract concept of climate. Weather, in Margaret Ronda's words, "stands as the master-sign of anthropogenic effects that are daily and systemic, visible and non-localizable."[25] Daily yet systemic, visible yet non-localizable: these are the paradoxes of climate change's imperceptible presence that weather enables us to think through. If climate is where weather is abstracted into a historical average, then weather is where that abstraction can be seen for what it really is: a set of material conditions that shape contemporary life. Weather is both a symptom and a symbol of the contemporary era of climate change, an imperfect yet irreplaceable method for grasping the otherwise invisible alteration of the climate.

This chapter is an attempt to theorize the relation of weather, climate, and the contemporary. To fully develop this theory, I have added one more item to the list: film. No aesthetic medium is more closely connected to the weather than film. On-screen, cinema has been synonymous with meteorological spectacle ever since the Lumière brothers' *Snow Dance* ("perhaps the earliest example of cinematic snow") was screened in 1896.[26] Off-screen, film production itself is inescapably entangled with the elements; to make a movie is to deal with the weather. Films shot on location involve extensive attempts to predict weather patterns; a preproduction memo from *True Grit* (Henry Hathaway, 1969), for example, "includes a meticulous two-page list . . . of the high and low temperatures and rainfall for every day of September and October for both 1966 and 1967." [27] Indeed, the very development of studio films is tied up with meteorological history, as the costs of dealing with inclement weather drove moviemaking indoors. As the film scholar Kristi McKim details in *Cinema as Weather*, "Film historians agree that weather became a defining factor in the rise of the studio film."[28] As a medium tasked with both representing weather and literally weathering it, film offers an indispensable site for reading weather that is simultaneously on-screen and behind the scenes, natural and manufactured, carefully controlled yet ultimately unpredictable. The history of cinema is a history of art's attempt to depict, to master, and to make the weather—and to do so in the midst of a historical moment when the weather we ourselves have made is becoming increasingly hard to either predict or control.

But why Westerns? It's a fair question. Today Westerns have a noticeably frail grip on the popular imagination, the consequence of a decline that began in the 1970s. In 1971, forty-four Westerns were released; in 1974, only nine; and since then, a "drop in production . . . so dramatic as to remove the Western from the list of major popular narrative genres altogether."[29] The Western is now just as likely to be the rarefied touchstone of art-house cinema as the sturdy backbone of a mainstream studio film.[30] The dramatic shift in both the popular fortunes and the cultural status of the genre was accompanied by a decisive historical shift. With the ends of both the Cold War and the American Century, the most influential framework for interpreting the Western—as a distinctive U.S. product of Cold War liberalism and nationalism—ceased to apply.[31] As one critic observes in the introduction to *Contemporary Westerns*, there is currently no "clear picture of the relationship between the post-9/11 American zeitgeist and the Western genre."[32]

My claim is that we can understand the contemporary persistence of the Western by rereading the genre in terms of ecological rather than political history. Just think of the issues around which almost every Western plot turns: "ranching and farming, water rights, mining techniques, land rush and the oil frontier, railroad[s]."[33] What more representative genre of fossil capitalism could there be than the prototypical genre of the coal-powered train (figure 4.1)? Taken together, these concerns shape the ecological unconscious of the Western. "Westerns stake a claim about the natural world's

FIGURE 4.1. The steam-engine Western (*High Noon*) as the genre of the Anthropocene.

relationship to American history," the film historian Scott Simmon argues in *The Invention of the Western Film.* "Is nature gentle and generous and thus in league with national advancement? Or leering and savage, opposed to us?"[34]

The Western's account of the natural world is most often communicated through its depiction of the land. The centrality of landscape to the classic Western is undisputed. "I think you can say that the real star of my westerns has always been the land," John Ford once remarked.[35] For Ford, this was a particular kind of land: the "deserts and canyons" that, according to Edward Buscombe, "in the last part of the nineteenth century . . . replaced mountains as the most beautiful and authentic American landscape."[36] Now the desert is so closely associated with the Western that, in answer to the question of why she wanted to make a Western, the director Kelly Reichardt could tell an interviewer, "I've always wanted to shoot in a desert."[37] For Tomkins, desert landscape is the genre's "whole point": "The typical western movie opens with a landscape shot. . . . In the beginning, say these shots, was the earth, and the earth was desert." The landscape of the Western is thus "a land defined by absence: of trees, of greenery, of houses, of the signs of civilization, above all, absence of water and shade."[38] The other thing that's absent from this land, it turns out, is time. In Tomkins's view, the Western's deserts suggest "a moment before time began."[39] It is indeed tempting to see in the landscapes of the Western an essentially timeless struggle between human society and the natural world, or, more precisely, between human time and nature's timelessness.[40] But this view isn't quite right. The seemingly primordial landscape of the Western contains its own kind of time: very, very, very slow time. As Buscombe describes it, "The thousand-feet-high outcrops of de Chelly sandstone rising starkly from the valley floor of Monument Valley surely call to mind an equally awesome sense of time etched into the rock by millions of years of erosion" (figure 4.2).[41] What looks at first like a distinction in the Western between time (culture) and timelessness (nature) is really a distinction between different measures of time: fast and slow, human and geological, social and glacial.

The Western gives us what the historian Fernand Braudel calls "history in slow motion."[42] Such historical slow motion doesn't apply only to geography and geology. It also applies to the climate. "Everything changes," Braudel reminds us, "even the climate."[43] How does the Western begin to

FIGURE 4.2. *The Searchers*: geological time in Monument Valley.

register the impossibly slow transformation of the climate? That is the question I seek to answer in the remainder of this chapter, by turning away from the genre's seemingly timeless landscapes and toward its increasingly foreboding skies. What follows is a meteorological history of the Western. The aim of this history is to show, first, how the classic Western became a prominent film genre for depicting strange variations in the weather; and to explain, second, how contemporary Westerns have adapted the genre's meteorological imaginary in order to represent the historical shift from the innocent days of anomalous weather to the imperiled age of a changing climate.

Through the changing meteorology of the Western, we may begin to see what it would mean to recover the frequently derided figure of weather as a vital concept for historicizing our contemporary moment. As the climate scientist Heidi Cullen suggests, "Weather is a timescale we can't stop."[44] In the unstoppable timescale of the weather, the contemporary Western discovers an aesthetic strategy for rethinking time, change, and climate change: a way of reimagining the relation between the imperceptibly slow motion of the climate crisis and the immediacy of contemporary life. The history of the Western, I argue, is a history of how global warming changes our weather, as well as a lesson in how the very concept of weather might in turn change our understanding of the temporality of climate change.

## THE COLD WEST

"Cold ain't it?" This question—posed to the doomed heroine of *The Great Silence* (Sergio Corbucci, 1967)—accentuates an unexpected weather pattern shaping the Western. We tend to think of the Western as a hot commodity; the classic midcentury Western was usually shot in the dry heat of Arizona or California, taking advantage of a stable desert climate that was obviously salutary for film production. But some of the most famous instances of the genre like it cold. How does the cold remake our assumptions about the cinema of the Old West? From the 1950s to the 1970s, both canonical and revisionist Westerns used winter settings to emphasize the tangibility and visibility of the weather. Across this range of winter Westerns, snow offers a record of the genre's need to grapple with a visibly hostile environment, revealing how the very attempt to make a Western was entangled in both the materiality and the mythology of the weather.

Everyone talks about the majestic landscape of *The Searchers* (John Ford, 1956), but almost no one talks about its weather. Nonetheless, weather plays a key role in the film, primarily in the stunning range of meteorological events the film depicts, as it shifts from sun-bleached desert to falling snow in the blink of an eye. Snow, in particular, plays a special role in *The Searchers*. In fact, snow is part of what gives the film its name: it is what prolongs the search. The film's main characters, Ethan and Marty, spend five years searching for Ethan's niece Debbie, who has been kidnapped by a Comanche tribe, and every time they seem close to finding her, they lose their way in the snow. First, they are caught in a blizzard that comes and goes without explanation; later, they find themselves in a week-long snowstorm that covers over the trail they had been following (figure 4.3). Marty acknowledges the frustrations of the snow in a voice-over: there may have been "other signs for us to follow but we'll never know, 'cause it snowed that day and all the next week." Snow is thus a narrative device in the form of a meteorological obstacle. Snowy weather structures the narrative of the film by making the search take long enough to be worth making a film about. While one function of snow in *The Searchers* is to take up time, its other function is to reassure both the characters and the audience that the time spent searching will be worth it. During the film's first blizzard, Marty, covered in snow, complains, "We're beat and you know it." Ethan responds, "We'll find 'em in the end, I promise you. We'll find 'em—as sure as the

FIGURE 4.3. Epic snow in *The Searchers*.

turning of the earth." This reference to the "turning of the earth" turns the natural cycle of the seasons—the very cycle that has covered them in snow in the first place—into a metaphor for a search for justice that is likewise natural and cyclical.[45] What comes around goes around: Debbie's disappearance is no different from the arrival of winter, both of which represent temporary points along a larger, inexorable orbit. In this way, the winter weather of *The Searchers* serves as both the foundation of the film's narrative form and the governing ideology of its vision of frontier justice, understood to be no less natural or inevitable than the coming and going of winter itself.

In addition to functioning as a narrative form and an organizing metaphor, snow plays a central role in *The Searchers'* self-made mythology as a classic Western. Ethan and Marty's search, stretched to epic proportions by the snow, becomes a metaphor for the film's self-consciously epic ambitions. In his book on the making of *The Searchers*, Glenn Frankel writes that the film's producer, C. V. Whitney, "had made himself clear: he didn't just want a movie; he wanted an epic."[46] Such epic ambitions were ultimately communicated through extreme variations in the weather. This explains why the weather in *The Searchers* looks so implausible. The film isn't trying to represent a single, diegetically coherent climate; it's trying to depict as many different impressive spectacles of weather as possible. To that end, *The Searchers* was shot in a variety of different climates, from Utah to Colorado to Alberta, Canada, and this pastiche of mismatched climates became central to the film's presentation of itself as an epic. *The Searchers* promised to be, in the words of its publicity materials, "the BIG-GEST, ROUGHEST, TOUGHEST, and MOST BEAUTIFUL PICTURE ever made."[47] The film's size, authenticity, and beauty all were tied to its depiction of extreme weather. Whitney's production company "boast[ed] grandiosely that *The Searchers* covered a wider range of geography and temperatures than any previous movie: 1,500 miles from Alberta, Canada[,] to Monument Valley, and more than 100 degrees Fahrenheit from the below-zero tundra of Canada to the blistering hot temperatures of summer in the valley."[48] If snow is the obstacle that Marty and Ethan must overcome to prove their heroic commitment to the search, it is also the obstacle the filmmakers themselves must overcome to demonstrate their heroic ability to make a properly epic film.

In revisionist Westerns of the same period, by contrast, snow was a way to question the very assumption of film's mastery of the natural world. One of the first Westerns set entirely in the harsh conditions of heavy snow was André de Toth's *Day of the Outlaw* (1959), which de Toth described as an attempt "to explore the bizarre situation of a group of outlaws on a getaway, terrorizing a small western village, and then, by a quirk of nature, becoming equally the prisoners of a white silence in the middle of nowhere." What de Toth calls "a quirk of nature" is really the cold truth of winter weather, which asserts its control over the characters. To emphasize that control, it was important to de Toth that the weather look real: "I wanted the weather, the rain and the snow to age on the buildings, not painters' spray and cotton wool for snow on the roofs. The weather and the natural snow were cheaper than studio material and labor."[49] De Toth's insistence on shooting the film outdoors in authentic winter conditions ended up creating a number of production problems. The film's star, Robert Ryan, "caught pneumonia which held up shooting for a week, then snowstorms caused further delays, and finally the money ran out."[50] At both levels of *Day of the Outlaw*—the film's production no less than its plot—winter becomes its own kind of prison. In both cases, the "white silence" of the snow has the last laugh.

The depiction of snow in *Day of the Outlaw* as both a physical and a metaphysical force was a touchstone in the development of the winter Western. De Toth's film had a particularly powerful influence on the Italian director Sergio Corbucci, who turned de Toth's throwaway comment on "white silence" into the premise of his great winter Western, *The Great Silence* (sometimes called *The Big Silence*). Set in Snow Hill County, Utah, in "the year of the great blizzard," *The Great Silence* tells the story of a mountain town terrorized by a mad bounty hunter named Loco and of a mute gunman, Silence, who tries and eventually fails to save the townspeople. *The Great Silence* is a story of bare survival, and sometimes not even that; one of its most radical images is the futile death of the hero in the film's last frame. The film is right at home in the snow-covered mountains, where the characters wear massive fur coats and the starving villagers are reduced to stealing and eating the sheriff's horse. "I'll be damned if I'm freezing to death up here," the sheriff insists upon arriving in Snow Hill and having his horse stolen. The sentiment is nothing if not prescient: later he is killed by Loco, who pushes him into a frozen lake. "Snow's appearance and temperature figuratively conjure death," among other things, Kristi McKim suggests in her history of cinematic weather.[51] Such figurative or symbolic connotations are hard to ignore in *The Great Silence*, a film in which blood, snow, silence, and death become interchangeable terms. The point of Corbucci's land of ice and snow is first to freeze and then to shatter the myths of the classic Western, replacing the genre's warmhearted depictions of heroism and justice with the cold realities of death by snow.

This short summary of the film makes Corbucci seem like an obvious successor to de Toth, as he strips away the trappings of the Western, subjecting the genre to the brute force of the climate. What is different about *The Great Silence*, however, is that its ostensible commitment to authenticity ends up foundering in the snow. Much of *The Great Silence* was filmed in the Italian Alps, Howard C. Hughes tells us in his encyclopedia of Italian Westerns, "near the ski resort of Cortina D'Ampezzo, in the Veneto region of Northern Italy," where Klaus Kinski's wife and daughter "enjoyed sledding in the snow on location."[52] This detail reveals a jarring mismatch between what's on-screen and what's off-camera, between starving in the mountains and sledding at a ski resort. If snow "figuratively conjure[s] death," as McKim puts it, in this case it literally conjured a vacation. The good times on location couldn't last forever, though, and so the mountains of northern Italy were soon replaced by the sound stages of Rome:

After the Cortina shoot, the crew returned to Italy. . . . The Elios town set in Rome was used for several Snow Hill scenes, including two night sequences and the build-up to the final duel. The scenes were shot at night so that the fake "snow" looked more convincing; shaving foam was used to give the street a snow-bound look. For the daylight scenes, the Elios set was swathed in fog, to disguise the fact that the surrounding countryside had no snow.[53]

By the end of the shoot, snow is no longer a symbol of authenticity or realism; it is pure artifice, and not particularly convincing at that. In the scenes shot in town, the snow sticks unnaturally to clothes and faces; it fails to melt when characters go indoors; and it just generally tends to look more or less like what it actually is: shaving cream (figure 4.4). The film's oscillation between the realism of its mountain exteriors and the artificiality of its close-up shots of snow adds an important dimension to Corbucci's distinctive meteorology. Here snow expresses not human finitude but meteorological fiction. This is a fiction that every film about the weather must

FIGURE 4.4. Snow, played by shaving cream, in *The Great Silence*.

reckon with. The snow in *The Great Silence* is less a symbol of the film's cold-blooded realism than a meditation on the dialectical relationship between the Western genre and the natural world—the tension between film's desire to record nature and its attempt to remake it. Rather than adding more realistic weather to the Western, *The Great Silence* reminds us how much the Western's very existence depends on its ability to control the weather. When Silence dies in the snow at the film's dark conclusion, the naturalist aspirations of the genre die with him. What *The Great Silence* ultimately kills off is the fantasy of Western filmmaking as a way to commune with nature.

If it's a real blizzard you want, you'll prefer Robert Altman's *McCabe & Mrs. Miller* (1971). As Robert MacLean writes in *Film Quarterly*, "*McCabe and Mrs. Miller* may be thought of as a film about snow."[54] It is hard to disagree. To think of the film in this way is to think primarily of its famous concluding sequence, in which McCabe and the evil mining company's hired bounty hunters pursue each other through a heavy blizzard. Eventually, everyone dies, including McCabe, who collapses in a snow drift, his face frozen over, gusts of snow sporadically blotting out our view of him (figure 4.5). Critics regularly read the final snow scenes of Altman's famous "anti-Western" as the perfect metaphor for the film's revision of the genre

FIGURE 4.5. The miraculous blizzard in *McCabe & Mrs. Miller*.

as a whole: death overtakes life, nature conquers culture, and McCabe's gift of gab is replaced by the inhuman voice of the howling wind.[55]

The thing about *McCabe*'s much-discussed snow, though, is that it actually wasn't supposed to be there. The 1970 version of the script says nothing about the film being set in snow, which is just as well, given that snow was sure to be unlikely on set in Vancouver, a location where, as Altman would later say, "it rained through the whole damned picture." The snow at the film's end—a real blizzard, which some critics misidentified as fake—was pure meteorological serendipity. Here is how Altman describes it:

Then this snow came along and it kept snowing. I said, "Let's shoot it in the snow." . . . I said, "It's snowing now and we got nothing to do, so let's do it." . . . [I]t snowed constantly for eight days. I mean it did not stop. The snow at times was up to my waist. The nature of the snow is such that as soon as you run a truck through or when an electrician walks through or a grip, there are the footprints and it's all screwed up. So we set up barriers. Suddenly we realized it didn't make any difference; we could walk through the snow and in five minutes it was covered up. We finished the last of that chase scene and we went up to start the church burning, which we did last, and it started to rain and in six hours you couldn't have gotten a bushel of snow. That was luck.[56]

Altman's story about the blizzard plays up the tension between weather and filmmaking. To film in the snow (with actors and electricians and grips traipsing through it) is to risk having it "all screwed up," which means having the weather reveal the presence of the filmmakers themselves. As it happens, de Toth had the same worry: "I didn't want the virgin snow to be defiled by the tracks of the poor electricians dragging cables and lamps."[57] Snow, emblem of nature's power (it covers everything), is also a maddeningly impressionable record of human presence, in the form of footprints and tire tracks. But where de Toth had to carefully manage the untouched appearance of his snow, Altman describes the good fortune of a snowstorm in which the traces left by the crew ultimately "didn't make any difference"; it was snowing so hard that every human imprint was immediately "covered up." Just as the snow blots out McCabe in the film's finale, it also erases the presence of the entire filmmaking apparatus that has set out to capture it.

In interviews, *McCabe*'s cinematographer, Vilmos Zsigmond, has similarly emphasized the serendipity of the snow: "We started shooting that [final] scene . . . then after lunchtime the snow started. A miracle."[58] For both Zsigmond and Altman, snow represents pure meteorological contingency: "luck," "a miracle." It is not surprising that Altman would be seduced by such contingency. The quintessentially Altmanian ethos of chance and improvisation shapes *McCabe & Mrs. Miller* through and through, from its ad-libbed dialogue to its purposefully inaudible sound editing to its intentional blurring of living and acting conditions (the actors and extras whom we see building up the makeshift town of Presbyterian Church on screen were also building the actual set for the film, while also living in the half-finished buildings during the filming). An extension of these naturalistic flourishes, the final blizzard becomes the ultimate example of *McCabe*'s account of a world that lies fully outside human control. Altman's improvisatory aesthetic doesn't just accommodate the randomness of the weather; it depends on it.

From the blur of real blizzards to the blurring of real and fake snow, the lesson of the winter Western is that filmmakers may make their own weather movies, but they do not make them in weather of their own choosing. When snow comes, Altman improvises, blurring the line between the climate control of cinema and the contingency of the weather. When snow doesn't come, Corbucci fakes it, revealing the artifice that underlies the Western's representation of nature. In both cases, snow becomes nothing less than a way of reflecting on the logistics of filmmaking itself.[59] Corbucci's fake snow embodies the chronically low production values that distinguished Rome's Cinecittà Studios from Hollywood's higher budgets, while Altman's blizzard expresses the improvisatory ideology that defined American independent cinema in the 1970s.[60] Snow is no less industrially reflexive in *The Searchers*, where it symbolizes the epic scope required to sell the film to the studio in the first place,[61] or in *Day of the Outlaw*, where it represents the practical difficulties of a director's stubborn insistence on shooting outdoors. In all four films, we see how the Western's confrontation with the weather becomes a site for meditating not on nature as such but on the nature of film production. Here weather represents nothing but itself. More precisely, it represents the dilemma of representing it, the spectacle of attempting to capture on film those weather conditions that are most difficult to film in. From this perspective, *The Searchers*, *Day of the Outlaw*, *The Great Silence*, and *McCabe & Mrs. Miller* all are stories about the same thing: the feats of planning, production, manipulation, and pure chance that are required to make a film both in and about inclement weather.

## THE WARMING WESTERN

The remainder of this chapter documents how the Western has transformed from a genre of epic weather into a genre of global warming. This is an argument about what happens to a genre about weather once it crosses into a historical moment in which humans realize that they have altered the very nature of the weather. The idea that people could influence the weather first entered popular discourse in the 1990s, largely by way of Bill McKibben's best seller *The End of Nature* (1989). McKibben's book was one of the earliest to lay out for a lay audience "the accepted scientific wisdom . . . that the increase in carbon dioxide and other trace gases will soon heat the world if it hasn't already done so."[62] "We have changed the atmosphere," McKibben announced, "and that will change the weather. The temperature and the rainfall are no longer to be entirely the work of some separate, uncivilizable force, but instead in part a product of our habits, our economies, our ways of life." Only ten years after *The End of Nature* was published, climate change had rapidly progressed from seeming like a "distant and speculative threat" to being a vivid contemporary reality.[63] As McKibben himself acknowledged in the introduction to the book's tenth anniversary edition, "A decade ago, those of us who were convinced that the climate was warming fast were out on a limb. A sturdy limb—the fact that carbon dioxide trapped heat near the planet seemed irrefutable—but a limb nonetheless." A decade later, by contrast, "the studies on global warming would fill an airplane hangar."[64] Almost all these studies came to the same conclusion, one summed up by the Intergovernmental Panel on Climate Change, whose 1995 report stated, "The balance of evidence suggests that there is a discernible human influence on global climate."[65]

If we consider the start of the twenty-first century as the moment not when climate change began per se but when it began to be a substantial part of public consciousness, we can understand how the Western, too, would begin to acquire new meaning during the same years, as it evolved from a genre concerning isolated changes in the weather to a genre concerning the worldwide crisis of a changing climate. At first glance, the recent spate of what I call *climate change Westerns*—including *The Assassination of Jesse*

*James by the Coward Robert Ford* (Andrew Dominik, 2007), *Sukiyaki Western Django* (Takashi Miike, 2007), *True Grit* (Joel and Ethan Coen, 2010), *Django Unchained* (Quentin Tarantino, 2012), *The Hateful Eight* (Tarantino, 2015), and *The Revenant* (Alejandro González Iñárritu, 2015)—may look a lot like the Westerns discussed in the previous section. These two sets of films do indeed have one obvious thing in common: an affinity for snow. Writing in the *New York Times*, Tarantino even cites *The Great Silence* as an explicit inspiration for *Django Unchained*: "'Silenzio' takes place in the snow—I liked the action in the snow so much, 'Django Unchained' has a big snow section in the middle of the movie."[66] (Tarantino's subsequent film, *The Hateful Eight*, can be read as the logical, if excessive, conclusion to his admiration for Corbucci.) My contention, however, is that these recent Westerns can be distinguished from earlier winter Westerns through their interest not in inclement but in *unseasonable* weather. The contemporary Western uses the increasingly unfamiliar patterns of the seasons to signify the larger historical catastrophe of a changing climate.

An increasingly visible consequence of climate change is the steady loss of normal seasons and, with them, our basic sense of seasonally regulated time.[67] "The seasons now are not proceeding cyclically," observes Gillen D'Arcy Wood.[68] It's not just that "summers are becoming unbearably hot," as Adrian Parr notes in *The Wrath of Capital*; it's also that the "leaves fall later in the year."[69] McKibben, too, notices a change in the way the seasons change: "Spring on average comes *a week earlier* across the Northern Hemisphere than it did just two decades ago."[70] As the concentration of greenhouse gases in the atmosphere grows and global temperatures continue to rise, explains Heidi Cullen, "the seasons [will] become almost unrecognizable."[71]

Unseasonality is thus an unavoidable concept for understanding the intersection of weather and climate in an age of global warming. It is also an inescapable fact for anyone trying to film a Western. Under conditions of climate change, it is getting harder and harder to make a movie in seasonally appropriate weather. Consider the well-documented tribulations in the making of Iñárritu's critically acclaimed (probably overrated) winter Western, *The Revenant*. As the film's star, Leonardo DiCaprio, explains in an interview: "We had a lot of complications while shooting, because it was the hottest year in recorded history. . . . Twice during the movie we had 7 feet of snow melt in a day—all of it, within five hours—and we were stuck with two or three weeks of no snow in a film that's all snow." With no snow in Calgary, where the film was originally scheduled to be shot, "we had to go to the southern tip of Argentina, to the southernmost town on the planet, to find snow." "That's what happens," DiCaprio concludes, "with climate change."[72] *The Revenant* thus offers a record of the ways that climate change changes the very conditions of making a Western. How the altered rhythms of the seasons affect both the production and the imagination of the contemporary Western is the subject of the pages that follow. In contemporary Westerns, the everyday epiphenomenon of the weather and the global crisis of an altered climate are brought together by the newly strange temporality of the seasons. If weather is always, in a certain sense, "a figure for change,"[73] the weather of the twenty-first-century Western dramatizes the change from predictable seasons to unfamiliar weather patterns—the transition from seasonal change to climate change.

The first thing we see in *The Assassination of Jesse James* is a shot of rolling clouds. The clouds tell us that this is a film preoccupied with atmospheric change, a story about shifts in the weather. Even Jesse James's mythic personality is figured in meteorological terms. "Rooms felt hotter when he was in them," says the narrator; "rains fell straighter. Clocks slowed." The atmospherics of the film seem, at first, to be largely internal, the heavy psychological weather of its two title characters, from Jesse's inscrutable intentions (the Ford brothers can never tell what Jesse is thinking, and so they worry he is planning to kill them) to Bob Ford's confused desires (he hates Jesse, and he also loves him). But changes in the weather play a more explicit role in structuring the narrative. The coming of winter at the film's midway point marks the sudden chilling of Jesse's friendships and his descent into solitude and paranoia; the arrival of spring at the end corresponds to the blooming of the Ford brothers' decision to kill Jesse. These seasonal shifts are further underscored by the film's visual grammar. An unmistakable series of parallel shots, for instance, track the slow arrival of winter. In the first shot, two men ride through a green field tinged with yellow light; in the second, they ride through a field dotted with snow; and in the third, a rider is half submerged in a full-blown blizzard (figure 4.6). The images are identically framed, shot through a window or from a porch, with a minor character (mirroring the viewer) either seen from behind or revealed in a reverse shot. The visual repetition highlights everything that stays the same in these scenes—the rider, the house, the approach—in order to underscore

FIGURE 4.6. Watching the seasons change in *The Assassination of Jesse James*.

the one thing that's in the process of changing: the season. In these shots, the inscrutable interiority of the characters is juxtaposed to the relentless time of the seasons. The unpredictable ebbs and flows of human emotion are dwarfed by the steady rhythms of the weather. Time and again, the film deploys meteorological imagery to put human subjectivity in its place. At one point, Jesse contemplates suicide while standing on a frozen lake; at another, Bob helps a friend bury a corpse in the snow and then assists in blessing the body. "Blessed are the—," says the friend, forgetting the last word, which Bob supplies for him: "—meek." On the word *meek*, the film cuts sharply from the claustrophobic forest burial to a wide-angle shot of fast-moving clouds rolling over the winter landscape, the sun setting in time-lapse off to the side. The cut tells us that meekness is the truth of human affairs when viewed from the cosmological perspective of meteorological time.

*Jesse James* is thus less about extreme weather than about the predictable cycles of the seasons. Seasonal time demands attunement to the continuous change of a climate. In this way, it is really change itself—the natural fact of ephemerality, the temporariness of the physical world—that lies at the heart of the film. Seasons change; passions cool; reputations rise and fall. The film seeks out a universal theory of these changes in seasonality, where wayward variation becomes formalizable as weather pattern. Pattern propels the film. There is the pattern of robbery and murder that made Jesse's reputation in the first place; the pattern that Bob and his brother detect in Jesse's killing off each member of his gang; and the pattern of fleeting celebrity itself, as Bob makes his name by killing Jesse and starring in a stage show based on the assassination, only to be killed in turn. The lesson of *Jesse James*, then, is that nothing lasts. While this lesson may apply to earthbound affairs, we first learn it, the film suggests, from watching the skies.

At the end of the film, though, these skies acquire a somewhat different texture. In one scene close to the end, we see Bob and his new love interest sitting on the shore of a lake, framed by the Colorado mountains. In the next scene, they are sitting together in a rowboat, once more against a backdrop of mountains. But here the natural setting has been drained of color, and in a moment, the camera pulls back to reveal why: they are no longer at the lake but in a photographer's studio, having their picture taken in front of a painted screen (figure 4.7, *top*). Having opened with moving clouds, the film ends with painted ones—a sky unmistakably of human making. This is one version of nature's end: the rhythms of the weather flattened into static image. The significance of the relation between the death of nature and technologies of representation is underscored by the way the painted screen and the photographer's studio parallel a key scene that has come just a few minutes earlier, in which Jesse's corpse is photographed first on an autopsy table and then on a bed of ice (figure 4.7, *bottom*). "The resulting

FIGURE 4.7. The painted sky (*top*), the photographed corpse (*bottom*), and the death of nature in *Jesse James*.

prints sold for two dollars a piece and were the models for the lithographed covers on a number of magazines," the narrator informs us as we see a crowd of eager customers rushing toward a photography studio. Demonstrating how the technology of the photograph manages to both capture and capitalize on Jesse's death, this scene predicts how (as we are about to witness in the shot of Bob in front of the painted mountains) aesthetic representation comes to record the death of nature itself.

The fact that both scenes cannot help but conjure the apparatus of the film camera—nowhere more than in the shot of Jesse's body reflected in the camera lens—suggests that *Jesse James* understands itself to be the latest point in the technological history of nature's end. The move indoors to escape the elements, the simulation of the weather inside the studio, the transfer of the natural landscape onto a screen: all the features of Bob's nature portrait combine to tell a story about the history of cinema itself. It is clear that for the film, this story about cinema's representation of nature is a distinctly melancholic one. This gives a rather different twist to the idea of industrial allegory that I argued was part of the earlier wave of winter Westerns, in which snow was a site for reflecting on the process of filmmaking. In *Jesse James*'s final depiction of weather's domestication by photography, in contrast, we find something like an allegory of industrialization—the technology of the camera lens as stand-in for the whole technological history of modernization and for modernization's wholesale remaking of the atmosphere. Whereas *McCabe & Mrs. Miller* recorded a blizzard so fierce that it was impervious to technological imprint ("we could walk through the snow and in five minutes it was covered up"), *Jesse James* reminds us that our technological capacity to represent the weather is inseparable from the industrialized history of our changing it. The film represents this decisive change in the weather as both a flattening into image and a passing into legend. The parallel between Jesse's frozen corpse and Bob's fake sky turns the film's own painstaking representation of seasonal weather into a kind of death-mask photography: less an image of a living climate than an homage to one that it realizes has already passed away.

*True Grit* similarly revolves around the rhythms of the seasons. The narrative arc of the film from injustice to justice is tracked by the seasonal movement from winter—as Mattie Ross "go[es] off in winter time to avenge her father's death"—to spring. Because spring represents the final blooming of justice, the bulk of the film takes place during winter. Snow is the first thing we see in the film, as the camera fades into a scene of snow falling on the dead body of Mattie's father, and it sporadically reappears as a kind of leitmotif at key moments in the story, first in the climactic sequence where Rooster Cogburn rushes to save Mattie's life after a snake bite and once more in the film's final scene. In this way, the snow in *True Grit* functions as both a visual motif and a framing device, the very first and very last thing the camera shows us. For as much as snow seems to be the visual accomplice to Mattie's quest for vengeance, it also suggests that her quest, like the winter itself, is only a temporary moment in a larger cycle. The film goes to great lengths to point out seasonal variation. "Ground's too hard," Rooster notes at one point; "if he wanted a decent burial he should have gotten himself killed in summer." Rooster himself does wait until summer to get himself killed. In the film's coda, when Mattie finds out that Rooster has died, she chalks it up to the change in the weather: "I believe the warm weather was too much for him." The passing of time that takes us from the main story to the coda and from fourteen-year-old Mattie to thirty-nine-year-old Mattie is here represented as a shift in the weather. The move from cold weather to warm or from winter to spring again calls to mind (as it did in *Jesse James*) those familiar meteorological metaphors of thaw, recovery, and rebirth: psychological closure both symbolized and secured by the seasons. As Mattie puts it in the film's final line, "Time just gets away from us." The evidence that it does so lies in the temporality of seasonally variable weather.

The concluding scene of *True Grit*, however, offers a more untimely vision of the weather. Having had Rooster's body shipped from Tennessee back to Yell County so he could be buried in the "family plot," Mattie now stands by his graveside on a hill under a tree. The sky is blue; the grass is green; and, strangely, the screen is filled with snowflakes (figure 4.8). The weather is not inclement or extreme. It is simply unseasonable. In other words, we simply cannot to tell what season it is. As it turns out, this is not the first time in the film when it's hard to say where the snow is coming from. Practically all the snow in *True Grit* poses a basic problem of provenance. For one thing, it never snows in the 1969 version of *True Grit* (though there is snow on the ground in the final farewell between Kim Darby and John Wayne, a brief and unexplained backdrop that may have inspired the Coens' alternative meteorology). For another, it doesn't snow very much in Yell County, Arkansas, where most of the film is set; indeed, the county

FIGURE 4.8. Unseasonable weather in *True Grit*.

averages less than three inches of snow a year. The intrusion of snow during Rooster's funeral can thus be read as a belated acknowledgment that
none of the weather in the film really belongs. From the first moment to
the last, the weather in *True Grit* is all wrong—from the wrong film, in the
wrong place, and at the wrong time. *True Grit* is less about seasonal change
than it is about unseasonableness as such, the radical disjuncture between
predictable seasons and untimely weather. This disjuncture, of course, also
defines climate change: a fact that has become depressingly familiar following a seemingly endless stream of news stories about unseasonable
weather, such as when the National Weather Service reported in 2013 that
an unprecedented May snowstorm in Arkansas was the latest into the year
it had ever snowed in the state's recorded history.[74] The snow that falls at
the end of *True Grit*—without any seasonal context, not a part of any known
climatic pattern—signifies the same incongruity. Out of season and without explanation, *True Grit*'s snow registers the turbulence wrought by a
changing climate, the discovery that snow no longer belongs to a stable seasonal pattern but now may fall in the most unlikely of places at the most
improbable times of the year.

Read together, *True Grit* and *The Assassination of Jesse James* are not so
much nostalgic re-creations of the old West as they are examples of how

the Western genre has been forced to adapt to the unseasonability of anthropogenic weather. Both movies include a self-conscious commentary on the relation between generic adaptation and meteorological change. Each film ends by dramatizing a key moment at which the old West is transformed from living history to fictionalized performance: Bob becomes the star of a play based on his life, while Rooster becomes a prop in a traveling Old West show. And each film connects this staged moment to a decisive change in the weather. In *True Grit*, it is "the warm weather" experienced during the show that proves "too much for Rooster." In *Jesse James*, it is the painted sky that situates Bob's newfound fame in an environment of purely human making. In both cases, the transformation of the *West* into the *Western* is inseparable from the transformation of the climate: the collapse of cyclical seasons into inimical weather, the replacement of the natural world by technological mediation. The steady timekeeping performed by the seasons is no longer available in an era of meteorological disruption and planetary warming. *True Grit* and *Jesse James* acknowledge this even as they indulge our desire to forget it. The form of that indulgence is nothing less than the generic form of the Western itself. The continued life of the genre, these films suggest, is a symptom of our nostalgia for a version of the weather that—like the Old West itself—has long since become an unrecoverable part of our past.

## SNOW GLOBALIZATION

If we want to understand the contemporary Western as a genre formally bound up with global warming, we also have to address the *global* part. In their essay "Writing the Anthropocene," Kate Marshall and Tobias Boes note that "anthropogenic climate change on a truly global level . . . can never be experienced—only local changes in weather patterns can."[75] Here is another way to read the tension between weather and climate: as a tension between the local and the global. From this perspective, climate change poses a dilemma not only of time but also of space: first, of how to scale up our thinking to the size of the entire planet; and second, of how to grasp the warming of that planet through the uneven geographical and geopolitical distribution of its effects. A systemic view of climate change is significantly complicated by the wide range of local weather patterns and geographical vulnerabilities. Today, however, such local differences and ostensibly isolated weather events make sense only with respect to the changing structure of the climate as a whole. How, then, can the Western get us from the local to the global in an era of climate change?

The genre that André Bazin famously called "the American film *par excellence*" has in fact had a surprisingly global career.[76] A map of the twentieth-century Western would include not just the United States but also Italy, Germany, Spain, France, China, Japan, and India, to offer only a partial list.[77] Here is one way to tell the story of the Western's globalization. As the popularity of Western cinema was declining in the United States in the early 1960s, the genre surfaced in Japan as Akira Kurosawa's *Yojimbo* (1961), a samurai film set against the John Ford–inspired backdrop of the American Western. One of *Yojimbo*'s greatest admirers was Sergio Leone, whose *A Fistful of Dollars* (1964) transplanted the plot of *Yojimbo* from Japan to the U.S.-Mexican border but otherwise copied Kurosawa's film almost shot for shot. (The similarity between the two films was so conspicuous that Kurosawa sued Leone for copyright infringement and won Japanese distribution rights for *A Fistful of Dollars*.)[78] *A Fistful of Dollars* was technically not the first Western made in Italy, but it was the first to make a marketable phenomenon out of what became known as the "spaghetti Western." Spaghetti Westerns were remarkably international affairs: *A Fistful of Dollars*, for example, was bankrolled by film studios in Italy, Spain, and West Germany; shot in Spain; and populated by "a cosmopolitan cast of German and Italian co-stars and Spanish extras" alongside its soon-to-be-famous American star, Clint Eastwood.[79] They were also explicitly made for an international audience. The films were post-synched, meaning they were not performed in any one language; actors often simply moved their lips, and in post-production the films were simultaneously dubbed into Italian, Spanish, French, German, and English to facilitate global distribution.[80] Eventually, the international popularity of the spaghetti Western came to the attention of Hollywood itself, which soon found itself making imitations—like *Hang 'Em High* (Ted Post, 1968)—and funding expansions—like Leone's *Once Upon a Time in the West* (1968)—of a subgenre of European productions that began with a copy of a Japanese film that itself was a rewriting of the American Westerns of the 1940s and 1950s. At this point, it becomes impossible to determine what exactly is being appropriated or by whom. Suffice it to say that by the end of the 1960s, the

Western was a genre fully shaped by the tension between its national roots and its global reach.

The unlikely protagonist of the story of the American-Japanese-Italian Western is a man named Django. Seeing the immense popularity of Leone's films and hoping to draw as much from the well as possible, in 1966 the Italian studio Cinecittà produced Sergio Corbucci's *Django*, which retold the story of *A Fistful of Dollars* (which you'll recall was already a retelling of *Yojimbo*), though with the unmistakable stylistic verve of the second most influential director to come out of the Cinecittà stable. *Django* was hugely successful, especially in Germany, and so "Italian studios began churning out 'Django' films that had little to do with Corbucci's original," with titles like *Son of Django* (1967), *A Few Dollars for Django* (1968), *Don't Wait for Django, Shoot* (1968), and *Viva Django* (1971).[81] By one estimate, there are more than fifty unofficial *Django* sequels, including many films that simply used the name in their titles as a marketing tool.[82] The market for *Django* remakes is apparently still going strong, as evidenced by Tarantino's *Django Unchained*, which grossed more than $162 million in the United States alone and managed to secure a cameo from none other than Franco Nero, the Italian actor who played the original Django. More interesting for our purposes, however, is that Tarantino also had a small speaking role in another remake of *Django* that came out some five years before his own: the Japanese director Takashi Miike's *Sukiyaki Western Django*. While *Django Unchained* reimagines the spaghetti Western as a narrowly U.S. product—a commentary on the legacy of slavery in the American South—*Sukiyaki Western Django* offers a more complex and disorienting meditation on the fate of the Western as a fully global form.

*Sukiyaki Western Django* feels less like a movie, let alone a Western, than like a work of performance art about the Western. From its title (*sukiyaki* is a Japanese dish to which *shirataki* [noodles] are added at the end, so the play is on "spaghetti") to its plot (which tells the Western's archetypal story of small-town conflict via references to both Japan's Genpei War and England's War of the Roses) to its dialogue (which transforms the multilingualism of the post-synched spaghetti Western into the spectacle of non-English-speaking Japanese actors reciting dialogue in deliberately stilted English), it is as if the film wants to fold into itself the Western's entire hidden history of transnational collaboration and appropriation.

(Miike's decision to have Tarantino speak some of his English lines with a cringeworthy Japanese accent represents perhaps the most explicit evidence of the film's awareness of the troubling dynamics of cultural appropriation, especially considering how much Tarantino himself had borrowed from Japanese cinema, for instance in the first *Kill Bill* [2003].) The contradictions of that history are embraced by the film's ending, which informs us with a paragraph of on-screen text that "a few years later, the kid, Heihachi"—the traumatized young boy who has seen his parents murdered but has otherwise played an extremely minor role in the story—"made his way to Italy and was known as a man called Django." On cue, the credits roll while the original *Django* theme song plays in the background, now sung in Japanese. The point of this cross-cultural finale is to reveal that *Sukiyaki Western Django* is not only a remake but also a prequel, the origin story of Corbucci's *Django* itself. As film history, this is a savvy claim. Given the debt that both *Django* and *A Fistful of Dollars* owe to *Yojimbo*, it is quite right to say that *Django* itself was, as it were, born in Japan before it making its "way to Italy." But considering that *Sukiyaki*'s plot is set "several hundred years after the battle of Dan-no-ura"—which took place in 1185—while *Django* is set sometime after the U.S. Civil War, this origin story is also an example of how Miike uses the Western genre as a means of contorting time and space.

The temporal, historical, and cultural disjunctions that shape *Sukiyaki Western Django* are neatly laid out in the film's opening prologue, a ridiculously fake scene in which an American cowboy is set upon by Japanese bandits in the Nevada desert. The scene is shot against a two-dimensional backdrop of Mount Fuji that is obviously painted onto a wall, with a setting sun hanging by a visible cable. The artificial setting, impossible geography, and dense allusiveness of the prologue establish one of the film's recurring themes. In *Sukiyaki*, the cinematic history of the global West is expressed, first and foremost, as a relation between genre and climate. In the first half of the film, that climate is the dry desert of the classic Western. As the film progresses, the desert slowly dissolves into mud, which eventually covers the characters. The mud is a direct reference to one of the most recognizable features of Corbucci's *Django*: its swamplike setting. "Instead of the sun-bleached towns of most spaghetti Westerns, *Django*'s was muddy and rain-sodden," a result of the rainy season in central Italy, which turned the set into "a desolate mud-flat."[83] The reappearance of

*Django*'s mud in *Sukiyaki* establishes the link between the two films in meteorological terms.

The allusive parallel inscribed in the mud gives way, in *Sukiyaki*'s final scene, to an abrupt change in the climate, from mud to a much different (though by now not all that surprising) weather pattern: snow (figure 4.9). The film's climactic shoot-out takes place in a blizzard, which begins out of nowhere and falls so heavily that it almost blots out the dueling characters,

FIGURE 4.9. From mud to snow: climate change in *Sukiyaki Western Django*.

the Eastwood-like unnamed stranger and the leader of the Genji clan, Yoshitsune. Given the rain, mud, and dirt that have defined the environment of *Sukiyaki* up to this point, snow seems a distinctly implausible occurrence. But while snow may not be likely in the Nevada desert, it is of course quite common in the mountains of Yamagata Prefecture, Japan, where *Sukiyaki* was shot, and where filming was delayed for almost a year because of blizzards. Whereas the mud in *Sukiyaki* seems to assert a kind of climatic and generic resonance with the original *Django*, the snow registers the meteorological difference of *Sukiyaki's* own making: the intrusion of the film's actual setting (Japan) into its fictional one (the United States). "Now this," says Yoshitsune, gazing up into the snow before the final showdown, "is what I call class." What is classy about the scene is simply the alignment of genre, geography, and climate: snow as the most suitable setting for the Japanese Western. Shifting the terrain of the spaghetti Western, the snow that falls at the end of *Sukiyaki Western Django* symbolizes the atmospheric difference that maps out the genre's global movement.

*Sukiyaki's* engagement with the cultural politics of the Western takes place as a meditation on the geopolitics of the weather. Weather offers a measure of both global continuity and local difference, as the shared mud of *Django* and *Sukiyaki Western Django* opens onto two markedly different versions of winter. On one hand are the winter rains of central Italy that produced Corbucci's distinctive swamp; on the other, the blizzards of Japan that frequently made Miike's film unfilmable. Same season, different weather. What is another word for this meteorological dialectic between the global and the local? It is the *climate* of climate change, a single planetary crisis expressed in a range of locally disparate but increasingly extreme weather patterns. Such patterns include dangerously more precipitation in the mountainous regions of Japan and dangerously less in the American West; they make it so that one of the hottest years ever recorded (2013) could include one of history's coldest winters. Here we confront a central conceptual challenge of global climate change: how to recognize these geographically and meteorologically varied effects (different weather in different places, highly variable weather in the same place) as part of a single, systematic transformation of the earth's climate. As is well known, global warming is not simply a question of warmth. Cold and snow are as much a part of our warming planet as heat and drought. The trick is to look at these wild fluctuations in the weather and be able to see a single process at work. That is the process of anthropogenic climate change that, through the unabated release of carbon dioxide into the atmosphere, is slowly but surely raising the earth's surface temperature. It is this global process masquerading as local difference that is on display in *Sukiyaki Western Django*. From its implausible placement of Mount Fuji to its cinematically allusive mud to its locally appropriate snow, *Sukiyaki* uses the global history of the Western to depict the multiple, divergent weathers that comprise a single changing climate. Tracking the genre's historical travels across a range of national weathers, *Sukiyaki* folds those different microclimates—desert and mountains, mud and snow—into its own improbable weather system. Miike's film makes the local forecast a matter of global concern. It does so by using the wayward geography of genre as a stand-in for the disparate system of climate. Indeed, what are genre and climate but two names for a global abstraction that takes various local forms? Record of so many regional weathers, catalog of the heterogeneities of the world's climate, the Western becomes, in *Sukiyaki Western Django*, the basis of a properly global view of global warming.

## REASONABLE DROUGHT

If snow has played a central role in the Western's climatological history, that may be because snow is central to the climate of the American West. As B. Lynn Ingram and Frances Malamud-Roam explain in *The West Without Water*, "The American West depends on snow-bearing winter storms for its water supply. In fact, the region is unique in the contiguous United States in its dependence on the winter snowpack in the high mountains for a natural reservoir. . . . Snowpack provides up to 80 percent of the annual water supply in this region."[84] While it continues to snow in the contemporary Western, however, snow is disappearing from the contemporary West. Since 2012, the West has been weathering one of the most devastating droughts in recorded history, as decreased precipitation and increased temperatures have radically diminished the Sierra Nevada snowpack, threatening the region's water supply. In April 2015, the snowpack in the Sierras was found to be at only 5 percent of its average level, the lowest measure taken since record keeping began in the 1950s.[85] One month later, it was effectively zero. Three months after that, the National Oceanic and Atmospheric Administration announced that July was the hottest single month of global temperatures ever recorded and that, taken together, the first seven months of 2015 were similarly record breaking. (Those records subsequently were broken by the first six months of 2016.) As the globe burns, the water supply dwindles, and the American West approaches a megadrought.

Snow and drought are thus inverse but inextricable concepts for understanding the contemporary consequences of climate change. As such, the contemporary Western cannot be read solely as a form for confronting changes in the weather. It must also be seen as a way to reckon with weather's increasing and disastrous absence—an absence known as *drought*. What does it mean to be a Western without water?[86] This is the question taken up by Kelly Reichardt's grueling masterpiece, *Meek's Cutoff* (2010). Reichardt's film tells the story of a group of pioneers traveling to the West who have gotten lost in the Oregon desert and spend the length of the film trudging across an unforgiving landscape searching for water. *Meek's Cutoff* is a preeminent example of what has come to be known as the aesthetic of "slow cinema" as well as a powerful feminist critique of the Western. Through the grim figure of Stephen Meek, the arrogant, violent, and racist guide who is responsible for getting the group lost (he insists that he knows a shortcut), the film punctures the idea of patriarchal authority so central to the conventional mythology of the West. Meek's mix of hubris and haplessness is juxtaposed to the communal awareness and determination of Emily Tetherow, who challenges Meek's authority in a way that none of the other men in the group is willing to do. Meek, self-advertised survivalist and guide, gets everyone lost; Emily, otherwise silenced by male authority, keeps them alive.

Alongside its commentary on gender roles and racial domination in the Old West, *Meek's Cutoff* is, from its first shot to its last, a film about water. For the first four minutes of the film, the only sound we hear is rushing water, as the pioneers lead their wagons and carry their belongings across a river, taking the time to fill water jugs and clean dishes. The immersive sonic and visual emphasis on water in the opening scene is something like the calm before the lack of a storm. Everything in the remainder of the film is structured around the simultaneous need for and absence of water. At one point the travelers find gold and exult, only to realize its utter uselessness; after all, you "can't drink gold." The search for water continues through the film's final, ambiguous scene, when the Native American whom the group has taken captive leads them to a lone tree growing inexplicably in the middle of the desert. The middle of the tree is green, but the top is dead. The liminal state of the tree—"A tree can't live without water, can it?" asks the young boy, Jimmy, to which another of the travelers replies, "That's just it. We're close, but we don't know what to"—mirrors the compromised condition of the people gathered around it. Both represent a form of biological life that is unsustainable in the waterless conditions of an inhospitable desert.

It is the desert that constitutes the film's visual and conceptual center. This is a desert not of sagebrush and tumbleweeds but of cracked, scorched earth (figure 4.10). Reichardt's landscape is so lifeless and barren that, as film scholar Elena Gorfinkel observes, it "gain[s] an apocalyptic charge, summoning an ecological imaginary of blight and ruin."[87] From its hopeless search for hydration to its apocalyptically arid landscape, *Meek's Cutoff* is a Western in which the West has been entirely drained of water. Seen through the meteorological lens of drought, the film's much discussed aesthetic of slowness—part of what Gorfinkel describes as "the slow tendency emergent in contemporary world cinema"[88]—becomes an expression of the temporality of dryness: the excruciating wait for rain that won't come and water that can't be found.

FIGURE 4.10. The Western without water: megadrought and *Meek's Cutoff*.

Through the total, terrifying absence of weather, *Meek's Cutoff* offers the starkest and most precise portrait yet of our climatological present. Together, the inhuman landscape and desperate life world of the film depict drought as simultaneously a large-scale geological phenomenon and an irreducibly human one. The same doubleness defines the drought that is currently remaking the American West. On one hand, evidence of the long-term climatic oscillation between dry and wet periods in the West goes back thousands of years, including indications of two severe, centuries-long megadroughts stretching from 900 to 1100 and from 1200 to 1400.[89] On the other hand, there is little scientific doubt that the extreme drought now afflicting the West is in part a product of anthropogenic climate change and the altered state of the earth's atmosphere. Situated between long-term climatic variability and human-induced climate change, today's drought marks the dried-out point at which geological time is transformed into contemporary crisis. Here, finally, it is not just the genre of the Western but the entire region of the West itself that testifies to the unequivocal presentness of climate change's unthinkable timescales. We have seen the future of climate change—and it is the contemporary West. As mountain snowpack melts and an unprecedented megadrought looms, the iconic region of the West may soon be rendered uninhabitable. Under such overheated conditions, faced with an altered climate and an alien landscape, the well of the Western genre may finally run dry. Or perhaps its role will simply be to make us realize, as Reichardt's Western does, that we did not miss the weather until it was gone.

# Chapter Five

# SURVIVAL

## Work and Plague

the virus of being at work has spread
CARL CEDERSTRÖM AND PETER FLEMING

## FROM TEXT TO WORK

The post-apocalyptic novel is preoccupied with how we occupy our time. What is there to do after the end of the world? How does one keep busy? These concerns, which shape much post-apocalyptic fiction, serve to remind us of one of the genre's more peculiar features: it isn't really about apocalypse. The end of the world is usually only the beginning of the story, and the story's end, more often than not, is yet another beginning, a seed of hope, if not the full flowering of some new form of social life. It's hard to say, in any case, what exactly ends in these stories of the end. That's because they aren't all that concerned with what ends; they're concerned with what survives the end. One reason that apocalyptic texts focus on surviving rather than ending is obvious enough. As narratives, they have to have something to narrate.[1] Still, there is something paradoxical about the narrative temporality of survival. Survival conveys both the radical jolt of historical rupture and the monotonous tempo of daily life. A counterintuitive form of futurity, survival is desperate for the mere continuation of the present. "Survival time," Lauren Berlant writes, is "the time of struggling, drowning, holding onto the ledge, treading water—the time of *not-stopping*" or, in other words, of not ending.[2] Survival invokes a world in which contemporary conditions are both the beginning of the end and the end of hoping for anything else.

The survival story is thus an experiment in monotony. Staying alive is about trying to keep things the way they are. The sameness at the heart of survival complicates the speculative power usually accorded to the genre of post-apocalyptic fiction. We tend to think of these fictions as fundamentally future oriented, keyed to images of catastrophe, rupture, and what the scholar of science fiction Peter Paik calls "revolutionary change."[3] Change: this, critics agree, is what the apocalypse genre is all about. Even those who think that the genre fails to describe how social change actually occurs tend to assume that something really does change in apocalyptic fiction.[4] Is that so obvious, though? The premise of this chapter is that what changes in post-apocalyptic stories is less significant than what stays the same. At minimum, we must admit that there is something decidedly non-apocalyptic about post-apocalyptic narratives. As Caren Irr remarks in her survey of twenty-first-century apocalypse novels, the genre is "not especially interested in assigning blame for the apocalypse or detailing its causes." Instead, Irr explains, these novels focus on "the day-to-day mechanics of survival."[5] Such "day-to-day mechanics" are a hedge against plotlessness. They give the genre, confronted with the prospect of a world in which there is literally nothing left to happen, something to narrate. The formal dilemma of the post-apocalyptic genre is how to pass the time, and the way it resolves this dilemma is through the banal regimens of survival. Survival, then, is not just what apocalyptic narratives are about; it's what makes them narratives in the first place. It also makes them a certain kind of narrative, one committed to endurance and routine—the most basic and repeatable gestures of daily existence—rather than to change. The tedious routines of survival require us to read the genre from a different angle: less as a speculative vision of the future than as a rendering of the monotonous rhythms that structure the contemporary.

This chapter shows how the peculiar rhythms of post-apocalyptic survival resonate with a more specific aspect of our present: the routines of contemporary work. The secretly entwined logics of survival and work afford us a glimpse not of a postcapitalist future but of a contemporary moment shaped by constant yet precarious labor. Amid the uncertainties and instabilities generated over the past several decades by post-Fordism and flexible accumulation, survival, I argue, emerges today as an ambivalent but indispensable form for imagining what it means to work—and what it means not to.

It is no simple task for art to represent work. As Kathi Weeks observes in *The Problem with Work*, there is a widespread "lack of interest in representing the daily grind of work routines in various forms of popular culture."[6] This is especially true in novels, concludes the novelist John Lanchester: "The world of work, especially of modern work, is significantly under-represented in fiction."[7] Why is this so? Lanchester speculates that it may have something to do with the "complexity" of contemporary office work. I would add that it is also connected to a deeper antinomy between the pillars of the novel form—detailed prose, developmental plots—and the repetitive logic of work. There is a fundamental tension between the grind of work and the grip of narrative, between what novels strive to be (interesting and eventful) and what work is—plotless and monotonous. The developmental teleology, or *Bildung*, of the novel form can't accommodate work's circular rhythms, which operate according to an entirely different narrative principle: the principle, in Franco Moretti's words, "of a peaceful and repeatable (and repeatable, and repeatable, and repeatable) everyday."[8]

The repeatable, monotonous form of work poses a problem for literary representation. It is a problem of how literature spends its time. Should a novel use its time describing the activity of work or the inner and outer lives of the person who happens to be working? We can think of this as a choice, in the representation of work, between *occupation* and *vocation*. Most literary characters tend to have vocations, jobs that tell us less about the nature of the work and more about the nature of the person who does it.[9] Vocation is a mode of identification and self-definition; it is a character trait. If literary characters' jobs are able to tell us something about who they are, that is only because the novel has avoided the more labor-intensive work of describing precisely what these characters do. By contrast, the idea of work as doing rather than being—as "an activity rather than an identity," in Weeks's words[10]—requires that we recast it in temporal terms. These are the terms of occupation rather than vocation. Occupation does not concern our character; it concerns the literal structuring of our time. It also restructures novelistic time. The aspiring novel of occupation is required to devote the bulk of its time to the tedious recounting of exactly how—and how much of—our time is occupied by work.

While the questions of how we occupy our time and how novels represent our occupations tend to be hidden behind developed characters and developmental plots, these questions rise to the surface in post-apocalyptic fiction. The post-apocalyptic genre is uneventful, repetitive, pedantic, and generic; for these reasons, it is uniquely poised to offer an exhaustive and exhausting record of the monotonous details of modern work. The post-apocalyptic novel forges what we might call an *occupational aesthetic*. This is an aesthetic concerned with work not as a mode of self-expression but as a temporal regime—the time-consuming, non-narrative grind of work. After the end of the world, it no longer matters what you do (and what you do certainly no longer reflects who you are); it matters only that you find something to do, over and over and over again, in order to survive.

The effects of survival as a narrative structure come to the fore in one of the most widely discussed apocalyptic novels of recent years, Cormac McCarthy's *The Road*, a novel so committed to the routines of bare existence that one of its Library of Congress subject headings is actually "Survival Skills." The struggle to survive is not merely a metaphysical conceit in *The Road*. It is the basic lifeblood of the book's prose. "Mostly he worried about their shoes. That and food. Always food": these are the preoccupations of both the protagonist (a harrowed father caring for his son) and the novel itself, which spends most of its time worrying about shoes, food, and other basic necessities. At its core, *The Road* is a story about performing the most quotidian tasks: building a fire, cooking food, scavenging for supplies, folding and unfolding a tarp ("He'd unfolded the tarp and propped one end of it up beneath the tree to try and reflect back the heat from the fire").[11] In reducing survival to a monotonous list of tasks and actions, McCarthy's pared-down style (often read in theological terms)[12] looks more like the style of survivalist efficiency. The sentences of *The Road* revolve around intuitive know-how and streamlined movement, all action verbs and coordinating conjunctions:

They collected old boxes and built a fire in the floor and he found some tools and emptied out the cart and sat working on the wheel. He pulled the bolt and bored out the collet with a hand drill and resleeved it with a section of pipe he'd cut to length with a hacksaw. Then he bolted it all back together and stood the cart upright and wheeled it around the floor. It ran fairly true. The boy sat watching everything. (16–17)

We sit watching everything, too, though there isn't much to see, just a man fixing a wheel on a shopping cart. The DIY tasks of survival, alongside the deliberateness of McCarthy's narration of them, do not necessarily make for interesting reading. But they do make an interesting point. In *The Road*, the will to survive is expressed as the inexhaustible willingness to do a certain kind of work.

"Out of an apocalypse," Evan Calder Williams writes in *Combined and Uneven Apocalypse*, "comes the hard work of the post-apocalyptic."[13] This is the secret not just of *The Road* but also of the vast number of post-apocalyptic novels whose formula McCarthy distills and perfects. The "hard work" of survival in these books is what work is supposed to look like after the end of work. The survival skills that McCarthy so painstakingly details picture the end of the world as the eradication of alienated labor. Although the destruction of society has taken much from the father in *The Road*, it manages to give him at least one thing back: the ability to work in direct, unalienated relationship to the ruined world around him. Such work is defined, first of all, by its variety. Over the course of the novel, the father demonstrates an impressive range of productive capacities: he is a decent cook, an effective handyman, a whimsical craftsman ("He'd carved the boy a flute from a piece of roadside cane" [77]), and an accomplished marksman (he "leveled the pistol and fired from a two-handed position balanced on both knees" [66]). As survival rewrites the teleology of plot as the repetition of routine tasks, *The Road* comes into focus as a portrait of a man constantly at work. Despite the hopelessness of its setting, *The Road* finds something reassuring in these labors. We know this because the prospect of old-fashioned hard work was already, before the apocalypse, the father's ideal way to spend his time:

There was a lake a mile from his uncle's farm where he and his uncle used to go in the fall for firewood. . . . The trees themselves had long been sawed for firewood and carried away. His uncle turned the boat and shipped the oars and they drifted over the sandy shallows until the transom grated in the sand. A dead perch lolling belly up in the clear water. Yellow leaves. They left their shoes on the warm painted board and dragged the boat up onto the beach and set out the anchor at the end of its rope. A lardcan poured with concrete with an eyebolt in the center. They walked along the shore while his uncle studied the treestumps, puffing at his pipe, a manila rope coiled over his shoulder. He picked one out and they turned it over, using the roots for leverage, until they got it half floating in the water. Trousers rolled to the knee but still they got wet. They tied the rope to a cleat at the rear of the boat and rowed back across the lake, jerking the stump slowly behind them. By then it was already evening. Just the slow periodic rack and shuffle of the oarlocks. The lake dark glass and windowlights coming on along the shore. A radio somewhere. Neither of them had spoken a word. This was the perfect day of his childhood. This is the day to shape the days upon. (12–13)

There is more than a little wistfulness in this memory of the silent, stolid tasks of subsistence, the hard work of harvesting firewood from tree stumps. But the real point of the scene is that one does not need a nuclear apocalypse to see the satisfying labors of survival as distinct from the alienating activities of modern capitalism. Because the trees have already been "carried away," the father and uncle are forced to do a different kind of work; they are not logging for profit but resourcefully reusing the leftover stumps. This is the kind of work "to shape the days upon," and it's a good thing the father thinks so, because it is exactly what his post-apocalyptic days *are* shaped upon. His days of building fires and repairing shopping carts with his boy perfectly recapitulate this "perfect day" of his own childhood—the silent performance and rote actions—and this alters, in a rather surprising way, the desperate affects we would normally associate with survival. Circumstances may be dire, but survival offers its own satisfactions in *The Road*, allowing the father to ceaselessly relive the "perfect day" of manual work.

The belief that the end of one kind of work implies the emergence of another—that the end of the world affords the possibility of a return to something like *real work*—props up any number of post-apocalyptic narratives. Consider, for instance, the back-cover copy that introduces each issue of the graphic novel series *The Walking Dead*:

How many hours are in a day when you don't spend half of them watching television? When is the last time any of us really worked to get something that we wanted? How long has it been since any of us really needed something that we wanted? The world we knew is gone. The world of commerce and frivolous necessity has been replaced by a world of survival and responsibility. An epidemic of apocalyptic proportions has swept the globe causing the dead to rise and feed on the living. In a matter of months society has crumbled, no government, no grocery stores, no mail delivery, no cable TV. In a world ruled by the dead, we are forced to finally start living.

Here the critique of contemporary capitalism is the critique of a world that encourages wants instead of needs, convenience instead of responsibility, and leisure instead of labor. Life under advanced capitalism appears as an endless waste of time (watching television, waiting for the mail). In response to the depredations of modernity, the apocalypse offers two solutions in one. First, having eradicated all the things we used to do with our time, it shows us how much time we've been wasting; and, second, having exposed us to the hard truth of "how many hours are in a day," it gives us something better to do to fill all those hours—the real work of survival. To "finally start living" is, in the terms of this passage, to start really working: "When is the last time any of us really worked to get something that we wanted?" The salubrious post-apocalyptic world of *The Walking Dead* mirrors that of *The Road*, as "commerce and frivolous necessity" are again replaced by "survival and responsibility," or more specifically, the responsibility of having to work in order to survive. These portraits evoke precapitalist society as Marx himself described it, where labor is not just man's "immediate *source of subsistence*, but . . . at the same time the manifestation of his *individual existence*."[14] In such circumstances, Marx wrote, "man not only effects a change of form in the materials of nature; he also realizes his own purpose in those materials."[15] The self-realizing potential of real work is at the center of both *The Road* and *The Walking Dead*, and not only in the content of their stories. In McCarthy's novel, the logic of unalienated labor functions as a formal principle. Just as the father in *The Road* sees his individual existence expressed in the work he indefatigably performs, so too does the novel find its own purpose, its very existence as a narrative, manifested in the work it tirelessly narrates. This, we could say, is the atavism of apocalypse: the end of the earth as back-to-the-land.[16] The point of the precapitalist nostalgia of the post-apocalyptic novel is that all the work it describes isn't actually work because it is something less alienated and more fulfilling: it is survival.

Survival, however, has a less sanguine side. Given its emphasis on continuity and continuation, the temporality of survival implies a more conflicted relation to the utopian future, a less optimistic belief in social transformation. While post-apocalyptic fiction is primarily focused on imagining the unalienated work of survival, it is also haunted by a more immediate problem: how to explain the continued *survival of work*. "The greatest habit of contemporary postindustrial life," Alan Liu suggests in his seminal study of the knowledge economy, is "work."[17] Indeed, one of the more vexing questions for contemporary economists is why an increasingly advanced and automated capitalist system continues to have so much work for people to do. It wasn't supposed to be this way. In 1930, John Maynard Keynes famously predicted that in a hundred years, economic prosperity would have us all working fifteen-hour weeks, free "from pressing economic cares," with our only problem being "how to occupy the leisure, which science and compound interest have won."[18] Of course, that's not how work has worked out. Jasper Bernes offers this historical synopsis:

In the 1960s and 1970s, work seemed to be losing its centrality within capitalism, as average hours fell and as commentators from both the Left and Right spoke of an imminent end of work brought about by automation. . . . Contrary to all expectations, however, what has emerged in the last few decades has been a profound renewal of work, evident not only in the mounting average workweek but in the absorption of nonwork activities by work.[19]

What, we are left to wonder, is the fate of the apocalyptic fantasy of the end of work in an age of what Bernes calls "the end of the end of work":[20] the end of the 1960s-era critique of alienation and routinization (which is absorbed into postindustrial management theory) and the beginning of a new age of intensified activity, extended hours, mandated flexibility, and stagnated wages? What happens when the self-motivated, highly adaptable, always-working protagonist of the post-apocalyptic survival story sounds a lot like the hero of the neoliberal workplace?[21] What happens when the "day-to-day tasks of survival"[22] in apocalypse fiction begin to echo what Weeks describes as the "enormous variety of tasks . . . that characterize the contemporary employment relation"?[23] And what happens when the post-apocalyptic genre's exhortation to start "really work[ing]" comes at a moment when almost all we do is work? Although *The Walking Dead* thinks that the question of "how many hours are in a day" is a question about all the time we waste, it isn't. It's a question about all the time we work. The capacity to confuse one for the other—endless work for no work at all—shows just how thoroughly the line between working life and waking life has been erased in contemporary culture. And it reveals the hidden cultural function of the narrative logic of survival, which both names and naturalizes the collapse of end into endlessness and of life into work.

My claim is that the very notion of survival skills acquires a markedly different valence in the era of postindustrial capitalism.[24] As "economic survival becomes more difficult," the autonomist critic Franco Berardi suggests, "we renew our affection for work."[25] Why is contemporary survival more difficult, and what does that difficulty have to do with our relation to work? The past several decades of flexible accumulation have put increased inequality and rising unemployment in lockstep with intensified work and protracted working hours. As Luc Boltanski and Eve Chiapello meticulously document in *The New Spirit of Capitalism*, today's managerial class aims at "pursuing maximum employment of technical resources twenty-four hours a day, with a minimum of stoppages and faulty work." At the same time, "the casualization of labour and the development of sub-contracting make it possible to *pay only the time actually worked*, and to subtract from paid time all slack periods, training time and breaks that used to be partially included in the definition of the fair working day." The result is an "increase in work intensity for the same wage." Under the banner of "adaptation, change, 'flexibility,'" many workers must work more intensely for less, while others cannot work at all.[26]

The debasements of flexibility and precarity have been accompanied, if not enabled, by a radical blurring of work time and non-work time. For Marx, the signal invention of modern capitalism was the limited workday: "In place of the pompous catalogue of the 'inalienable rights of man' there steps the modest Magna Carta of the legally limited working day, which at last makes clear 'when the time which the worker sells is ended, and when his own begins.'"[27] Since the 1970s, however, the difference between the time we sell and the time we own has become significantly harder to discern. The past several decades have witnessed the increasing indistinguishability of work and leisure. This is largely the result of new technologies that paved the way for the mobile workplace, allowing us, as Bernes explains, "to work anywhere and anytime and therefore work *always*, endlessly." One of the signal products of post-Fordism is thus the "24/7 of the inescapable job."[28] The more that work comes to colonize our lives, the more our most basic, everyday activities are folded into our work. The blurring of life into work casts a substantially different light on the centrality of subsistence work to post-apocalyptic fiction. While the point of the skills necessary to survive the apocalypse is that they can be distinguished from the alienated work of late capitalism, the point of postindustrial work is that such a distinction is increasingly difficult to make. At a moment when the "ideal of nonalienated labor . . . has passed out of the realm of utopian fantasy and into the workplace"—as Sarah Brouillette describes the ideology of creative work[29]—we might wonder whether literary fantasies of the end of the world of work can really be said to depict the end of anything at all.[30]

Some post-apocalyptic novels have begun to wonder the same thing. In the remainder of this chapter, I focus on two novels, Ben Marcus's *The Flame Alphabet* and Colson Whitehead's *Zone One*, that seek a different understanding of the relation between the narration of survival and the nature of postindustrial work. Against the ideology of creative work—the tendency, as Brouillette describes it, to imagine "contemporary labor" as an "act of self-exploration, self-expression, and self-realization"—the routine form of the apocalyptic novel serves to remind us of something else: the now often hidden forms of "routine, standardized, mechanized production" that remain the engine of the global economy.[31] Drawing on the mechanical monotonies of the survival story, Marcus and Whitehead expose the monotonous routines that structure our basic relationship to labor. In doing so, they offer a timely reminder of "the scandalous fact of mindless alienated work."[32] The routines required to narrate life after the end of the world become, in *The Flame Alphabet* and *Zone One*, the grounds for grasping the structural conditions of a world defined by work. Rendering survival as a formal problem, these tedious novels of the apocalypse attempt to untangle one of the central contradictions of contemporary life: that we cannot survive the endless work we do, and we cannot survive without doing it.

## ODD JOBS

Ben Marcus's *The Flame Alphabet* is a novel about the onset of an epidemic caused by the toxicity of children's speech. It is also a novel about work. Sam, the novel's narrator, responds to the unfolding horrors of the plague by occupying himself with an unending stream of menial tasks. Under the ˙gn of what he calls "smallwork," Sam collects data, performs amateur ˌmistry experiments, cooks ineffective medicines. There is the upkeep ᵊ Jewish hut where he and his wife, Claire, worship in secret ("We could

do some work on the land, build an addition onto the hut"); the maintenance of the primitive technological device that connects them to their
rabbi's radio sermons ("A small box of maintenance tools was entrusted to
us"); the extensive effort required to use that device ("I found the labor
dispiriting"); and the diligent discharge of housework ("I took charge of what
remained of our dwindling domestic project, the blending of food into
shakes, the cleaning of all our gray traces").[33] In her account of the manic,
exhausted worker of the contemporary economy, Sianne Ngai suggests
that the worker's "continuous succession of activities" cultivates "a certain
indifference" to the specificity of those activities.[34] That is certainly the case
here. It doesn't matter what Sam is doing so long as he's doing something.
The premise of *The Flame Alphabet* is not that the collapse of capitalist
society will leave us with nothing. It's that it will leave us with nothing to
do but work. Although Marcus's novel gestures toward issues of language
(what is it?) and family (what good is one?), its real interest, I think, is how
the end of these things—the sudden disappearance of the basic markers
of humanity—exposes a deeper, apparently inexhaustible compulsion to
work. With no one to talk to and no family to care for, Sam throws himself
into the one thing he has left: "I'd want to resume my work as soon as we
relocated" (124).

The most noticeable thing all this work produces is what feels like an
endless supply of tediously detailed descriptions of work:

I conducted perimeter and fence line ambient air quality tests and sent in the re-
sults for analysis. Sediments of speech, airborne now, might indicate different toxicity thresholds throughout the area. The numbers that returned offered no insight I could use. . . . This after administering a full broad-spectrum heavy-metals
panel inconclusive on us both. This after following the standard collection protocol for poisoning, testing our blood, hair, saliva, and nails. . . . I performed smallwork with salts, knowing little of how to modify my tonic, knowing nothing of a
delivery system through poultice applications on the sweeter nerves inside of my
arms, the so-called Worthen site, proceeding only with some unmodified antisei-
zure agents as a foundational syrup. (54–55)

On the kitchen counter I looped tubes between a trio of breakers, and I flipped the
circuit to the furnace so I could plug in the micro finer, which pulverized whatever organic matter I required as ballast, without causing a brownout. . . . With an

induction burner I reduced solutions of saline, blended anti-inflammatory tablets, atomized powder from non-drowsy time-release allergy vials, and milled an arsenal of water-charged vitamins, particularly from the B group, along with the binding agents and hardened shavings of an herb dust I'd crushed in the mortar. The salted protein sheets, rolled out from bulk supplies of medical gelatin, I stretched on the dish rack until they resolved as clear as glass, and once they'd hardened I cut them into batons and hollowed out their middles so they could be injected with medicine. (71)

Like McCarthy, Marcus understands that the *sine qua non* of the post-apocalyptic novel is monotonous particularity, the banal spectacle of specialized know-how translated into gesture and action. But Marcus stretches such descriptions to their breaking point, marshaling ever more insignificant details that add little or no meaning to the passage. What exactly are "salted protein sheets"? What is involved in "fence line ambient air quality tests"? What, you might wonder on the very first page of the novel, is "a Drager Aerotest breathing kit," and why, for that matter, is Sam carrying around "a copper powder for phonic salting, plus some rubber bulbs and a bootful of felt" (3)? Marcus never says. At first, this may not seem all that unusual. All science fiction novels throw the reader into a strange, disorienting world that is gradually defined and familiarized over the course of the narrative. What makes Marcus's novel different is that it never bothers to define anything; indeed, most of the unfamiliar terms that appear in these passages will never be mentioned again. Taking note of Marcus's apparent indifference to fleshing out his invented world, Lee Konstantinou, writing in the *Los Angeles Review of Books*, concludes that Marcus's novel "devolves into a kind of technobabble."[35] For Konstantinou, Marcus gives us purely superficial science fiction, empty words unredeemed by even the bare minimum of imaginative effort to explain them. But there's something unexpectedly illuminating about Konstantinou's description, which helps us get a better grip on the meaning of all this meaninglessness. Technobabble, after all, is not just any kind of empty discourse. It is the empty discourse of white-collar work: the trumped-up jargon of professional expertise that serves as a rhetorical alibi for the otherwise rote and pointless tasks of the office. Read this way, *technobabble* is the perfect word to describe Marcus's novel. *The Flame Alphabet* fails to give any meaning to its

pseudoscientific descriptions because its aim is not to describe a meaningful sci-fi world but to depict the meaninglessness of the world of work.

To put a finer point on it, the reason that passages like the ones I just
quoted fail to have much meaning to the reader is because the work they
describe has no meaning or purpose in the novel. Sam's work literally
produces nothing. "Oh, right," the novel's villain LeBov taunts Sam. "You're
not productive at all" (218). His experiments extract no usable medicines.
His trials are "inconclusive." Those "ambient air quality tests . . . offered no
insight I could use." Sam's smallwork is effectively busywork: not the effi-
cient skills of McCarthy's seasoned survivalist but pointless tasks that produce nothing of use. In fact, with much of Sam's smallwork, it turns out
that he himself isn't entirely clear about why he's doing it. He's just following instructions. Eventually Sam discovers that the person giving him these
instructions is not his rabbi, as he has assumed, but LeBov, who essentially
subcontracted the work to him. "I needed it done," LeBov tells Sam, "and
there you were, needing to do it" (129). Needing work done and needing to
work: it would be hard to find a more concise formulation of the capitalist
labor contract, which turns the worker's free time into the "freely" given
consent to be exploited by someone else. To say that Sam works with little
concern for what he is doing or why he is doing it is simply to say that he is
the epitome of the worker, defined—like every worker—by his alienation
from the work that he does.

The funny thing about Sam's lack of knowledge about his own work is
that much of the work he does in *The Flame Alphabet* could reasonably be
described as knowledge work, or the management of information. Sam
spends the first half of the novel collecting data about the speech fever, a
reminder that what is happening is first and foremost a crisis of understanding: "We were ignorant of the illness plateau, the comprehension
ratio we'd soon surpass. . . . About the child radius we were naïve" (23). The
illness is largely a matter of measurements and statistics, ratios and radi-
uses. The result verges on a kind of information overload. The meaningless
tasks that Sam performs throughout the novel are matched by the opacity
of the vast data he amasses, which he never figures out how to interpret.
Nevertheless, he remains determined to collect the information anyway.
Here the apocalyptic crisis becomes the most literal kind of information
economy: a situation in which one's survival depends entirely on how much

information about the epidemic one has. Yet Sam's need to know is not driven solely by the necessity of staying alive. Rather, he tells us, the need to work in this way—to take measurements, log trials, track data—arises out of "pure, scientific ambition . . . a technical, professional need" (21). LeBov understands the stakes of this "professional need" even better than Sam: "There's a territory of wisdom we don't own, and that's troubling" (203). The technocratic world of professional expertise and the private ownership of specialized "wisdom" are the two faces of a knowledge economy that survives, however unexpectedly, amid the apocalyptic ruins of *The Flame Alphabet.*

The significance of knowledge work in the novel is indicated not just by the new tasks of the contemporary information economy but also by the exemplary site where such tasks are carried out: the office. Lo and behold, in the second half of the novel, Sam finds himself—and it is hard to overstate how improbable this is in this kind of story—working in an office. Having been either rescued or captured by LeBov and taken to Forsythe, the research facility and power center of the disintegrating world, Sam is given a desk job. He describes his "first day of work in the research wing, in a private office with a view" (165), where he sits "at my desk each day" (169). What does he do there? The data collection of the novel's first half is here replaced by work of a more scholarly or "creative" sort. Sam now works directly with language, as he has been tasked with investigating and testing different alphabets in the hope of inventing a new method of communication. But his work in scripts, like his work in "solid medicines" and "smokes," is both menial and meaningless. They are tasks given to him simply to occupy his time. Sam realizes this: "Nothing had come of my projects today, as usual. More slogging, more obviously failed scripts, more redundant work that was doomed in advance" (193). From the laborious "logging" of trials and tests that comprises the novel's first half to the "redundant" "slogging" of its second, all the work that fills the pages of *The Flame Alphabet* is "doomed in advance" because it is done for no other reason than the need to have something to do. The irony of Sam's knowledge work, in other words, is that it is no more knowing and no less mindless than any other kind of work.

Marcus uses the office setting to connect the social form of white-collar work to the narrative form of the post-apocalyptic novel. As Sam himself puts it, work at Forsythe is defined primarily by its "grueling familiarity"

(189) and "the most killing forms of banality" (191). What I described earlier as the grueling monotony of reading about all this work thus turns out to be a reflection of the monotony of doing it. Nevertheless, the time Sam spends at Forsythe does give us a glimpse of the deeper meaning work has for him. While Sam produces nothing of use or value, his office work does allow him to reproduce the comforting rhythms of the capitalist working day. When Sam first arrives at Forsythe as a test subject, he notes his basic temporal disorientation: "With no smallwork to perform, the time of day failed to matter" (154). It is only after being put back to work that he regains the basic measures of capitalist time: workday, workweek, weekend. Now his days have a predictable structure: "At Forsythe one worked, one ate, one rested, and on occasion one consensually fucked a stranger . . . if the [recreation] room was empty I sat down when the workday ended and enjoyed the shows" (173). Sam's work is aimed at producing nothing but the concept of the "workday" itself, which makes his pointless routines meaningful not by giving them a point but by giving them a form—the familiar framework of nine-to-five work. The key to this particular way of ordering time is that it separates work from "recreation." And the key to its role in *The Flame Alphabet* is that it allows Sam to believe that there is still such a thing as a "working shift" (183), and therefore such a thing as the time when that shift will be over.

In *The Flame Alphabet*, alienated work is the only hope for regimenting the endless time that follows the end of the world. This remains true even after Sam abandons the ersatz civilization of the office. In the final section of the novel, Sam escapes Forsythe and, in accordance with the routine conventions of the post-apocalyptic genre, establishes a new life alone in the woods. Even here, though, he cannot escape the meaninglessness of office work. There is still the meaningless jargon of the postindustrial workplace—"A remote perspective was best, sheared of sentimentality, which impedes a productive workflow" (279)—and there is still the recognition that even the most elemental tasks of survival (collecting firewood, cooking meals) are merely "errands to kill the day" (262). Out here in the woods, work is not a means of subsistence; it's simply a way to kill time. The urgency of survival is replaced for Sam by the numbing repetition of unnecessary errands: "[F]or errands there is the gathering of goods and tools even as the surplus spoils in my cold locker, plunder spilling down the hillside. Mostly I grab what I already have. I hoard. I stockpile" (262). *Hoard, stockpile, surplus*: these unexpected watchwords underscore the fundamental re-dundancy of Sam's work. Why hoard what you "already have"? Because there is nothing else to do; because scheduled errands are the only way Sam has to structure his time. Of course, he admits, he could be more enterpris-ing: "I suppose with my time I could farm and hunt and subsist through harvest, but all of those food products on the shelves in empty stores off the quiet freeway make such labors unnecessary" (262). Against the fantasies of harvest and subsistence, which imply (as in, say, *The Road*) a more respon-sible use of one's time, Marcus offers a stark reply. While post-apocalyptic survival has certainly made it more necessary to work, it has not made work any more affectively necessary, any more fulfilling or affirming. What survives at the end of this novel of the world's end is only a particular kind of meaningless work ("errands to kill the day") and a particularly mean-ingless way of talking about it ("productive workflow"). The routines of survival are, in *The Flame Alphabet*, inseparable from the logic of late cap-italist work. Another way to put this is to say that what survives the end of capitalism here is capitalism—a world where other people's work obviates the need for you to work yourself, where "all those food products on the shelves . . . make such labors unnecessary." This is not as paradoxical as it sounds. The point of *The Flame Alphabet* is that our primary technology for imagining this end, the survival story, is premised on a kind of work and invested in a kind of work ethic that imply the survival of the system itself. No matter how sincere our desire to imagine a world without capi-talism, the post-apocalyptic narrative leaves us, like Sam, unable to imag-ine a life without work.

Having noticed the inescapability of work in *The Flame Alphabet*, though, what are we actually seeing? This is no insignificant question for a novel preoccupied with how clear a view its protagonist is able to have of the crisis unfolding around him. The sea of misinformation that spreads in the initial panic about the plague has created a "massive pit of confusion we all swam in" (52), and no one swims in deeper waters than Sam, who consistently demonstrates a "complete inability to understand what's go-ing on" (129). Yet as I suggested earlier, we risk misunderstanding the nov-el's interest in incomprehension if we fail to understand misunderstand-ing as the worldview of alienated work. Like a worker in a cubicle or on an assembly line, Sam is not privy to the final product of his productive ef-forts. The key to work in *The Flame Alphabet* is that it represents a sphere in which action is divorced from understanding: "Laughably amateur modifications, yet ones I hardly understood. I needed to believe [Rabbi] Thompson that my own understanding played no role. I could execute a procedure without knowing why. I had to believe, per [Rabbi] Burke, that my own insights, if I even had them, were an impediment to survival" (55). The refusal of insight and understanding that threads through *The Flame Alphabet* is no celebration of indeterminacy. It is simply a description of the epistemological conditions that work makes possible.

The necessity of unknowing is quite literal for Sam, who is working with a raw material—language—that would kill him if he could actually read it. To prevent this, Sam labors in "working conditions I thought of as *controlled ignorance*" (169, italics in original). The conditions of ignorance are secured by

a scroll of self-disguising paper—paper with small windows factored in that could be enlarged with a dial—that allowed you to see only the script character you were presently reading, and nothing else, not even the word it belonged to. It broke the act of reading into its littlest parts, keeping understanding at bay. . . . Unless you opened the window at your peril, this device revealed only part of a letter at a time, and even of that part it revealed so little that you might never guess that this mark on a page was participating in the larger design of an entire letter, which joined others in a set of interlocking designs called words, that would coalesce on the page to *mean* something, and thus bring a reader to his knees. (166)

This description of work broken into the smallest and most absurd increments ("only part of a letter at a time") makes clear how much Sam's work depends on literally not being able to see the bigger picture, "the larger design." What kind of society requires that we not see how all its "interlocking designs" fit together? What is a society in which our "own understanding play[s] no role"? It is a society founded on the division of labor. As Franco Moretti explains in *The Bourgeois*, the capitalist "culture of work" has its origins in this division: "The legitimacy and productivity of modern work are not just intensified but *established* by their blindness to what lies around it."[36] This explains why Sam works so hard but understands so little. His blindness to everything around him is simply what it means to be a worker, who must "execute a procedure without knowing why." Understanding is, by definition, above the pay grade of the worker. If "insight" is "an impediment to survival," as Rabbi Burke tells Sam, that is because survival is inseparable from work and because the ability to work depends on an inability to understand: controlled ignorance. The "price to pay for" work, Moretti concludes, is "totality":[37] the capacity to see the bigger picture. To work is to be free from the burden of having to understand the work you happen to do. It is also to be free from having to understand the larger truth of a society in which work is what you are required to do.

The difficulty of understanding the totality of the working world is not Sam's alone. It is also one that *The Flame Alphabet* recognizes as part of its own contemporary moment. While I've been arguing that the problem of work is most forcefully articulated in the novel's form—its generic structure (the tedium of the survival story) and linguistic style (the monotony of description)—there is one particularly strange plot detail that demands our attention. In the early, uncertain days of the illness, everything that is known about language toxicity is discovered first, Marcus repeatedly tells us, in Wisconsin:

When the affliction crystalized on a map, colors coding the victim radius, the image was pretty, a golden yellow core radiating out of inner Wisconsin. Whatever was happening seemed to happen there first. (53)

Something had happened in Wisconsin. Wisconsin had experienced an incident. There was, according to reports, a complete absence of speech originating from Wisconsin. This was no longer a poison from children. In Wisconsin all language, no matter the source, was toxic. (118)

The Wisconsin area has unfortunately been a reliable precursor. We believe that what happens there will soon, we do not know when, happen here. . . . We unfortunately have to expect this escalation to spread. (118)

Why Wisconsin? Is it only the New York writer's handy synecdoche for the alien manners of the Midwest? Perhaps. But in a novel about work, Wisconsin must also stand for the midwestern Rust Belt as a whole, ground zero for the devastating process of deindustrialization that reshaped American work in the latter half of the twentieth century. Moreover, when we narrow our gaze from the past several decades to the past few years, we realize there is an even more specific problem for which Wisconsin proved to be a "reliable precursor": something that, once it "happen[ed] there," could suddenly seem capable of happening anywhere; something that could even give rise to magazine articles with titles like "What's Happening in Wisconsin Explained," whose writers worried, "How could this spread?"[38] What was the plague poised to spread from Wisconsin? That would be the neoliberal assault on unions, collective bargaining, and workers' rights that was written into law as Act 10 by the Wisconsin state legislature in 2011 (one year before the publication of Marcus's novel) in what had been up until then one of the most reliably pro-labor states in America. The bill was a "reliable precursor" indeed: a year after Wisconsin passed its "budget repair bill" in the face of massive protests, both Indiana and Michigan passed "right-to-work" laws (followed by Wisconsin's own right-to-work act, this time aimed at private-sector unions, in 2015). This is not to suggest that the history of de-unionization began in the state of Wisconsin in 2011; after all, there are twenty-four right-to-work states in the United States, a result of the Labor Management Relations Act (or Taft-Hartley Act, 1947), which imposed significant restrictions on unions. But the much-publicized Wisconsin bill unquestionably heralded the rising cultural tides and political fortunes of antiunion legislation in those areas of the country—particularly the Rust Belt—that until then had strongly resisted it.

If Marcus's post-apocalyptic novel envisions the end of anything, then, it is not the end of work but the end of *protections* regarding work—the specter of work without limits, or work without end. The incomprehension and misunderstanding that darken Marcus's novel are really about something much more specific: the challenge of recognizing the increasingly catastrophic labor conditions that are less the stuff of science-fictional fantasy than of contemporary history. Wisconsin may represent the sudden visibility of the attack on unions, but it also reminds us of the relative darkness in which such attacks—the wholesale dismantling of worker protections, livable wages, and social safety nets—have been taking place for the past half century. In *The Flame Alphabet*, the problem of narrating the endlessness of work is inseparable from the problem of diagnosing the labor crisis that has been unfolding around us for decades: a crisis of more hours, less time off, heightened precarity, and the receding ability to have a say in negotiations over even these basic parameters of working life. "Do you think I fucking work *alone*?" LeBov asks Sam (221, italics in original). What looks at first like "a little suburban catastrophe" is in fact, LeBov explains, "a human machine the size of the world" (221). The name of that machine— a machine made of human workers, a system the exact size of the world— is capitalism. To scale it down, whether to the level of family ties or state laws, is to misunderstand how it works. And to think it doesn't continue to hum, even in our fantasies of the apocalyptic future, is to fail to listen closely enough.

## ROT BY ROTE

Work survives in the post-apocalyptic novel. It does so by exploiting the ambiguity inherent in survival, which is both a response to catastrophically changed conditions and the rhythm of a life staying the same. The logic of survival puts some pressure on storytelling itself. What is a story in which nothing ever changes? Can a narrative be made of nothing but redundancy? These are the questions put to us by *Zone One*, Colson Whitehead's splendidly uneventful novel of the zombie apocalypse. Whitehead grinds the genre to a halt, turning the usual hyperactivity of the zombie chase into a Proustian exercise in languorous recollection. The memories are Mark Spitz's, who recalls the bygone rituals of the pre-apocalyptic world while dutifully cleaning up the post-apocalyptic one. Mark Spitz is a "sweeper" employed by the new government in Buffalo to aid "reconstruction" by helping make New York City habitable again. His job is not to fight zombies, just to laboriously double-check that the city really is rid of them (and to neutralize the occasional straggler). The building that Mark Spitz and his team are sweeping when the novel opens is, naturally, an office building, and the first thing he senses on entering it is the aura of undying work: "[T]he pure industry of this place still persisted. Insisting on itself. He felt it in his skin even though the people were gone and all the soft stuff was dead." Of course, something else persists in the building as well: the zombified inhabitants of the Human Resources Department. Accidentally opening the door to their office, Mark Spitz finds himself literally attacked by Human Resources—the phrase itself promoted to metonym: "He tried to heave Human Resources off him"—an experience that only confirms the sense Mark Spitz already had about the kind of people who work in HR: "Surely this one possessed the determination befitting a true denizen of Human Resources. . . . The plague's recalibration of its faculties only honed the underlying qualities." Considered from this perspective, standing in an abandoned office building fighting off zombies is not so unfamiliar an experience. In fact, it reminds Mark Spitz a lot of his "first office job" in a mail room, whose "only downer," he tells us, "was the ogre head of Human Resources, who'd been relentless about Mark Spitz's paperwork, downright insidious about his W-this, W-that."[39] The idea here is that the new post-apocalyptic world is basically indistinguishable from the pre-apocalyptic world. This is the running joke and central conceit of *Zone One*. The plague did not transform or unmake the modern world; it "only honed" its elemental features. The lingering sense of apocalyptic sameness explains a number of things about the novel, not least why, to Mark Spitz, having the zombies of Human Resources chase you for your flesh does not ultimately feel all that different from having the "ogre" of Human Resources hound you for your W-2. In *Zone One*, you can't spell horror without HR.

The eerie sameness of the post-apocalyptic world is, for Whitehead, a direct consequence of the instinct to survive. Survival is first and foremost a rule of repetition, an image of things kept constant, if not an ideology of preservation: "If she survived, she'd doubtless continue to be a grade-grubber in that coming, reborn world they crawled toward, paying her bills in a timely fashion once goods and vital services and autopay reappeared" (29). The survivor's impulse to "continue to be" the way she was both predicts and guarantees the larger continuities of the entire socioeconomic system, the inevitable reappearance of "goods and vital services." Indeed, reappearance is both the principle and the product of this system. The novel consistently emphasizes the repetitive nature of late capitalist life: "The reunions were terrific and rote, early tutelage in the recursive nature of human experience" (5); "their lives had been an interminable loop of repeated gestures" (62); "It was a banality no one could elude" (71). The banal, "interminable loop" of daily life guarantees the survival of both persons and systems. *Sameness*, Whitehead reminds us, has long been the watchword of a globalized world whose current imperative to rebuild itself is itself just more of the same.

The "recursive nature" of civility and social interaction parallels more literal sites of capitalist replication, which the novel dutifully records: chain restaurants ("He had been here before and not been here before. That was the magic of the franchise" [191]), mass culture ("it was still appointment television" [17]), brands so familiar that Whitehead doesn't feel the need to give us their names ("That juggernaut clothing empire" [46]; "The coffee company started in the Pacific Northwest" [184]). These examples offer a single account of a world made generic—unspecific, universal, endlessly substitutable. This suggests that the best way to understand the repetitions of late capitalism may be through the mechanisms of genre itself. What is genre but an explanation of how it is possible to see the same thing over and over again? And what is genre fiction but the primal scene of those "repeated gestures" that enable capitalism's continued survival, no less than our own?

When he used to watch disaster flicks and horror movies he convinced himself he'd survive the particular death scenario. . . . He was the only cast member to heed the words of the bedraggled prophet in Act I, and the plucky dude who slid the lucky heirloom knife from his sock and sawed at the bonds while in the next room the cannibal family bickered over when to carve him for dinner. He was the one left to explain it all to the skeptical world after the end credits, jibbering in blood-drenched dungarees before the useless local authorities, news media vans, and government agencies who spent half the movie arriving on the scene. I know it sounds crazy, but they came from the radioactive anthill, the sorority girls were dead when I got there, the prehistoric sea creature is your perp, dredge the lake and you'll find the bodies in its digestive track, check it out. By his sights, the real movie started after the first one ended, in the impossible return to things before. (165–66)

These "disaster flicks and horror movies" do not impart the skills and strategies of survival so much as they reveal the generic, repeatable character of catastrophe and survival alike. What genre films teach us about disaster is that it happens over and over again. The "impossible return to things before" is only the grounds for being able to tell the story again. It may well be the case, as Whitehead's narrator tells us, that "the plague didn't let you in on its rules; they weren't printed on the inside of the box" (107). But the real point is that, like every genre, the plague has rules. You just "had to learn them one by one" (107). The way Mark Spitz learns them is by watching all those monster movies. He discovers the generic secret of apocalypse—which is also the secret to his own survival of it—in genre.

Readers, in turn, discover the same secret in *Zone One* itself, which is yet another iteration of what has rapidly become one of our most ubiquitous

and least inventive genres, the zombie story. Whitehead's particular interest in the genre, though, is less about the allegorical possibilities of the
zombie and more about the rules of the generic game.[40] The unwritten (but
of course constantly written) rules of the story that Whitehead is telling are
what the novel has the most to say about. If nothing in the novel does not
seem utterly predictable, that is because no plot turn can possibly surprise
us. Whitehead writes as if we've heard it all before, and we probably have:
"The new micro-societies inevitably imploded, on the island getaways, in
reclaimed prisons, at the mountaintop ski lodge accessible only by sabo-
taged funicular, in the underground survivalist hideouts finally summoned
to utility" (110). The tossed-off, unelaborated style of these examples under-
scores how familiar they are. In a story like this, they basically go without
saying, and so the novel sets about saying as little about them as possible.
The thoroughly generic character of the zombie story compels the novel to
confess its own generic mechanisms: "At their core, Last Night stories were
all the same. They came, we died, I started running" (138). This pithy description of the structure shared by every Last Night story—the characters'
stories about where they were when the world ended—doubles as an apt
summary of zombie stories in general and *Zone One* in particular: they are
all the same.

Narrative sameness—the real law of genre—is how *Zone One*'s formu-
laic form works to frame its depiction of late capitalism and its account of
the capitalist essence of survival. Survival is a genre with its own repeatable rules. And it is a mode of existence that is itself based on the generic
and the repeatable:

They'd all done the same things during the miseries. Manhattan was a template
for other feral cities and Mark Spitz was a sort of template, too, he'd figured out.
The stories were the same, whether Last Night enveloped them on Long Island or
in Lancaster or Louisville. The close calls, the blind foraging, the accretion of loss.
Half starved on the roof of the local real estate office, crouching so they wouldn't
be seen from the street and have the ravenous dead clot around the only exit. Comforted in a stainless-steel restaurant cabinet and waiting for morning to break,
when it was time to split for the next evanescent refuge. (108)

Everything here is a "template," inviting reuse. Everything can be copied:
"Manhattan," "Mark Spitz," the "things" he'd done to survive, and the

"story" he lives to tell about it. Indeed, the trick of the second half of the passage is that it turns what sound like highly particular narrative details into purely exemplary ones. "Crouching so *they* wouldn't be seen": what sounds like one person's singular story is really everybody's, plural. The generic structure of the survival story discloses the generic nature of survival itself. Everyone has "done the same things" in order to survive, and everyone-doing-the-same-things is just another way to describe the survival of an entire system of social relations. The paradox of survival in Whitehead's novel is that it expresses not the end of the familiar late capitalist world but the uncanny persistence of capitalist familiarity. Even "gentrification had resumed" (35), Mark Spitz observes early on, though before it can, something more elemental must take hold. This is a process that, following the novel's description of its own narrative form, we can only call *genre-fication*: the principle of endless reiteration that makes survival itself one more version of the self-replicating logic of capitalism.

*Zone One* thus recasts the narrative of survival as a "theater of the mundane" (132). But be warned: it is not just the narratives that have a role on this stage. It is also the critics tasked with commenting on them. Accordingly, now would be the moment to announce that the lesson of *Zone One* must be that *it is easier to imagine the end of the world than the end of capitalism*. At the very least, it is easier to imagine the end of the world than it is to imagine the end of critics saying this about end-of-the-world fiction.[41] This is *Zone One*'s whole point; like so much else in the novel, the familiar theoretical dictum is "a banality no" critic can "elude" (as if we too "were programmed . . . to utter such things at the correct triggers" [71]). Such banality or cliché is what is channeled through genre, which reveals in the recursivity of form the afterlife of undead interpretation. Convention begets convention. Whitehead's "theater of the mundane"—a stage on which both the novel and its criticism play their parts—is nothing less than a staging of genre itself. Genre is the cultural logic of systemic perpetuation. It is the model for how social forms survive.

The chain stores, unnamed brands, and generic cultural references that litter *Zone One* are rooted in the "recursive nature" of genre itself and in the novel's attempt to come to grips with the cultural significance of its own generic status. The workings of genre direct our attention to a particular social form whose survival in the novel is more stubborn and more uncanny than any other: work. The generic banality and sheer uneventfulness that shape *Zone One* are, in the end, symptoms of the "recurring epidemic" of work itself. At the most obvious level, this is made clear by the constant confusion of workers and zombies. Early on, Mark Spitz mistakes a group of zombies for dispirited workers: "He didn't recognize their faces, only that deflated curl of the shoulders that marked Sunday night's recurring epidemic: Back to work" (84). Later, it is work that explains the behavior of the zombies: "The dead continued to commute, so hardwired was the custom" (233). Even the terrifying hordes of the living dead appear to Mark Spitz (here, in a recurring dream) as a stand-in for the city's hordes of working living: "[He] stepped out to the sidewalk into the rush-hour stream of the dead on their way home, the paralegals, mohels, resigned temps, bike messengers, and slump-shouldered massage therapists, the panoply of citizens in the throes of their slow decay" (133). In "The Zombie Manifesto," Sarah Juliet Lauro and Karen Embry suggest that the zombie is "a model of posthuman consciousness," registering "our doubts about humanity."[42] In these passages from *Zone One*, however, the conventional tension between humans and zombies is clearly less remarkable than what they have in common. Which is what, exactly? If both are what we might call *creatures of habit*, Whitehead's emphasis falls squarely on the *habit* part. In *Zone One*, the habits that make humans creaturely—that make them either "post-" or less than human—are forged in the cauldron of work: in the mindless, repetitive, unconscious patterns (Sunday night, morning commute, rush-hour stream) imposed on us by our jobs.

It is no surprise, then, that one of the first things to reappear in *Zone One*'s post-apocalyptic world is the very "concept" of the workweek: "This was the fourth day of rain, Friday afternoon, and a conditioned part of him submitted to end-of-the-week lassitude. . . . Hard to believe that reconstruction had progressed so far that clock-watching had returned, the slacker's code, the concept of weekend" (9). The "clock-watching" monotony that makes one weekday indistinguishable from the next and one office job the same as another is ultimately the secret of apocalyptic form. The form of Whitehead's novel is shaped above all by the "rhythms of . . . work flow" (253). Life goes on, systems regenerate: these principles constitute the practical truth of reconstruction, which is the real story of *Zone One*. "Systems," the novel insists, "die hard" (201). What dies the hardest, we find, is the workday, which day after day keeps coming back to life: "[T]he minute you bury the miserable day it rises from its coffin the next morning, this monster" (183). Work's recursive structuring of our time—"Monday-morning despair, hump-day torpor, and a fragile strain of muted Friday-afternoon euphoria" (253)—is what allows us to believe in the recursivity or repeatability of the whole world. The undying routines of work are the grounds for thinking that the social system itself can likewise be resurrected—that, come Monday, everybody will be back to work.

But reconstruction doesn't simply borrow the recursive ideology of the working day. It also depends, quite literally, on getting people to go back to work: on convincing someone like Mark Spitz to agree to be a sweeper. Society isn't going to clean up itself. If *Zone One* makes survival sound an awful lot like a job, that's because it is one. Work is what the sweepers must to do to help the social order survive, and work is what they know a surviving social order will continue to require them to do. Thus, as the opening set piece of the novel so elegantly demonstrates, even Human Resources has a role after the apocalypse—not as carriers of the zombie virus but as overseers of menial employment. Mark Spitz understands this. That's why his first thought upon hearing the zombies shuffling around in the HR office is not about zombies at all. It is the thought that "when this is all over," he should probably "come back and ask for a job" (16). It's a good idea, and one that suggests that Whitehead's zombies may carry a more allegorical message after all. Without a job, Mark Spitz can plainly see, you're as good as dead.

## OFFICE 365

What in the world does the end of the world have to do with office work? On the face of it, not much. The primary lure of survivalism is its promise of escape from the confines of the cubicle, its vision of a return to good old-fashioned work. ("When is the last time any of us really worked," *The Walking Dead* wanted to know.) Yet for all their emphasis on end times and all their interest in survival instincts, *Zone One* and *The Flame Alphabet* evince a strange affinity for the office, from Sam's "private office" at Forsythe to Mark Spitz's repeated tours of abandoned office buildings. For Whitehead and Marcus, the work of survival remains inseparable from postindustrial or white-collar work. At the simplest level, this scuttles the idea that survival skills could offer some sort of reprieve from the alienations of the office. Refusing the lingering nostalgia for Fordism and the survivalist tendency to "make a fetish of manual labor," as Derek Nystrom puts it,[43] these novels remind us of the one thing that manual work and mental work have in common: they are both work. But what is it about the office that seems so inescapable? The question is put to us not only by Marcus's and Whitehead's versions of the post-apocalyptic novel but also by another genre that has risen to prominence in recent years: the office novel. In books like Joshua Ferris's *Then We Came to the End* (2007), Ed Park's *Personal Days* (2008), Sam Lipsyte's *The Ask* (2010), Helen DeWitt's *Lightning Rods* (2011), and David Foster Wallace's *The Pale King* (2011), we confront the office as a defining feature of contemporary life and a new topic of literary investigation. In an age when white-collar work is modeled on the "creative" work of artists and writers, it cannot be surprising to find writers of literary fiction beginning to turn their attention to the ignominies and monotonies of office work.[44] For many of these writers, the office represents a particular nexus of time and work. Put simply, office work is what it looks like for work to be a complete waste of our time. In Ferris's *Then We Came to the End*, for instance, the open secret of the ostensibly creative advertising work that the novel depicts—and the secret, too, of the form of Ferris's novel—is that it is unbearably boring: "Is this boring you yet? It bored us every day. Our boredom was ongoing, a collective boredom, and it would never die because we would never die."[45] This boredom—a boredom so inescapable and "collective" that it requires a collective, first-personal-plural narrator—is what makes the office novel seem so tenuously literary, almost a contradiction in terms. Ferris's narrators know this. Their story, they admit, is one "set in the pages of an Office Depot catalog, of lives not nearly as interesting as an old man and the sea, or watery-world dwellers dispelling the hypos with a maniacal peg leg" (327–28). The dull lives played out in the office do not seem destined for the annals of literature; the great American novel has not tended to be a novel of office workers.[46]

What seems most unliterary about the office is that it is "not nearly as interesting" as almost anything else a novel could be about. "'The stock exchange is a poor substitute for the Holy Grail,'" Moretti writes, quoting the economist Joseph Schumpeter, "and business life—'in the office, among columns of figures'—is doomed to be 'essentially unheroic.'"[47] The novel form itself appears anathema to the monotony of office work. This is the paradox that office novels like Ferris's seek to examine in the dull light of day. Asked to share some stories about a recently deceased co-worker, the people in Ferris's office can think of nothing to say: "To be honest, what we remembered most about Brizz was his participation, along with the rest of us, in the mundane protocols of making a deadline" (82). Instead of interesting stories, the office offers only "mundane protocols." These monotonous routines cancel the prospect of good stories, and they even obstruct the possibility of meaningful accomplishment. Work in *Then We Came to the End* doesn't so much keep people busy as require them to *look* busy: "Looking busy was essential to our feeling vital to the agency, to mention nothing of being perceived as such by the partners, who would conclude by our labors that it was impossible to lay us off" (175); "We worked in the creative department developing ads and we considered our ad work creative, but it wasn't half as creative as the work we'd put in to pad our time sheets" (27). The vicious circle of late capitalist office work—there is nothing to do, so one must look busy in order to be allowed to keep doing it—dictates the form of Ferris's novel, which becomes a sort of *One Thousand and One Nights* for the office set. The novel is really just a compendium of the gossip, rumors, and digression-filled stories that the co-workers must keep telling if they want to look busy, or simply keep themselves occupied, on the days (which is most of them) when there is no real work to do. In the most extreme case, a ten-page secondhand anecdote about how a fired employee, Chris Yop, got revenge by disassembling his chair culminates in the revelation that the story has been only a way to kill time, not just for those who work in the office but also for the novel that dutifully seeks to tell their story:

"But Chris Yop wasn't what I came in here for, was it?" said Marcia.
"I don't think so," said Benny.
"What was it?" she asked herself. "Why'd I stop by?"
"I don't know," he replied, intrigued, hopeful.
"Oh my god," she said out of the blue. "Can you believe it's only three-fifteen?"

––––––

Some days felt longer than other days. Some days felt like two whole days. Unfortunately those days were never weekend days. Our Saturdays and Sundays passed in half the time of a normal workday. In other words, some weeks it felt like we worked ten straight days and had only one day off. . . . Everybody was trapped in this contradiction but nobody ever dared to articulate it. They just said, "Can you believe it's only three-fifteen?"

"Can you believe it's only three-fifteen?" Amber asked Larry Novotony.
(276–77)

Time, it seems, is never more homogeneous and more empty (pace Benedict Anderson) than it is at the office. In that case, all the office novel can
do is tell the story of the impossible attempt to fill all that time with insignificant stories. Read in this way, the office novel offers a commentary both
on the "unheroic" or un-novelistic nature of white-collar work and on the
deeper formal tension embedded in the genre itself: between the novelist
whose job it is to stretch out narrative time and the office workers who
would give almost anything to escape the interminable time of their job.

What's most paradoxical about *Then We Came to the End*'s status as a
novel is that novels themselves are something that few contemporary workers actually have the time to read—"who, working our hours, had time to
read books?" (371). The point is well taken. But it does raise a further conundrum: How do we explain the relation between extreme boredom and
unrelenting busyness? Today's office workers are indeed expected to work
longer hours than ever before. As Andrew Hoberek points out in *The Twilight of the Middle Class*, "white collar labor" has become "the frontline of
efforts to overturn the forty-hour week."[48] The relentless, all-consuming
time of work also calls to mind what Sianne Ngai has described as the *zany*
character of contemporary labor, the frantic, nonstop performances required of post-Fordism's flexible workers. Zaniness, Ngai proposes, is what
happens when "the ultimate standard for judging the worth of persons and
things becomes, simply, 'activity.'" The requirement of constant activity or
"incessant doing" leads to the hyperactivity of the zany performance, its
"stressed out, even desperate quality."[49] Of course, the stress and despera-
tion of Ferris's characters are expressed in an entirely different way, not
through zany hyperactivity but in the "mundane protocols" of "collective
boredom." That makes sense; these characters are office workers, not service workers. What does it mean, though, for an office worker to have simultaneously too much time to fill at the office ("Can you believe it's only
three-fifteen?") and too little time "to read books"? Between the feeling of
busyness and the unfolding of time, we may begin to see zaniness and routine as two sides of a single coin. While zany performance seems to be a
source of endless variation—Ngai: "the worker's role expands to become a
grotesque metarole, one containing all 'roles'"—it is actually the opposite:

a site of endlessness itself. Being zany is what it looks like to *never be able to stop working*. Hyperactive performance hides constant repetition. The ability to take on any role and perform any task makes one "finally indifferent to their individual specificity."[50] The indifference to our own work activities brings us back to the "mundane protocols" and banal routines that rule Ferris's office. These routines—the repeated schedules, tasks, meetings, and deadlines of life in the office—are represented in the novel not as the individual experience of the worker but as the impersonal temporal rhythms of the ever-expanding workday. If zaniness is the performative "affect" that emerges from the "cross-coupling of play and work," routine is the narrative form that uncouples them.[51] Draining the dubious play and pleasure out of work, routine attests to the iron grip that work has on practically all of our time.

The "dull, interminable hours" (9) of the office in *Then We Came to the End* finally explain the unlikely kinship between the office novel and the post-apocalyptic novel. Ferris, Marcus, and Whitehead all are equally concerned with how to represent the monotonies of nonstop work that once characterized assembly-line labor but are now commonly associated with office work. This slip from the factory floor to the office cubicle makes the forms of monotony and routine especially useful for thinking beyond what Brouillette calls the ideological "split between elite, fulfilling mental work and the banal, meaningless manual tasks performed by service workers and production lines."[52] Monotony and routine serve to remind us of the temporal logic that all seemingly different kinds of work, from the most "fulfilling" to the most "banal," share: the measurement and monetization of time that defines capitalist work as such. I recognize that my emphasis throughout this chapter on a concept like routine could be taken to imply a qualitative and moralizing distinction (routine work is bad, less routine work would be better!). But it implies no such thing. In my argument, routine is not what makes work unbearable.[53] Routine is what defines it as work in the first place. It does so by providing a rhetorical and narrative form for the temporal realities of work: the time that governs both the tasks we are continually required to perform and the value that is routinely extracted from them. Capitalism, of course, is what it means for time to be money. Routine, in turn, shows us what it means for capitalism to become synonymous with our time. As a figure for representing the most basic repetitions of the capitalist system—the ceaseless transformation of time into value—routine is not a contingent quality or a subjective experience. It is another name for the system itself.

## THE END OF WORK

*Then When We Came to the End* is not simply about the interminable time of work. It is also about the fear of no longer having any work to fill our time. Not just work's endlessness, but work's end: Ferris's novel is ultimately a novel about layoffs. The fear of getting fired structures the book's plot from beginning to end. "Layoffs were upon us" (16), we learn at the start, and the firings continue until the book's final pages: "In the last week of August 2001, and in the first ten days of that September, there were more layoffs than in all the months preceding them" (356–57). Layoffs are what inspire the novel's "creatives" to do their most creative work ("At first we called it what you would expect—getting laid off, being let go. Then we got creative. We said he'd gotten the ax, she'd been sacked, they'd all been shit-canned" [35]), and they are also the implacable reality that cuts through the dissimulation of advertising work: "The only words that ever meant a goddamn were, 'We're really very sorry about this, but we're going to have to let you go'" (329). The "end" that looms over *Then We Came to the End* is neither the literal end of the century (even though the novel's first main section is entitled "Enter a New Century") nor the ideological end of a certain vision of the American Century (even though the novel's climax revolves around September 11). It is the end of stable employment. As Alan Liu recounts in *The Laws of Cool*,

Downsizing began in the 1980s, but only during its second phase in the 1990s—when middle managers were laid off in unprecedented numbers—did it emerge from the older concept of cyclical "layoffs" (primarily in the blue-collar ranks but also in some professional sectors) as a systemic phenomenon that went to the heart of company identity. . . . Evidence that downsizing was indeed structural rather than cyclical lay in the unabated continuation of downsizing even as the U.S. economic recovery and expansion entered its seventh and eighth years in 1997–1998.[54]

The threat of massive layoffs that organizes *Then We Came to the End* reflects the emergent conditions of structural downsizing and white-collar precarity. As Liu emphasizes, these conditions were neither contingent nor cyclical but a new structural and systemic fact of the information economy. This fact—masked briefly by the dot-com bubble—makes Ferris's characters suddenly, anxiously aware that "any of us could be let go at any time" (44).

Here is the other thing the post-apocalyptic novel and the office novel have in common: both are attempts to grapple with an unthinkable catastrophe. Whereas the post-apocalyptic novel responds to the end of the world with the work of survival, the office novel suggests that literary representations of work must take into account the catastrophic fact of precarious white-collar employment. (In the 1990s, Liu notes, "as many as 80 percent of middle managers were vulnerable in companies undergoing re-engineering.")[55] Compared with the nearly apocalyptic experience of being fired, the humiliations of the office may not sound so bad after all. Ferris's narrators admit, "It was a shrill, carping, frenzied time, and as poisonous an atmosphere as anyone had ever known—and we wanted nothing more than to stay in it forever" (356). The implausible fantasy of keeping one's job forever (by the time *Then We Came to the End* ends, everyone has been laid off) reminds us that there is another, less salubrious meaning to be heard in that ostensibly utopian catchphrase "the end of work." It may not mean the end of capitalism. It may simply mean *unemployment*. The fantasy of being freed from the tyranny of the wage collapses into the reality of what Margaret Ronda describes as "the unceasingly difficult circumstances, social invisibility, and lack of mobilization of those 'set free' from waged life."[56] Indeed, what is the end of the world but an allegory for the horrific "freedom" of mass unemployment, the sudden disappearance of every job on earth?

In that case, the plague at the center of both *The Flame Alphabet* and *Zone One* is not just "the virus of being at work."[57] It is also the epidemic of unemployment. In Mark Spitz's view, the shambling gait of the walking dead resembles nothing so much as the ruined life of the unemployed. The shuffling zombies look like

a version of something that predated the anguishes . . . one of those laid-off or ruined businessmen who pretend to go to the office for the family's sake, spending all day on a park bench. . . . The city had long carried its own plague. Its infection had converted this creature into a member of its bygone loser cadre, into another one of the broke and the deluded, the mis-fitting, the inveterate unlucky. (148)

The "plague" that turns people into zombies is only a repetition of the "infection" that turned the employed into the unemployed. One way or another, both infections will spread. The fear of contagious unemployment explains Mark Spitz's odd gratitude for the obviously thankless job of being a sweeper: "I'm grateful. Buffalo has given us some busywork to keep our minds off things. Dig a drainage ditch for the camp, shuck the fucking corn. . . . You have to admit, it passes the time" (271). Even after the apocalypse, it turns out, not having a job is neither to be freed from work nor to be free to work for yourself; it is simply to be out of work. Unemployment is also the open secret of *The Flame Alphabet*. Why is Sam so grateful for all the smallwork he has to do? Why, for that matter, does he "nee[d] to do it" in the first place? Because he isn't doing anything else. Sam, always around the house even before the apocalypse, does not appear to have had a job.

In *Zone One* and *The Flame Alphabet*, we witness the apocalyptic fantasy of the end of work come to an end in an age of mass unemployment. Turning the work of survival into the survival of work, Marcus and Whitehead force us to confront the most devastating truth about work: that the only thing worse than having to do it is not having any to do. Part of what it means to survive today, after all, is just to be lucky enough to have a job. If, say, you happened to live in a major U.S. city whose unemployment rate was above 8 percent every month from February 2009 to December 2013, you too may have had "to figure out how to survive. Hunt-and-gather rent money, forage ramen" (*Zone One*, 17).[58] Such survival skills (hunting, gathering, foraging) are not the sole province of those wandering post-apocalyptic wastelands. They are also the anguished activities of those with uncertain employment. This is a useful reminder that our most basic survival skill may simply be the ability to get work. Marcus and Whitehead recognize this; for them, the essence of the post-apocalyptic genre is less a dire vision of the future than a simple drama of putting people back to work.

Still, survival remains a deeply contradictory figure. It offers no solution to our current predicament and no respite from our contemporary condition. But it at least explains the contradictory temporalities that make that condition so relentlessly contemporary, continuously pulling the speculative future back into the routine orbit of the present. Survival makes the period of the contemporary both equivocal and implacable, a moment in history whose hardships are clear and whose alternatives are anything but.

If the relation between work and survival thus feels uniquely or definitively contemporary, that is because it explains how the contemporary's own ceaseless repetition—the crushing permanence of present conditions— comes to seem like both a problem we need to solve and a solution we are willing to live with. Caught between the dreadful routines of our jobs and the deeper dread of losing them, survival is the compromise we are consigned to by a world in which our work means nothing to us and in which we are made to mean nothing without work.

# HOW TO HISTORICIZE THE PRESENT

The arbitrary period of the decade. The questionable context of revival. The indeterminate temporality of waiting. The ephemeral atmosphere of the weather. The economic compromise of survival. These concepts, I've argued, are central to understanding what the idea of the contemporary means to us today. Yet even as *Contemporary Drift* has worked to theorize these concepts, it has also been at pains to emphasize their basic shortcomings as ways of writing the history of the present. These "alternative measures of time and history," I wrote in the introduction, are also "ambivalent and limited ways of historicizing." They are not self-evident periodizing terms, I suggested, but at best "provisional historical frameworks." Instantiated through such frameworks, the history of the contemporary would seem to be similarly provisional and problematic. From the decade's arbitrariness to the weather's epiphenomenal status, from revival's stale repetitions to waiting's worrisome uncertainty, the concepts that organize *Contemporary Drift* suggest that the figures we use to imagine contemporary history are also figures for the limits of historical imagination in the present.

My continued insistence on the split personality of each of these concepts may be read as a brief for the necessity, if not simply the inevitability, of a properly dialectical account of the contemporary. Yet for as much as this book has highlighted (starting with its title) the "problem" of understanding our own contemporary moment, *Contemporary Drift* has not, finally, been content to settle for the negative. If I began this book by emphasizing the difficulties posed by the concept of the contemporary, I did so in order to present them not as foregone conclusions but as puzzles to be solved. We fail to understand our contemporary if we don't begin by acknowledging that it really is more difficult to historicize than other periods are. We also fail to understand it if we simply leave it at that. While the theses I laid out in the introduction describe what makes the contemporary so challenging as an object of analysis, the preceding chapters have sought not to confirm those challenges but to do just the opposite: to perform the hard but hardly impossible task of producing positive knowledge about our contemporary moment.

Such knowledge flashes up, for instance, in the figure of the decade, which is more than a symbol of our inability to periodize the present; it is an index of literature's response to the triumphalist ideology of post–Cold War consumer capitalism. Revival, likewise, is not just a theoretical lesson in the elusive nature of context but also an urgent reminder of the political and economic continuities that knit together the postwar world system. Waiting, meanwhile, is not a capitulation to deferred knowledge but a narrative form that reflects the epistemological conditions of twenty-first-century risk society. Weather, too, is more than a figure of flux; it is a representation of the temporal and historical quandaries posed by climate change. And survival is not a simplistic image of a utopian future but a way of narrating the ambivalence of a contemporary world shaped by the twin poles of constant work and looming unemployment. Each term turns a negative into a positive, a gap in history into a historical claim. Through the problems of periodization posed by the decade, we confront the new historical period marked by the end of the Cold War. In the difficulty of situating a cinematic revival, we discover the unexpectedly continuous context of our long twentieth-century situation. From the indeterminacy of waiting, we derive a lesson about the nature of knowledge in an era of boundless risk. Buffeted by the temporary circumstances of the weather, we manage to grasp the true temporal scale of the crisis of climate change. Seduced by the equivocal prospect of survival, we are forced to face the deeper truths of laboring in a postindustrial society. In each case, what looks at first like an ambivalent or problematic way of conceptualizing contemporary history turns out to be a complex cultural record of our determinate—though still in the process of being determined—historical conditions.

There is, to be sure, something paradoxical about the concept of the contemporary, something contradictory about its status as an unfinished and undistanced category of historical experience. In this book, I have sought to demonstrate how the contemporary's paradoxes may serve as narrow but not impassable openings onto historical knowledge. Throughout *Contemporary Drift*, that knowledge has centered on the crisis-ridden conditions of our economically and ecologically threatened era, an age defined from every angle by inequality, immiseration, dispossession, and disaster. In trying to say something about the dire circumstances of contemporary capitalism, this book has also sought to reflect on the peculiar nature of this type of historical knowledge—not just the facts such knowledge comprises but also the path by which we arrive at it. It is a circuitous path indeed, one whose numerous detours toward the negative (the impossibility of periodizing, the endlessness of waiting, the inescapability of work) risk taking us nowhere. But it is a path that, however tortuous, does lead us to a point from which we can catch a clearer glimpse of our contemporary moment. This is no mean feat. Without the privilege of critical distance, without the time-tested judgment of hindsight, without the power to foresee the future course of current events, we are still able to know something about the history of our contemporary. This, finally, is what it means to historicize the present.

Faced with the question of whether we really can historicize our own contemporary, this book's answer has been a lengthy but unambiguous yes. How, in that case, does the contemporary challenge what we think it means to historicize? Here, too, we must hold out for something more than negation or contradiction. I would suggest that the story of how we acquire positive knowledge about the contemporary—the story I have sought to tell in *Contemporary Drift*—is not a story about giving up on the distanced insights and totalizing aspirations of historicism. It is, on the contrary, a story about the improbable resilience of the historicist imagination. It is about how the formal conventions of contemporary artworks allow us to envision the historical coherence of the contemporary world. It is the story of how we learn to practice historicism by other means.

# NOTES

## INTRODUCTION

1. There are several valuable exceptions, including, in literary studies, Roger Luckhurst and Peter Marks, eds., *Literature and the Contemporary: Fictions and Theories of the Present* (London: Longman, 1999); and a recent cluster of essays, Héctor Hoyos and Marília Librandi-Roch, eds., "Theories of the Contemporary in South America," special issue, *Revista de Estudios Hispánicos* 48, no. 1 (2014). In art history, see Terry Smith, *What Is Contemporary Art?* (Chicago: University of Chicago Press, 2009); Richard Meyer, *What Was Contemporary Art?* (Cambridge, Mass.: MIT Press, 2013); Peter Osborne, *Anywhere or Not at All: Philosophy of Contemporary Art* (London: Verso, 2013); and Terry Smith, Okwui Enwezor, and Nancy Condee, eds., *Antinomies of Art and Culture: Modernity, Postmodernity, Contemporaneity* (Durham, N.C.: Duke University Press, 2008).

2. John Sturrock, "Editor's Introduction," in *The Oxford Guide to Contemporary Writing*, ed. John Sturrock (Oxford: Oxford University Press, 1996), vii.

3. The journal and professional organization Post45 (founded in 2006) is the most explicit example of how the post-1945 boundary dictates the study of contemporary literature. On the relation between 1945 and 1989 as periodizing markers, see Amir Eshel, *Futurity: Contemporary Literature and the Quest for the Past* (Chicago: University of Chicago Press, 2013). For examples of the recent use of the post-2000 cutoff, see Timothy Bewes, ed., "The Contemporary Novel: Imagining the Twenty-First Century," special issue, *Novel: A Forum on Fiction* 45, no. 2 (2012); and David James and Andrezej Gąsiorek, eds., "Fiction Since 2000: Postmillennial Commitments," special issue, *Contemporary Literature* 53, no. 4 (2012). Finally, for a parallel account of these periodizing questions from the perspective of art history, see Osborne's description of the "three periodizations of contemporary art": "art since 1945," art since "the early 1960s," and "art after 1989" (*Anywhere or Not at All*, 18–22).

4. *Oxford English Dictionary*, "Contemporary," A.4, A.1. It is interesting to note that the *OED* did not actually add this meaning to the entry on "Contemporary" until 1972. Roger Luckhurst and Peter Marks point this out in their introduction to *Literature and the Contemporary*, 1.

5. For a more detailed account of this history, see Meyer, *What Was Contemporary Art?*; and Osborne, *Anywhere or Not at All*.

6. Daniel Grausam acknowledges as much when he points out that "much of what we still call 'contemporary' fiction is no longer meaningfully contemporary" (*On Endings: American Postmodern Fiction and the Cold War* [Charlottesville: University of Virginia Press, 2011], 6).

7. Smith, for instance, suggests that the decades-long "shift . . . from modern to contemporary art" was "nascent during the 1950s, emergent in the 1960s, contested during the 1970s, but unmistakable since the 1980s" (*What Is Contemporary Art?* 5).

8. Meyer, *What Was Contemporary Art?* 13.

9. Gordon Hutner, "Historicizing the Contemporary: A Response to Amy Hungerford," *American Literary History* 20, nos. 1–2 (2008): 420.

10. For a longer history of the "ideal of critical distance" (4) and "the *aspiration* to a distanced view" (6), see Amanda Anderson, *The Powers of Distance: Cosmopolitanism and the Cultivation of Detachment* (Princeton, N.J.: Princeton University Press, 2001). In modern historical thought, the necessity of distance is enshrined in everything from Hegel's famous" owl of Minerva"—which, taking flight at dusk, suggests that historical knowledge always comes after the fact—to Braudel's principle of "unconscious history," which insists that people in the present are never fully aware of their own historical significance. Georg Wilhelm Friedrich Hegel, *The Philosophy of Right*, trans. S. W. Dyde (London: George Bell and Sons, 1896), xxx; Fernand Braudel, *On History*, trans. Sarah Matthews (Chicago: University of Chicago Press, 1980), 39.

11. Rita Felski, " 'Context Stinks!' " *New Literary History* 42, no. 4 (2011): 574.

12. Amy Hungerford, "On the Period Formerly Known as Contemporary," *American Literary History* 20, nos. 1–2 (2008): 416.

13. Ibid.

14. Braudel, *On History*, 36.

15. In his history of the discipline, Gerald Graff quotes a 1948 college textbook claiming, "The literature of the youth's own century is more easily understood by him. He can read it rapidly without being perplexed by historical background or outmoded style." As Graff goes on to note, by the middle of the century this sentiment would come to seem "an apparent solution . . . to the problem of apathetic students" taking English classes (*Professing Literature: An Institutional History* [Chicago: University of Chicago Press, 1987], 195–96). Before it was the solution, though, it was the problem: the reason contemporary literature hadn't been included as part of the discipline before then was that it didn't seem to require scholarly commentary. The presumed self-evidence of modern and contemporary fiction was long thought to make its study "unacademic," in the words of William Lyon Phelps, one of the field's earliest defenders (*Essays on Modern Novelists* [New York: Macmillan, 1910], 246).

16. For a description of how the "visual art-producing institutions (art schools, museums, galleries, auction houses, publishers, educators) have ramped up to industrial levels, and are putting out more new art, sooner and with less vetting, to booming crowds of consumers," see Smith, *What Is Contemporary Art?* 250–51. For an

examination of the problems posed by a publishing situation that is currently giving us "fifty thousand new novels in the U.S. every year" and rising, see Matthew Wilkens, "Contemporary Fiction by the Numbers," *Post45: Contemporaries*, March 11, 2011, http://post45.research.yale.edu/2011/03/contemporary-fiction-by-the-numbers/.

17. As Lauren Berlant puts it, "The present is something given back to us by those who reflect on it; not available to experience as such, the sense and the sense experience of the present are effects of critical practice" ("Critical Inquiry, Affirmative Culture," *Critical Inquiry* 30, no. 2 [2004]: 447). Along similar lines, Osborne suggests that because the contemporary "is beyond possible experience," it "exists only 'in the idea'" (*Anywhere or Not at All*, 22).

18. While genre has conventionally been thought of as a problem of classification (is this a Western or isn't it?), critics have become increasingly attuned to genre's capacity to help us think differently about history. For Wai Chee Dimock, genre illuminates the continuities of literature across "deep time" (*Through Other Continents: American Literature Across Deep Time* [Princeton, N.J.: Princeton University Press, 2006], 84). For Rita Felski, genre is "hospitable to theorizing transtemporal connections, repetitions, and translations" ("'Context Stinks!'" 581). For Caren Irr, genre depicts "the historically mutable character of literary form" (*Toward the Geopolitical Novel: U.S. Fiction in the Twenty-First Century* [New York: Columbia University Press, 2014], 13). For Vilashini Cooppan, "genre describes a moving mode of literary history" shaped by a "combination of temporal oscillation and spatial expansion" ("Hauntologies of Form: Race, Genre, and the Literary World System," *Gramma: Journal of Theory and Criticism* 13 [2005]: 75). And for Franco Moretti, genres are "Janus-like creatures, with one face turned to history and the other to form" (*Graphs Maps Trees: Abstract Models for Literary History* [London: Verso, 2007], 14). Across this wide spectrum of thinkers, genre emerges as a crucial site for retheorizing historicity and rethinking the historical protocols of literary study.

19. Virginia Jackson renders this point with particular power: "Genres became modes of recognition—complex forms instantiated in popular discourse, relying on what we could or would recognize *collectively, in common*—and so subject to historical change and cultural negotiation" ("The Function of Criticism at the Present Time," *Los Angeles Review of Books*, April 12, 2015, https://lareviewofbooks.org/essay/function -criticism-present-time, italics in original).

20. Lauren Berlant, *Cruel Optimism* (Durham, N.C.: Duke University Press, 2011), 16.

21. Fredric Jameson, *Postmodernism or, The Cultural Logic of Late Capitalism* (Durham, N.C.: Duke University Press, 1991), 18.

22. Andrew Hoberek, "Introduction: After Postmodernism," in "After Postmodernism: Form and History in Contemporary American Fiction," ed. Andrew Hoberek, special issue, *Twentieth-Century Literature* 53, no. 3 (2007): 240.

23. Ibid., 238.

24. In the past twelve years, genre has been the topic of special issues of *New Literary History* ("Theorizing Genre I" 34, no. 2 [2003] and "Theorizing Genre II," 34, no. 3 [2003]) and *PMLA* ("Remapping Genre" 122, no. 5 [2007]), as well as the edited series Selected Essays from the English Institute (2011). Genre has also become relevant to an impressively broad range of literary-critical methodologies, including Marxism (Franco Moretti), sociology (Jeremy Rosen), postcolonial theory (Vilashini Coopan), actor-network theory (Rita Felski), and affect theory (Lauren Berlant).

25. The question about the detective novel shouldn't be all that surprising. One of the more familiar sights in postmodern fiction from the 1960s to the 1980s was a writer like Thomas Pynchon or Paul Auster updating the hard-boiled tradition with a new commitment to epistemological relativism and metaphysical indeterminacy. Between Pynchon and Chabon (who won the 2001 Pulitzer for *The Amazing Adventures of Kavalier and Clay*), however, one important thing did change: the cultural status of hard-boiled fiction itself. In the 1990s, hard-boiled fiction traded in its origins in pay-per-word pulp magazines like *Black Mask* for the handsome omnibus editions of the Library of America, which published Raymond Chandler's complete works in 1995, followed by two volumes of "American noir" authors in 1997, and the complete works of Dashiell Hammett in 1999. Such a vertiginous shift from countercultural to canonical must play a part in any history of hard-boiled detective fiction.

26. For a particularly provocative theory of the relation between genre and art under the conditions of total commodification, see Nicholas Brown, "The Work of Art in the Age of Its Real Subsumption by Capital," *nonsite.org*, March 13, 2012, http://non site.org/editorial/the-work-of-art-in-the-age-of-its-real-subsumption-under-capital.

27. Tania Modleski writes, "Although Harlequin Romances, Gothic novels, and soap operas provide mass(ive) entertainment for countless numbers of women . . . very few critics have taken them seriously enough to study them in any detail" (*Loving with a Vengeance: Mass Produced Fantasies for Women*, 2nd ed. [New York: Routledge, 2008], 1).

28. Stephanie Harzewski, *Chick Lit and Postfeminism* (Charlottesville: University of Virginia Press, 2011), 6.

29. Michael Z. Newman and Elena Levine, *Legitimating Television: Media Convergence and Cultural Status* (New York: Routledge, 2012), 10–11.

30. As Modleski wryly observes: "One cannot find any writings on popular feminine narratives to match the aggrandized titles of certain classic studies of popular male genres ('The Gangster as Tragic Hero') or the inflated claims made for, say, the detective novel which fill the pages of the *Journal of Popular Culture*" (*Loving with a Vengeance*, 1).

31. For an exemplary case study of the relation of "Asian horror film," "global Hollywood," and "the temporality of transnational generic appropriation and exchange" (193), see Bliss Cua Lim, *Translating Time: Cinema, the Fantastic, and Temporal Critique* (Durham, N.C.: Duke University Press 2009), 190–244. For Lim, genre is an especially useful category to the extent that it is able to track "the 'international exchange' between national cinemas, domestic and overseas audiences, cult aficionados, film producers, studio distributors, critics, and promoters" (192)—a dizzying series of transnational relations and exchanges that are, needless to say, definitive of the culture of globalization.

32. In a different though extremely generative context for thinking about the "drag" of time, Elizabeth Freeman theorizes the double meaning of "drag" (as a kind of time and a kind of queer performance) as "a way of thinking about identity and social change relationally across time—about 'drag' as a *productive* obstacle to progress, a usefully disorienting pull backward, and a necessary pressure on the present tense" (*Time Binds: Queer Temporalities, Queer Histories* [Durham, N.C.: Duke University Press, 2010], 64–65, italics in original). For Freeman, "temporal drag" thus becomes "a way of connecting queer performativity to disavowed political histories."

Although this book does not explicitly engage debates in queer theory, it does draw inspiration from the powerful ways of rethinking history, historicism, and temporality explored by critics like Freeman, Valerie Rohy, Kathryn Bond Stockton, Jack Halberstam, and Carolyn Dinshaw. For a broad discussion of issues in queer temporality and queer historicism, see "Theorizing Queer Temporalities: A Roundtable Discussion," *GLQ: A Journal of Lesbian and Gay Studies* 13, nos. 2–3 (2007): 177–95.

33. Quoted in Graff, *Professing Literature*, 124.

34. Phelps, *Essays on Modern Novelists*, 245.

35. Graff, *Professing Literature*, 124.

36. John Crowe Ransom, "Criticism, Inc." *Virginia Quarterly Review* 13, no. 4 (1937), http://www.vqronline.org/essay/criticism-inc-0.

37. Graff, *Professing Literature*, 206.

38. Ibid., 195–208.

39. An additional point to make here is that the discipline of English ceased to be the study of history around the same time it became the teaching of creative writing. For the seminal literary history of the creative writing program, see Mark McGurl, *The Program Era: Postwar Fiction and the Rise of the Creative Writing Program* (Cambridge, Mass.: Harvard University Press, 2009). McGurl acknowledges that his own book—as a study of contemporary literature—was made possible by an earlier group of critics, including Ihab Hassan, Tony Tanner, and Jerome Klinkowitz, who effectively "established the viability of academic criticism of contemporary literature" (31). What McGurl does not mention, however, and what clearly demands a more thorough accounting, is that the work of these critics emerged directly alongside—and, I would venture, as a result of—the explosion of creative writing programs in the 1960s.

40. Amy Hungerford, for instance, makes the surprising but plausible observation that still today, some scholars of post-1945 literature continue to "evinc[e] discomfort at writing about the literature of the late century" ("On the Period Formerly Known as Contemporary," 418).

41. Lefebvre writes in the third and final volume of his epic *Critique of Everyday Life*: "Two ways of studying daily life and its alterations might be envisioned: either a periodical publication or a series of works over time attempting regular updates. The first, doubtless preferable, was not feasible for material (editorial) reasons" (*Critique of Everyday Life*, vol. 3, *From Modernity to Modernism [Towards a Metaphilosophy of Daily Life]*, trans. Gregory Elliott [London: Verso, 2005], 9).

42. Walter Benjamin famously called for "the notion of a present which is not a transition, but in which time stands still and comes to a stop" ("Theses on the Philosophy of History," in *Illuminations*, trans. Harry Zohn and ed. Hannah Arendt [New York: Schocken Books, 1968], 262).

43. The phrase appeared in Marx's 1844 letter to Arnold Ruge; the letter is reprinted as "For a Ruthless Criticism of Everything Existing" in *The Marx-Engels Reader*, 2nd ed., ed. Robert C. Tucker (New York: Norton, 1978), 12–15. On "the status of the present" as the "ultimate dilemma" of Marxist thought, see Fredric Jameson, "Marxism and Historicism," in *Ideologies of Theory* (London: Verso, 2008), 478.

44. In *Discipline and Punish*, for instance, Foucault writes, "I would like to write the history of this prison. . . . Why? Simply because I am interested in the past? No, if one means by that writing a history of the past in terms of the present. Yes, if one

means writing the history of the present" (*Discipline and Punish: The Birth of the Prison*, trans. Alan Sheridan [New York: Vintage, 1995], 31).

45. Sylviane Agacinski, *Time Passing: Modernity and Nostalgia*, trans. Jody Gladding (New York: Columbia University Press, 2003), 5, italics in original.

46. Berlant, *Cruel Optimism*, 4, 213.

47. Osborne rightly points out that "it has only been in the last ten years . . . that 'contemporary' has begun to emerge into the critical daylight," triggering "the recent rush of writing trying to make some minimal theoretical sense of the concept" (*Anywhere or Not at All*, 17).

48. Paul Rabinow, *Marking Time: On the Anthropology of the Contemporary* (Princeton, N.J.: Princeton University Press, 2008), 1; Terry Smith, *What Is Contemporary Art?* 256, italics in original; Giorgio Agamben, "What Is the Contemporary?" in *What Is an Apparatus?* trans. David Kishik and Stefan Pedatella (Stanford, Calif.: Stanford University Press, 2009), 46.

49. Of course, the question of the present is not confined to the twentieth history. The history of the historical present can be traced back to at least the eighteenth century, when, as James Chandler argues, "European intellectual culture underwent radical historiographical transformations." Those transformations, Chandler suggests, "involved a certain unprecedented self-consciousness about" the nature of the present as a historical period (*England in 1819: The Politics of Literary Culture and the Case of Romantic Historicism* [Chicago: University of Chicago Press, 1998], 100, 90). My argument here, then, is not that the late twentieth century is the first time we have been preoccupied with the present. Instead, my claim is that this is the moment when the question of the present has become at once a new source of intense cultural anxiety and a newly codified subject of study in the institution of the academy.

50. Ulrich Beck, Anthony Giddens, and Scott Lash, *Reflexive Modernization: Politics, Tradition and Aesthetics in the Modern Social Order* (Stanford, Calif.: Stanford University Press, 1994).

51. McGurl, *Program Era*, 12.

52. On postmodernism and the "perpetual present," see Fredric Jameson, "Postmodernism and Consumer Society," in *The Anti-Aesthetic: Essays on Postmodern Culture*, ed. Hal Foster (New York: New Press, 1998), 143–44. On "24/7 capitalism," see Jonathan Crary, *24/7: Late Capitalism and the Ends of Sleep* (London: Verso, 2013).

53. On recent changes in the measure of work time, see chapter 5. On the acceleration of the present, see Hartmut Rosa, *Social Acceleration: A New Theory of Modernity*, trans. Jonathan Trejoy-Mathys (New York: Columbia University Press, 2013); and Judy Wajcman, *Pressed for Time: The Acceleration of Life in Digital Capitalism* (Chicago: University of Chicago Press, 2015). The pervasive sense of acceleration has predictably led to a renewed critical interest in slowness. For a study of aesthetic alternatives to our "accelerated now" (4), see Lutz Koepnick, *On Slowness: Toward an Aesthetic of the Contemporary* (New York: Columbia University Press, 2014).

54. On the "temporal dimension" of finance, see Robin Blackburn, "Finance and the Fourth Dimension," *New Left Review* 39 (2006): 39–70. On the temporality of climate change, see chapter 4.

1. DECADE

1. Fredric Jameson, *A Singular Modernity: Essay on the Ontology of the Present* (London: Verso, 2002), 25.

2. For a survey of periodization's "unfashionable" place in scholarship, see Fredric Jameson, "Periodizing the 60s," in *The Ideologies of Theory* (London: Verso, 2008). On periodization's "unsophisticated" and undertheorized idea of totality, see Eric Hayot, *On Literary Worlds* (New York: Oxford University Press, 2012), 156. On the "paranoid" logic of periodization and its "imperfect" work of deletion, see Graham Thompson, "Periodizing the '80s: The 'Differential of History' in Nicholson Baker's *The Mezzanine*," *Modern Fiction Studies* 57, no. 2 (2011): 315. The assessment of periodization as "intolerable and unacceptable in its very nature" comes from Jameson, *Singular Modernity*, 28.

3. Virginia Jackson, "Introduction: On Periodization and Its Discontents," in *On Periodization: Selected Essays from the English Institute*, ed. Virginia Jackson (ACLS Humanities E-Book, 2010), para. 17.

4. Jameson, *Singular Modernity*, 29.

5. Andrew Hoberek, ed., "After Postmodernism: Form and History in Contemporary American Fiction," special issue, *Twentieth-Century Literature* 53, no. 3 ( 2007); Jason Gladstone and Daniel Worden, eds., "Postmodernism, Then," special issue, *Twentieth-Century Literature* 57, nos. 3–4 (2011).

6. Brian McHale, "What Was Postmodernism?" *Electronic Book Review*, December 2007, http://www.electronicbookreview.com/thread/fictionspresent/tense.

7. Perry Anderson, *The Origins of Postmodernity* (London: Verso, 2002), 44–45.

8. Bran Nicol, introduction to *Postmodernism and the Contemporary Novel: A Reader*, ed. Bran Nicol (Edinburgh: Edinburgh University Press, 2003), 1.

9. Hans Bertens, *The Idea of the Postmodern: A History* (London: Routledge, 1995), 3.

10. Stefan Morawski, *The Troubles with Postmodernism* (London: Routledge, 1996), 1.

11. Fredric Jameson, *Postmodernism, or, The Cultural Logic of Late Capitalism* (Durham, N.C.: Duke University Press, 1991), xxii.

12. Jeffrey T. Nealon, *Post-Postmodernism, or, The Cultural Logic of Just-in-Time Capitalism* (Stanford, Calif.: Stanford University Press, 2012), ix.

13. Ibid., 51, xi, 52.

14. Karl Marx, *The German Ideology*, in *The Marx-Engels Reader*, 2nd ed., ed. Robert C. Tucker (New York: Norton, 1978), 175.

15. For a different reading of the double negative, see Eric Cazdyn, *The Already Dead: The New Time of Politics, Culture, and Illness* (Durham, N.C.: Duke University Press, 2012), 170–71.

16. Andrew Hoberek, "Introduction: After Postmodernism," in "After Postmodernism: Form and History in Contemporary American Fiction," special issue, *Twentieth-Century Literature* 53, no. 3 (2007): 241.

17. Steven Biel, "Lewis Allen's 'Only Yesterday' and the Idea of the Decade," *Journal of American Studies* 25, no. 2 (1991): 260.

18. This would seem to confirm Eric Hayot's observation that "periods get shorter as we get closer to the present" (*On Literary Worlds*, 157).

19. Jameson, *Postmodernism*, 286–87.

20. Biel, "Lewis Allen's 'Only Yesterday,'" 259.

21. Phillip E. Wegner, *Life Between Two Deaths, 1989–2001: U.S. Culture in the Long Nineties* (Durham, N.C.: Duke University Press, 2009); Samuel Cohen, *After the End of History: American Fiction in the 1990s* (Iowa City: University of Iowa Press, 2009); Jay Prosser, ed., *American Fiction of the 1990s: Reflections of History and Culture* (London: Routledge, 2008); Leigh Claire La Berge, *Scandals and Abstraction: Financial Fiction of the Long 1980s* (New York: Oxford University Press, 2015); Adam Kelly *American Fiction in Transition: Observer-Hero Narrative, the 1990s, and Postmodernism* (London: Bloomsbury Academic, 2013); Jeremy Green, *Late Postmodernism: American Fiction at the Millennium* (New York: Palgrave Macmillan, 2005), 3; Nealon, *Post-Postmodernism*, 4.

22. La Berge, *Scandals and Abstraction*, 3.

23. Amy Kaplan, *The Social Construction of American Realism* (Chicago: University of Chicago Press, 1988), 8, 9.

24. Erich Auerbach, *Mimesis: The Representation of Reality in Western Literature*, Fiftieth Anniversary Edition, trans. Willard R. Trask (Princeton, N.J.: Princeton University Press, 2003), 480.

25. Ibid., 485, 491, 459.

26. Jerome Klinkowitz, *The New American Novel of Manners: The Fiction of Richard Yates, Dan Wakefield, and Thomas McGuane* (Athens: University of Georgia Press, 1986), 2.

27. Kent Puckett, *Bad Form: Social Mistakes and the Nineteenth-Century Novel* (Oxford: Oxford University Press, 2008), 11, 6.

28. Nancy Bentley, *The Ethnography of Manners: Hawthorne, James, Wharton* (Cambridge: Cambridge University Press, 1995), 2.

29. Ibid., 112, 113.

30. Klinkowitz, *New American Novel of Manners*, 4.

31. Bret Easton Ellis, *Glamorama* (New York: Vintage, 1998), 527. Subsequent references are cited in the text.

32. Daniel Mendelsohn, "Lesser Than Zero," review of *Glamorama*, by Bret Easton Ellis, *New York Times*, January 24, 1999, http://www.nytimes.com/books/99/01/24/reviews/990124.24mendelt.html; James Wood, "Human, All Too Inhuman," review of *White Teeth*, by Zadie Smith, *New Republic*, July 24, 2000, http://www.newrepublic.com/article/books-and-arts/human-all-too-inhuman; Padmaja Challakere, "Aesthetics of Globalization in Contemporary Fiction: The Function of the Fall of the Berlin Wall in Zadie Smith's *White Teeth* (2000), Nicholas Royle's *Counterparts* (1996), and Philip Hensher's *Pleasured* (1998)," *Theory and Event* 10, no. 1 (2007).

33. Walter Benn Michaels, *The Shape of the Signifier: 1967 to the End of History* (Princeton, N.J.: Princeton University Press, 2004), 150.

34. Roland Barthes, "The Reality Effect," in *The Novel: An Anthology of Criticism and Theory 1900–2000*, ed. Dorothy J. Hale (Malden: Blackwell, 2006), 234, italics in original).

35. Bret Easton Ellis, *American Psycho* (New York: Vintage, 1991), 5, 29. Subsequent references are cited in the text.

36. Jameson, for instance, sees the obsession with fashion as a symptom of postmodernism's failure to "think historically." According to this well-known account, postmodern culture "approached the 'past' through stylistic connotation, conveying 'pastness' by the glossy qualities of the image, and '1930s-ness' or '1950s-ness' by the

attributes of fashion" (*Postmodernism*, 19). In response to Jameson's dim view of fashion, we might recall Walter Benjamin's more dialectical account: "Fashion has an eye for what is up-to-date, wherever it moves in the thicket of what was. It is the tiger's leap into that which has gone before" ("Theses on the Philosophy of History," in *Illuminations*, trans. Harry Zohn and ed. Hannah Arendt [New York: Schocken Books, 1968], 261).

37. Puckett, *Bad Form*, 87, italics in original.

38. Frances Ferguson, *Pornography, the Theory: What Utilitarianism Did to Action* (Chicago: University of Chicago Press, 2004), 147.

39. Zadie Smith, *White Teeth* (New York: Vintage, 2000), 197. Subsequent references are cited in the text.

40. On post-1945 immigration and "the political economy of racism" in Britain, see Ashley Dawson, *Mongrel Nation: Diasporic Culture and the Making of Postcolonial Britain* (Ann Arbor: University of Michigan Press, 2007).

41. Ruth Jennison, *The Zukofsky Era: Modernity, Margins, and the Avant-Garde* (Baltimore: Johns Hopkins University Press, 2012), 40.

42. Fredric Jameson, "Postmodernism and Consumer Society," in *The Anti-Aesthetic: Essays on Postmodern Culture*, ed. Hal Foster (New York: New Press, 1998), 127–28.

43. As Green points out, many of the best-known "attempts to theorize postmodernism have relied on the list" (*Late Postmodernism*, 20). Jeff Nealon also comments on this particular aspect of Jameson's writing style: "the heavy volume of seemingly passing references . . . that would seem to have very little or nothing in common" (*Post-Postmodernism*, 5).

44. It is notable, by contrast, that the one section in the main narrative whose title makes reference to the decade—"End of the 1980s" (371)—concludes with one of *American Psycho*'s best-known passages, which in the context of the section title seems to refer to the *impossibility* of historical self-reflection: "I gain no deeper knowledge about myself, no new understanding can be extracted from my telling. There has been no reason for me to tell you any of this. This confession has meant nothing" (377).

45. Joshua Clover, *1989: Bob Dylan Didn't Have This to Sing About* (Berkeley: University of California Press, 2009), 5, xiii.

46. Biel, "Lewis Allen's 'Only Yesterday,'" 259.

47. Marshall Brown, "Periods and Resistances," in "Periodization: Cutting Up the Past," special issue, *Modern Language Quarterly* 62, no. 4 (2001): 313.

48. Michael North, "Virtual Histories: The Year as Literary History," in "Periodization: Cutting Up the Past," special issue, *Modern Language Quarterly* 62, no. 4 (2001): 412.

49. James Chandler, *England in 1819: The Politics of Literary Culture and the Case of Romantic Historicism* (Chicago: University of Chicago Press, 1998), 67.

50. Ibid., 74, italics in original.

51. North, "Virtual Histories," 412.

52. Virginia Woolf, "Mr. Bennett and Mrs. Brown," in *Essentials of the Theory of Fiction, 3rd ed.*, ed. Michael J. Hoffman and Patrick D. Murphy (Durham, N.C.: Duke University Press, 2005), 22.

53. Charles Jencks, *The New Paradigm in Architecture: The Language of Post-Modernism* (New Haven, Conn.: Yale University Press, 2002), 9.

54. Wegner, *Life Between Two Deaths*, 27.

55. Amy Hungerford, "On the Period Formerly Known as Contemporary," *American Literary History* 20, nos. 1–2 (2008): 418.

56. Francis Fukuyama, "The End of History?" in *Globalization and the Challenges of a New Century*, ed. Patrick O'Meara, Howard D. Mehlinger, and Matthew Krain (Bloomington: Indiana University Press, 2000), 161–62, italics in original.

57. Ibid., 178.

58. Francis Fukuyama, *The End of History and the Last Man* (New York: Avon Books, 1992), 311, 330.

59. Ibid., xxii–xxiii, 305.

60. On the peculiar rhythm of reading *American Psycho*—oscillating between "the boredom of reading repeated consumerist jargon" and the unexpected "shock of reading repeated violence"—see C. Namwali Serpell, *Seven Modes of Uncertainty* (Cambridge, Mass.: Harvard University Press, 2014), 209. On the end of ideology and the "triumph of . . . posthistoricism" in *Glamorama*, see Michaels, *Shape of the Signifier*, 181.

61. North, "Virtual Histories," 407.

62. Cohen, *After the End of History*, 3.

63. See, for example, Philip Wegner, *Life Between Two Deaths*, in which he reads texts of the 1990s as uncanny anticipations of September 11. For a more robust theory of how catastrophic events are strategically preempted and "premediated" in post-9/11 media culture, see Richard Grusin, *Premediation: Affect and Mediality After 9/11* (New York: Palgrave Macmillan, 2010).

64. Naomi Mandel, introduction to part II of *Bret Easton Ellis: American Psycho, Glamorama, Lunar Park*, ed. Naomi Mandel (New York: Continuum, 2011), 65.

65. Nor is it made any more plausible by the fact that the plots of both *White Teeth* and *Glamorama* involve acts of terrorism, considering that the fundamentally pre-September 11 point of both novels is that these terrorist plots achieve nothing and change nothing.

## 2. REVIVAL

1. On film noir as "a recurring pattern of both modernity and postmodernity," see James Naremore, *More Than Night: Film Noir in Its Contexts* (Berkeley: University of California Press, 1998), 277.

2. For the seminal critique of the postmodern "nostalgia film," see Fredric Jameson, *Postmodernism, or, the Cultural Logic of Late Capitalism* (Durham, N.C.: Duke University Press, 1991), 19–21. For the formative articulation of "corporate art" and "studio authorship," see Jerome Christensen, *America's Corporate Art: The Studio Authorship of Hollywood Motion Pictures* (Stanford, Calif.: Stanford University Press, 2012).

3. Bliss Cua Lim, *Translating Time: Cinema, the Fantastic, and Temporal Critique* (Durham, N.C.: Duke University Press, 2009), 190–91.

4. The original films, screened in succession in 1946, were *The Maltese Falcon, Double Indemnity, Laura, Murder, My Sweet*, and *The Lost Weekend*.

5. Naremore, *More Than Night*, 37.

6. Fred Pfeil, "Home Fires Burning: Family *Noir* in *Blue Velvet* and *Terminator 2*," in *Shades of Noir*, ed. Joan Copjec (London: Verso, 1993), 229.

7. Sianne Ngai, *Ugly Feelings* (Cambridge, Mass.: Harvard University Press, 2005), 299.

8. Robert Pippin, *Fatalism in American Film Noir: Some Cinematic Philosophy* (Charlottesville: University of Virginia Press, 2012), 39.

9. Ibid., 27.

10. As J. P. Telotte notes in his seminal study of the genre, "we would typically begin any list of the basic *noir* conventions with that narrative combination of voice-over and flashback" (*Voices in the Dark: The Narrative Patterns of Film Noir* [Urbana: University of Illinois Press, 1989], 40). On film noir as exemplary of the more general popularity of voice-over in the 1940s, see Sarah Kozloff, *Invisible Storytellers: Voice-Over Narration in American Fiction Film* (Berkeley: University of California Press, 1988), 34. On "movie and television revivals of film noir" as one of the few places where voice-over has continued to persist since its midcentury heyday, see Kaja Silverman, *The Acoustic Mirror: The Female Voice in Psychoanalysis and Cinema* (Bloomington: Indiana University Press, 1988), 52.

11. The null content of the noir voice-over has not gone unnoticed by critics. Joan Copjec, for instance, notes that Neff's voice-over does not "describe or attempt to describe the world that the narrator inhabits" ("The Phenomenal Nonphenomenal: Private Space in *Film Noir*," in *Shades of Noir*, ed. Joan Copjec [London: Verso, 1993], 186). For Copjec, the de-privileging of the voice's content offers a psychoanalytic lesson about the objectlessness of desire. We can also understand the emptying out of the voice as part of a larger media history, one in which, as Friedrich A. Kittler argues, film's technological subsumption of the radio and the phonograph alters the very nature of spoken communication. "Henceforth," writes Kittler, "speech knows only tautology and contradiction, the two empty, informationless extremes of truth values" (*Discourse Networks 1800 /1900*, trans. Michael Metteer, with Chris Cullens [Stanford, Calif.: Stanford University Press, 1990], 239).

12. Michel Chion, *Audio-Vision: Sound on Screen*, ed. and trans. Claudio Gorbman (New York: Columbia University Press, 1994), 32.

13. Ibid.

14. Quoted in Mladen Dolar, *A Voice and Nothing More* (Cambridge, Mass.: MIT Press, 2006), 67. Elsewhere, Chion calls this type of listening "causal listening," which he claims is "the most common" kind ("The Three Listening Modes," in *The Sound Studies Reader*, ed. Jonathan Sterne [London: Routledge, 2012], 48).

15. Chion uses the term *nondiegetic* "to designate sound whose supposed source is not only absent from the image but is also external to the story world" (*Audio-Vision*, 73). The noir-styled science-fiction of *Blade Runner* (Ridley Scott, 1982) offers a useful historical lesson about the nature of nondiegetic voice-over. *Blade Runner*'s voice-over was the source of an infamous controversy: Scott did not originally intend the film to have one (nor did Harrison Ford have any desire to record one), but the studio insisted that one be added to the theatrical release. (Scott managed to remove the voice-over only in his 1991 "director's cut"; it is similarly missing from the "final cut" released in 2007.) In *Blade Runner*, the voice-over is thus quite literally superadded, supplementary: we know that Deckhard narrates the film, but we never see him in the act of narrating, never see the source of his voice. Deckhard's narration is radically external to the space-time of the film. *Blade Runner* thus reminds us of how drastically acousmatic

sound can be cut off from its source and how normal it is to watch a film whose voice-over has no literal, locatable place in it.

16. Naremore, *More Than Night*, 87.

17. The original ending to *Double Indemnity* involved a scene in which Neff is put to death in a gas chamber. Ultimately, Wilder decided to cut the scene because he deemed it "'unnecessary.'" However, Naremore suggests he may have felt "pressure from both the studio and the Breen Home Office, which insisted that the gas chamber sequence was 'unduly gruesome'" (*More Than Night*, 81–82).

18. David Simpson, *Situatedness, or, Why We Keep Saying Where We're Coming From* (Durham, N.C.: Duke University Press, 2002), 3.

19. Ian Baucom, *Specters of the Atlantic: Finance Capital, Slavery, and the Philosophy of History* (Durham, N.C.: Duke University Press, 2005), 43.

20. Simpson, *Situatedness*, 20.

21. Lauren Berlant, *Cruel Optimism* (Durham, N.C.: Duke University Press, 2011), 195.

22. For a philosophical history of the situation from Nietzsche and Schopenhauer to Husserl and Heidegger to Jaspers and Sartre, see Simpson, *Situatedness*, 146–91. Jean-Paul Sartre, perhaps the preeminent philosopher of the situation, develops his thoughts on the situation in *Being and Nothingness*, trans. Hazel E. Barnes (New York: Washington Square Press, 1984), and *Search for a Method*, trans. Hazel E. Barnes (New York: Vintage, 1963).

23. Simpson, *Situatedness*, 20.

24. Jameson, *Postmodernism*, 185, italics in original.

25. Christopher Nealon, "Reading on the Left," *Representations* 108 (2009): 25.

26. Simpson repeatedly ties situatedness to the paradigmatic figure of the speaking subject: "*Let me situate my argument*"; "*let me tell you where I'm coming from*" (*Situatedness*, 1, 20, italics in original).

27. Baucom, *Specters of the Atlantic*, 43.

28. Rita Felski, "'Context Stinks!'" *New Literary History* 42, no. 4 (2011): 573, 574.

29. Eric Hayot, *On Literary Worlds* (New York: Oxford University Press, 2012), 158.

30. Ted Underwood, *Why Literary Periods Mattered: Historical Contrast and the Prestige of English Studies* (Stanford, Calif.: Stanford University Press, 2013), 158.

31. Friedrich A. Kittler, *Gramophone, Film, Typewriter*, trans. Geoffrey Winthrop-Young and Michael Wutz (Stanford, Calif.: Stanford University Press, 1999), xxxix.

32. Copjec, "Phenomenal Nonphenomenal," 186.

33. Joan Copjec, *Imagine There's No Woman: Ethics and Sublimation* (Cambridge, Mass.: MIT Press, 2004), 161.

34. Quoted in Ed Sikov, *On Sunset Boulevard: The Life and Times of Billy Wilder* (New York: Hyperion, 1998), 283–84.

35. Ibid., 301.

36. Mary Ann Doane, *The Emergence of Cinematic Time: Modernity, Contingency, the Archive* (Cambridge, Mass.: Harvard University Press, 2002), 164.

37. J. Hoberman, *An Army of Phantoms: American Movies and the Making of the Cold War* (New York: New Press, 2011), 118.

38. Edward Dimendberg, *Film Noir and the Spaces of Modernity* (Cambridge, Mass.: Harvard University Press, 2004), 211, 210.

39. Dolar, *Voice and Nothing More*, 63.

40. Marc Vernet, "*Film Noir* on the Edge of Doom," in *Shades of Noir*, ed. Joan Copjec (London: Verso, 1993), 1.

41. J. Hoberman, "Dark Night Returns," review of *Sin City*, Dimension Films, *Village Voice*, March 22, 2005, http://www.villagevoice.com/2005-03-22/film/dark-night-returns.

42. Garrett Stewart, *Framed Time: Toward a Postfilmic Cinema* (Chicago: University of Chicago Press, 2007), 111.

43. Ibid., 8, 89, 106.

44. Copjec, "Phenomenal Nonphenomenal," 183.

45. Silverman, *Acoustic Mirror*, 52.

46. Quoted in Alice Bennett, *Afterlife and Narrative in Contemporary Fiction* (New York: Palgrave Macmillan, 2012), 99.

47. Brian Richardson, *Unnatural Voices: Extreme Narration in Modern and Contemporary Fiction* (Columbus: Ohio State University Press, 2006).

48. Roland Barthes, "To Write: An Intransitive Verb?" and "Discussion: Barthes—Todorov," in *The Languages of Criticism and the Sciences of Man: The Structuralist Controversy*, ed. Richard Macksey and Eugenio Donato (Baltimore: Johns Hopkins University Press, 1970), 143, 155.

49. Edgar Allan Poe, "The Facts in the Case of M. Valdemar," in *The Portable Poe*, ed. Philip Van Doren Stern (New York: Penguin, 1977), 276, 277, italics in original.

50. "Discussion: Barthes—Todorov," 156, italics in original.

51. *The Man Who Wasn't There* is surprisingly faithful to James M. Cain's novel (also the source of the 1946 film), retaining even smaller details like the decision to try Doris alone for the murder Ed committed, the climactic role of the car accident, Ed's ironic conviction not for the murder he did commit but for the one he didn't, and, most significantly, the revelation that Ed has been narrating all along from "the death house," where he is awaiting execution (James M. Cain, *The Postman Always Rings Twice* [New York: Vintage, 1992], 115). Even the characters' altered names don't stray very far from the Cain corpus. "Nirdlinger"—the name of the department store where Doris works and whose owner, Big Dave Brewster, Ed kills—is borrowed from Cain's other classic novel of the same period, *Double Indemnity*, in which Walter Huff meets, conspires with, and is killed by Phyllis Nirdlinger; so even the Coens' decision to change Cain's names in *The Man Who Wasn't There* simply repeats the change that Billy Wilder made to the names in his film version of *Double Indemnity*.

52. Frank Miller, *Frank Miller's Sin City*, vol. 4, *That Yellow Bastard* (Milwaukie, Ore.: Dark Horse Books, 2005), 218–23.

53. Soderbergh also imposed a number of technical constraints on the film's production, such as the use of era-appropriate camera equipment, in order to replicate the feel of 1940s studio films (of which *Casablanca* is the signal example).

54. Vernet, "*Film Noir* on the Edge of Doom," 4.

55. Nicholas Brown, "The Work of Art in the Age of Its Real Subsumption by Capital," *nonsite.org*, March 13, 2012.

56. Hayot, *On Literary Worlds*, 8.

57. Amy Hungerford, "On the Period Formerly Known as Contemporary," *American Literary History* 20, nos. 1–2 (2008): 416.

58. Sianne Ngai, *Our Aesthetic Categories: Zany, Cute, Interesting* (Cambridge, Mass.: Harvard University Press, 2012), 251n60.

59. Ibid., 17.

60. Compared with Ngai's coordination of the eighteenth, nineteenth, and twentieth centuries, my humble attempt to bridge sixty short years of postwar U.S. history can hardly register as provocative! That it might still seem so is a testament to historicism's overwhelming yet unacknowledged influence and to its deeply ingrained desire for the smallest units of specificity possible.

61. As Andrew Hoberek argues, postmodernism itself can be read as a symptom of "the bitter discovery of [the middle class's] lack of agency and inability to navigate the world" (*The Twilight of the Middle Class: Post-World War II American Literature and White Collar Work* [Princeton, N.J.: Princeton University Press, 2005], 129).

62. The increasingly anxious relation between individuals and systems is a central part of the story that Mark McGurl tells about postwar fiction in *The Program Era*. For McGurl, the writing that comes out of creative writing programs after World War II is characterized by an intense anxiety about the status of the individual within the bureaucratic institution of the university. The institutionalization of creative activity is just one way that social life in the postwar period is shaped by the radical blurring of what McGurl calls "the distinction between agency and structure" (*The Program Era: Postwar Fiction and the Rise of the Creative Writing Program* [Cambridge, Mass.: Harvard University Press, 2009], 388).

63. Underwood, *Why Literary Periods Mattered*, 158.

64. Stephen Greenblatt, *Shakespearean Negotiations* (Berkeley: University of California Press, 1988), 1.

65. Walter Benn Michaels, *The Shape of the Signifier: 1967 to the End of History* (Princeton, N.J.: Princeton University Press, 2004), 137.

66. Ibid.

67. Baucom, *Specters of the Atlantic*, 323.

68. Michaels, *Shape of the Signifier*, 137; Alan Liu, *Local Transcendence: Essays on Postmodern Historicism and the Database* (Chicago: University of Chicago Press, 2008), 3.

69. Hayot, *On Literary Worlds*, 151, italics in original.

70. Alan Liu, "The Power of Formalism: The New Historicism," in *Local Transcendence*, 44, 55, 57.

71. David Simpson, *The Academic Postmodern and the Rule of Literature: A Report on Half-Knowledge* (Chicago: University of Chicago Press, 1995), 51, 180.

## 3. WAITING

1. Shoshana Felman, "Turning the Screw of Interpretation," *Yale French Studies* 52 (1975): 176, italics in original.

2. Stephen Best and Sharon Marcus, "Surface Reading: An Introduction," in "The Way We Read Now," ed. Sharon Marcus and Stephen Best, with Emily Apter and Elaine Freedgood, special issue, *Representations* 108 (2009): 18.

3. Ibid., 9, 13, 17.

4. C. Namwali Serpell, *Seven Modes of Uncertainty* (Cambridge, Mass.: Harvard University Press, 2014).

5. Dorothy J. Hale, "Aesthetics and the New Ethics: Theorizing the Novel in the Twenty-First Century," *PMLA* 124, no. 3 (2009): 903.

6. Bruno Latour, "Why Has Critique Run Out of Steam? From Matters of Fact to Matters of Concern," *Critical Inquiry* 30, no. 2 (2004): 227.

7. Many of these keywords appear in Best and Marcus, "Surface Reading." For more detailed treatments of the turn to sociology, see James F. English, "Everywhere and Nowhere: The Sociology of Literature After 'the Sociology of Literature,'" *New Literary History* 41, no. 2 (2010): v–xxiii; of "the descriptive turn," see Heather Love, "Close but Not Deep: Literary Ethics and the Descriptive Turn," *New Literary History* 41, no. 2 (2010): 371–91; and of quantitative analysis, see Matthew Jockers, *Macroanalysis: Digital Methods and Literary History* (Urbana: University of Illinois Press, 2013).

8. Colleen Lye and Jed Esty persuasively suggest that things like surface reading and the quantitative turn reveal a wariness of more complex theoretical questions in the face of institutional pressures in the academy to produce interdisciplinary empirical research: "The more interdisciplinarity has become a normative expectation across disciplines, the more impossible the theoretical labor of mediation has seemed— specifically, the question of the dialectical relation between literature and history" ("Peripheral Realisms Now," *Modern Language Quarterly* 73, no. 3 [2012]: 277).

9. As the historians of science Naomi Oreskes and Erik M. Conway recount, the realization of corporations in the 1960s was "that you could use *normal* scientific uncertainty to undermine the status of actual scientific knowledge" (*Merchants of Doubt: How a Handful of Scientists Obscured the Truth on Issues from Tobacco Smoke to Global Warming* [New York: Bloomsbury, 2010], 34, italics in original).

10. Ronald R. Thomas, *Detective Fiction and the Rise of Forensic Science* (Cambridge: Cambridge University Press, 1999), 2, 7.

11. Dennis Porter, *The Pursuit of Crime: Art and Ideology in Detective Fiction* (New Haven, Conn.: Yale University Press, 1981), 254.

12. Sean McCann, *Gumshoe America: Hard-Boiled Crime Fiction and the Rise and Fall of New Deal Liberalism* (Durham, N.C.: Duke University Press, 2000).

13. Sean McCann and Michael Szalay, "Do You Believe in Magic? Literary Thinking After the New Left," *Yale Journal of Criticism* 18, no. 2 (2005): 438.

14. Sir Arthur Conan Doyle, "A Case of Identity," in *Sherlock Holmes: The Complete Novels and Stories* (New York: Bantam Classics, 1986), 301; Thomas Pynchon, *The Crying of Lot 49* (New York: Harper Perennial, 1966).

15. Porter, *Pursuit of Crime*, 251.

16. Paul Auster, *The New York Trilogy: City of Glass, Ghosts, The Locked Room* (New York: Penguin, 1990), 124.

17. Mark McGurl, "Ordinary Doom: Literary Studies in the Waste Land of the Present," *New Literary History* 41, no. 2 (2010): 329, italics in original.

18. Ulrich Beck, *Risk Society: Towards a New Modernity*, trans. Mark Ritter (London: Sage, 1992), 19.

19. Ibid., 22, 72, 73, italics in original.

20. As Annie McClanahan reminds us, the widespread rhetoric of unpredictability "appeared across the ideological spectrum, from George W. Bush to Jean Baudrillard" ("Future's Shock: Plausibility, Preemption, and the Fiction of 9/11," *symploke* 17, nos. 1–2 [2009]: 43n.4).

21. Brian Massumi, "Potential Politics and the Primacy of Preemption," *Theory and Event* 10, no. 2 (2007). On the history of preemption as a legal doctrine, see McClanahan, "Future's Shock," 48–52.

22. Brian Massumi, "The Future of the Affective Fact: The Political Ontology of Threat," in *The Affect Theory Reader*, ed. Melissa Gregg and Gregory J. Seigworth (Durham, N.C.: Duke University Press, 2010), 53.

23. To be sure, the constant anticipation of geopolitical catastrophe has been a part of American and European culture throughout the twentieth century, from the specter of total war in World War I to the fear of mutually assured destruction during the Cold War. The key difference is that these earlier anxieties concerned a specific threat. The inexhaustible uncertainty of contemporary risk society, in contrast, represents a moment in which almost everything has become a possible threat. On modernist literature's response to total war, see Paul K. Saint-Amour, *Tense Future: Modernism, Total War, Encyclopedic Form* (Oxford: Oxford University Press, 2015).

24. Franco Moretti, "Clues," in *Signs Taken for Wonders: Essays in the Sociology of Literary Forms*, rev. ed., trans. Susan Fischer, David Forgacs, and David Miller (London: Verso, 1988), 148, italics in original.

25. Tzvetan Todorov, *The Poetics of Prose*, trans. Richard Howard (Ithaca, N.Y.: Cornell University Press, 1977), 44.

26. Moretti, "Clues," 150.

27. Ibid.

28. P. D. James, *Talking About Detective Fiction* (Knopf: London, 2009), 169–70.

29. Fredric Jameson, "The Synoptic Chandler," in *Shades of Noir*, ed. Joan Copjec (London: Verso, 1993), 33.

30. Peter Brooks, *Reading for the Plot: Design and Intention in Narrative* (Cambridge, Mass.: Harvard University Press, 1984), 19, 23.

31. Frank Kermode, "The Use of the Codes," in *The Art of Telling: Essays on Fiction* (Cambridge, Mass.: Harvard University Press, 1983), 87.

32. Robert A. Rushing, *Resisting Arrest: Detective Fiction and Popular Culture* (New York: Other Press, 2007), 9, italics in original.

33. According to Slavoj Žižek, "We are immensely disappointed if the denouement is brought about by a pure scientific procedure. . . . But it is even more disappointing if, at the end, after naming the assassin, the detective claims that 'he was guided from the very beginning by some unmistakable instinct'" (*Looking Awry: An Introduction to Jacques Lacan Through Popular Culture* [Cambridge, Mass.: MIT Press, 1991], 49).

34. S. S. Van Dine, "Twenty Rules for Writing Detective Stories," *American Magazine*, September 1928.

35. Robert A. Rushing, "Traveling Detectives: The 'Logic of Arrest' and the Pleasures of (Avoiding) the Real," *Yale French Studies* 108 (2005): 89–90.

36. Edgar Allan Poe, *The Murders in the Rue Morgue: The Dupin Stories* (New York: Modern Library, 2006), 3.

37. Ibid.

38. The most famous unanswered question in *The Big Sleep* is what happened to the Sternwoods' driver, Owen Taylor, whose body is found in a Buick floating in the ocean. See Raymond Chandler, *The Big Sleep* (New York: Vintage, 1992). On this plot point, Jameson recounts the following irresistible (possibly apocryphal) anecdote:

> The story of Humphrey Bogart's argument with Howard Hawks is well known; very late at night, after much drinking, during the filming of *The Big Sleep* the two men argue about the status of the dead body in the Buick in the ocean off the Lido pier: murder,

suicide, or some third thing? They finally phone Chandler himself, still awake and drinking at that hour; he admits he can't remember either. ("Synoptic Chandler," 33)

39. For Porter, detective fiction is defined by delay. "The appeal" of the genre, he writes, "depends on the fact that closure . . . does not occur right away but only after significant delay." Delay is necessary, Porter suggests, because "the longest kept secrets are the ones we most desire to know" (*Pursuit of Crime*, 30, 51).

40. A different account of waiting as deferral is offered by Jacques Derrida, who came to gloss the politics of deconstruction as a kind of "messianic" waiting, a constant openness to what he called "democracy *to come*." Derrida articulates his sense of the "to-come" (*á venir*) most fully in *Rogues: Two Essays on Reason*, trans. Pascale-Anne Brault and Michael Naas (Stanford, Calif.: Stanford University Press, 2005). Derrida's messianic commitment to the "to-come" rather than the here-and-now produced a wide range of theoretical and political responses. A characteristically skeptical response was offered by Terry Eagleton, who derided Derridean messianism as "a promise which would betray itself in the act of fulfillment, a perpetual excited opennnes to the Messiah who had better not let us down by doing anything as determinate as coming" ("Marxism Without Marxism," in *Ghostly Demarcations: A Symposium on Jacques Derrida's Specters of Marx*, ed. Michael Sprinker [London: Verso, 1999], 87).

41. Amy Hungerford, *Postmodern Belief: American Literature and Religion Since 1960* (Princeton, N.J.: Princeton University Press, 2010), xxi.

42. Vikram Chandra, *Sacred Games* (New York: Harper Perennial, 2007), 838. Subsequent references are cited in the text.

43. Michael Chabon, *The Yiddish Policemen's Union* (New York: Harper Perennial, 2007), 344. Subsequent references are cited in the text. Chabon's novel is both a detective story and a historical counterfactual: it takes place in an alternate present in which the state of Israel does not exist and the Jews have been temporarily settled in Sitka, Alaska. The story is set in the months before "Reversion," when Sitka's sixty-year " 'interim status' as a federal district" (29) is poised to expire, at which point the land will revert to the U.S. government and the Jews will once again be diasporically scattered across the globe.

44. Beck, *Risk Society*, 28, 73, italics in original.

45. Siegfried Kracauer, "Those Who Wait," in *The Mass Ornament: Weimar Essays*, trans. and ed. Thomas Y. Levin (Cambridge, Mass.: Harvard University Press, 1995), 129, 138, italics in original.

46. Ibid., 139.

47. Walter Benjamin, "Theses on the Philosophy of History," in *Illuminations*, trans. Harry Zohn and ed. Hannah Arendt (New York: Schocken Books, 1968), 264.

48. Hungerford, *Postmodern Belief*, xiii, 134, xxi.

49. Ibid., 83.

50. D. A. Miller, *The Novel and the Police* (Berkeley: University of California Press, 1988), 207.

51. For a more detailed discussion of the speaking dead as a problem in literary and narrative theory, see chapter 2.

52. Felman, "Turning the Screw of Interpretation," 215.

53. China Miéville, *The City and the City* (New York: Del Rey, 2009), 25. Subsequent references are cited in the text.

54. Benedict Anderson, *Imagined Communities: Reflections on the Origin and Spread of Nationalism* (London: Verso, 1983).

55. China Miéville, *Between Equal Rights: A Marxist Theory of International Law* (Chicago: Haymarket, 2006).

56. Giorgio Agamben, *Homo Sacer: Sovereign Power and Bare Life*, trans. Daniel Heller-Roazen (Stanford, Calif.: Stanford University Press, 1998), 15.

57. On the relation between the U.S. and British governments' responses to September 11, see Kent Roach, *The 9/11 Effect: Comparative Counter-Terrorism* (Cambridge: Cambridge University Press, 2011). A primary difference is the two nations' divergent answers to the question of law. Roach explains, "If an overriding theme of the American response to 9/11 is a frequent reliance on extra-legalism and executive measures, the overriding theme of the British response is a commitment to a legislative war on terrorism that is prepared to impose robust limits and derogations on rights normally enjoyed in the nonterrorist context" (238).

58. Nathan K. Hensely notes that "Stanford University Press confirms that by fall 2009 it had sold in the neighborhood of thirty thousand copies since its 1998 translation from the Italian, a number that will sound fantastic to anyone passingly familiar with today's academic publishing market" ("Allegories of the Contemporary," in "The Contemporary Novel: Imagining the Twenty-First Century," ed. Timothy Bewes, special issue, *Novel: A Forum on Fiction* 45, no. 2 [2012]: 278).

59. Giorgio Agamben, *State of Exception*, trans. Kevin Attell (Chicago: University of Chicago Press, 2005), 4.

60. Ibid., 9, 18, 187, 20.

61. Ibid., 25.

62. Ibid. 166.

63. This intellectual genealogy is made more explicit in *State of Exception*, in which the zone of indistinction is retranslated (by Kevin Attell) as "zone of undecidability" (86). Nevertheless, while Agamben is very much a thinker of indeterminacy and paradox, it is worth noting that he does, in *Homo Sacer*, suggest that deconstruction may go too far, "threat[ening] thinking" with "the possibility that thinking might find itself condemned to infinite negotiations" (54).

64. Agamben, *Homo Sacer*, 187.

65. "Mystical" is Jacques Derrida's term, in "Force of Law: The 'Mystical Foundation of Authority,'" in *Acts of Religion*, ed. Gil Anidjar (New York: Routledge, 2002), 228–98.

66. Lee Spinks, "Except for Law: Raymond Chandler, James Ellroy, and the Politics of Exception," *South Atlantic Quarterly* 107, no. 1 (2008): 125.

67. Ibid., 128, 135.

68. Best and Marcus, "Surface Reading," 1–2.

69. Emily Apter and Elaine Freedgood, afterword to "The Way We Read Now," ed. Sharon Marcus and Stephen Best, with Emily Apter and Elaine Freedgood, special issue, *Representations* 108 (2009): 145, italics in original.

70. Kevis Goodman, *Georgic Modernity and British Romanticism: Poetry and the Mediation of History* (Cambridge: Cambridge University Press, 2004), 3.

71. I am thinking here of Goodman's reading of the day-long life span of the newspaper, through which she rereads Benedict Anderson's well-known account of the newspaper as a relation between everydayness and history:

There are really two issues intertwined in Anderson's description: where the first concerns the openness of this outward-oriented subjectivity engaged by the daily paper, the second is the altered perception of history invited by the rapid obsolescence of editions or installments of news. The newspaper's speeding up of communication renders ongoing history as a process in flux; time contracts such that "now" is always on the verge of expiring into "then." (*Georgic Modernity*, 70)

This last remark brings us back to Apter and Freedgood's account of "the way we read now," in which they suggest that "now is" *already* "then." For Goodman, by contrast, the "now" is only "on the verge" of passing away. The daily-ness of the daily paper thus provides a model of time that recognizes the fleetingness of the present yet is still able, if only for an instant (or perhaps for a whole day), to fix it in place.

72. D. A. Miller reminds us that novel reading is a thoroughly time-bound enterprise, one drawn out even further by a wandering mind or distracted eye: "Another open secret that everyone knows and no one wants to: the immense amount of daydreaming that accompanies the ordinary reading of a novel" (*Novel and the Police*, 215).

73. Antonis Balasopoulos, "Ghosts of the Future: Marxism, Deconstruction, and the Afterlife of Utopia," *Theory and Event* 12, no. 3 (2009): 1–19.

74. Walter Benjamin, *The Arcades Project*, trans. Howard Eiland and Kevin McLaughlin (Cambridge, Mass.: Belknap Press of Harvard University Press, 1999), 107.

## 4. WEATHER

1. The great critic of the spaghetti Western, Christopher Frayling, suggests that we might think of Sergio's Leone's Westerns as studies in "the effects of intense heat" (*Spaghetti Westerns: Cowboys and Europeans from Karl May to Sergio Leone* [London: Tauris, 1998], 188).

2. Jane Tomkins, *West of Everything: The Inner Life of Westerns* (New York: Oxford University Press, 1992), 71.

3. Dipesh Chakrabarty, "The Climate of History: Four Theses," *Critical Inquiry* 35, no. 2 (2009): 197.

4. David Archer, *The Long Thaw: How Humans Are Changing the Next 100,000 Years of Earth's Climate* (Princeton, N.J.: Princeton University Press, 2009), 11.

5. Paul J. Crutzen and Eugene F. Stoermer, "The 'Anthropocene,'" *Global Change Newsletter*, May 2000, 17–18. See also Paul J. Crutzen, "Geology of Mankind," *Nature*, January 3, 2002, 23.

6. Dipesh Chakrabarty, "Climate and Capital: On Conjoined Histories," *Critical Inquiry* 41 (2014): 3, 1.

7. Walter Benjamin, "Theses on the Philosophy of History," in *Illuminations*, trans. Harry Zohn and ed. Hannah Arendt (New York: Schocken Books, 1968), 263.

8. Archer, *Long Thaw*, 2.

9. Timothy Morton, "Ecology Without the Present," *Oxford Literary Review* 34, no. 2 (2012): 229, 235, 233.

10. See, for instance, Wai Chee Dimock's "attempt to rethink the shape of literature against . . . the 'deep time' of the planet Earth" (*Through Other Continents: American*

*Literature Across Deep Time* [Princeton, N.J.: Princeton University Press, 2006], 6). For a more general survey of the geological turn in literary and cultural studies, see Mark McGurl, "The New Cultural Geology," *Twentieth-Century Literature* 57, nos. 3–4 (2011): 380–90.

11. Fredric Jameson, "Afterword: A Note on Literary Realism," in *A Concise Companion to Realism*, ed. Matthew Beaumont (Chichester: Wiley-Blackwell, 2010), 281.

12. Crutzen and Stoermer, "'Anthropocene,'" 17.

13. Andreas Malm, "The Origins of Fossil Capital: From Water to Steam in the British Cotton Industry," *Historical Materialism* 21, no. 1 (2013): 56, 58.

14. Andreas Malm, "The Anthropocene Myth," *Jacobin*, March 30, 2015, https://www.jacobinmag.com/2015/03/anthropocene-capitalism-climate-change/.

15. On the idea of the "Capitalocene," see Jason W. Moore, *Capitalism in the Web of Life: Ecology and the Accumulation of Capital* (London: Verso, 2015).

16. For further accounts of climate change as a crisis not of humankind in general but of capitalism in particular, see Adrian Parr, *The Wrath of Capital: Neoliberalism and Climate Change Politics* (New York: Columbia University Press, 2013); and Naomi Klein, *This Changes Everything: Capitalism vs. the Climate* (New York: Simon & Schuster, 2014).

17. Walter Benjamin, *The Arcades Project*, trans. Howard Eiland and Kevin McLaughlin (Cambridge, Mass.: Belknap Press of Harvard University Press, 1999), 101–2, 106.

18. To my mind, the best and most surreal demonstration of this problem comes from Don DeLillo's classic satire of environmental risk, *White Noise* (New York: Viking, 1985), as the narrator Jack Gladney and his son Heinrich debate whether it's raining outside:

> "He wants to know if it's raining *now*, at this very minute?"
>
> "Here and now. That's right."
>
> "Is there such a thing as now? 'Now' comes and goes as soon as you say it. How can I say it's raining now if your so-called 'now' becomes 'then' as soon as I say it?" . . .
>
> "Rain is a noun. Is there rain here, in this precise locality, at whatever time within the next two minutes that you choose to respond to the question?"
>
> "If you want to talk about this precise locality while you're in a vehicle that's obviously moving, then I think that's the trouble with this discussion."
>
> "Just give me an answer, okay, Heinrich?"
>
> "The best I could do is make a guess."
>
> "Either it's raining or it isn't," I said.
>
> "Exactly. That's my whole point. You'd be guessing. Six of one, half dozen of the other." (23–24)

19. Frances Ferguson, "Climate Change and Us," *diacritics* 41, no. 3 (2013): 33.

20. B. Lynn Ingram and Frances Malamud-Roam, *The West Without Water: What Past Floods, Droughts, and Other Climatic Clues Tell Us About Tomorrow* (Berkeley: University of California Press, 2013), 2.

21. Gillen D'Arcy Wood, "Constable, Clouds, Climate Change," *Wordsworth Circle* 38, nos. 1–2 (2007): 32.

22. Climate Central, *Global Weirdness: Severe Storms, Deadly Heat Waves, Relentless Drought, Rising Seas, and the Weather of the Future* (New York: Vintage, 2012), 30.

23. Archer, *Long Thaw*, 92.

24. Climate Central, *Global Weirdness*, 29.

25. Margaret Ronda, "Mourning and Melancholia in the Anthropocene," *Post45: Peer Reviewed*, June 10, 2013, http://post45.research.yale.edu/2013/06/mourning-and -melancholia-in-the-anthropocene/.

26. Kristi McKim, *Cinema as Weather: Stylistic Screens and Atmospheric Change* (London: Routledge, 2013), 46.

27. Ibid., 55.

28. Ibid., 52.

29. Robert T. Self, *Robert Altman's "McCabe & Mrs. Miller": Reframing the American West* (Lawrence: University Press of Kansas, 2007), 51.

30. The past two decades have given us an array of acclaimed independent Westerns, from Jim Jarmusch's *Dead Man* (1999) to Kelly Reichardt's *Meek's Cutoff* (2010). Those same years brought us a series of studio Westerns that turned out to be major box-office flops, including *Cowboys and Aliens* (2011) and *The Lone Ranger* (2013).

31. On the relation between Westerns and the Cold War, see Stanley Corkin, *Cowboys as Cold Warriors: The Western and U.S. History* (Philadelphia: Temple University Press, 2004). For the seminal reading of the frontier myth and twentieth-century American politics, see Richard Slotkin, *Gunfighter Nation: The Myth of the Frontier in Twentieth-Century America* (New York: Harper Perennial, 1992).

32. Andrew Patrick Nelson, "Introduction: The American Western, 1990–2010," in *Contemporary Westerns: Film and Television Since 1990*, ed. Andrew Patrick Nelson (Lanham, Md.: Scarecrow Press, 2013), xvii.

33. Robin L. Murray and Joseph K. Heumann, *Gunfight at the Eco-Corral: Western Cinema and the Environment* (Norman: University of Oklahoma Press, 2012), 19. Murray and Heumann's book provides an exhaustive analysis of this list of issues. For an even broader taxonomy of "Western ecological films" and of the environmental issues they address—including "dust and flood," "the forest," "the oil field," mining, and nuclear power (21–22)—see John Shelton Lawrence, "Western Ecological Films: The Subgenre with No Name," in *The Landscape of Hollywood Westerns: Ecocriticism in an American Film Genre*, ed. Deborah A. Carmichael (Salt Lake City: University of Utah Press, 2006), 19–50.

34. Scott Simmon, *The Invention of the Western Film: A Cultural History of the Genre's First Half-Century* (Cambridge: Cambridge University Press, 2003), 115.

35. Quoted in Deborah A. Carmichael, "The Living Presence of Monument Valley in John Ford's *Stagecoach* (1939)," in *Landscape of Hollywood Westerns*, ed. Carmichael, 226.

36. Edward Buscombe, "Inventing Monument Valley: Nineteenth-Century Landscape Photography and the Western Film," in *The Western Reader*, ed. Jim Kitses and Gregg Rickman (New York: Limelight Editions, 1998), 120.

37. Joy Dietrich, "O Pioneers! Kelly Reichardt's Anti-Western," *New York Times Style Magazine*, April 7, 2011, http://tmagazine.blogs.nytimes.com/2011/04/07/o-pio neers-kelly-reichardts-anti-western/?_r=0.

38. Tomkins, *West of Everything*, 85, 69–70.

39. Ibid., 70.

40. Robert B. Pippin makes a similar point when he argues that the defining conflict of the Western genre is "the conquest by labor, persistence, violence, and technology

of an extraordinarily hostile, inhospitable natural world." Pippin goes on to note, fittingly, that "Ford's Monument Valley landscapes make this point with immediate, visually compelling power" ("What Is a Western? Politics and Self-Knowledge in John Ford's *The Searchers*," *Critical Inquiry* 35, no. 2 [2009]: 228).

41. Buscombe, "Inventing Monument Valley," 126.

42. Fernand Braudel, *The Mediterranean and the Mediterranean World in the Age of Philip II*, trans. Siân Reynolds (Berkeley: University of California Press, 1995), 1:23.

43. Ibid., 267.

44. Heidi Cullen, *The Weather of the Future: Heat Waves, Extreme Storms, and Other Scenes from a Climate-Changed Planet* (New York: Harper, 2010), 10.

45. Ironically, the only unnatural thing in this scene is the setting itself. Edward Buscombe points out that this first of the film's snow scenes was in fact shot on a sound stage at the RKO-Pathé Studio, in *BFI Film Classics: The Searchers* (London: British Film Institute, 2000), 31.

46. Glenn Frankel, *The Searchers: The Making of an American Legend* (New York: Bloomsbury, 2013), 251.

47. Ibid., 304.

48. Ibid., 251.

49. André de Toth in conversation with Anthony Slide, *De Toth on De Toth: Putting the Drama in Front of the Camera*, ed. Anthony Slide (London: Faber & Faber, 1996), 142, 142–43.

50. Franklin Jarlett, *Robert Ryan: A Biography and Critical Filmography* (Jefferson, N.C.: McFarland, 1990), 103.

51. McKim, *Cinema as Weather*, 135.

52. Howard C. Hughes, *Once Upon a Time in the Italian West: The Filmgoer's Guide to Spaghetti Westerns* (London: Tauris, 2005), 196.

53. Ibid., 196.

54. Robert MacLean, "The Big-Bang Hypothesis: Blowing Up the Image," *Film Quarterly* 32, no. 2 (1978–1979): 2.

55. For an extended reading of the film along these lines, see Self, *Robert Altman's "McCabe & Mrs. Miller."*

56. Quoted in McKim, *Cinema as Weather*, 153–54.

57. *De Toth on De Toth*, 142.

58. Allan Tong, "Old, Faded Pictures: Vilmos Zsigmond on *McCabe & Mrs. Miller*," *Filmmaker Magazine*, August 12, 2014, http://filmmakermagazine.com/87150-old-faded-pictures-vilmos-zsigmond-on-mccabe-mrs-miller/#.VdjomXiJnFJ.

59. This is one version of what Jerome Christensen calls *studio allegory* (*America's Corporate Art: The Studio Authorship of Hollywood Motion Pictures* [Stanford, Calif.: Stanford University Press, 2012]). See also J. D. Connor, *The Studios After the Studios: Neoclassical Hollywood (1970–2010)* (Stanford, Calif.: Stanford University Press, 2015).

60. Lawrence Webb argues that "during the industrial crisis of the early 1970s, the fragmentation and decentralization of the production process weakened the studios' control over the corporate identity of their output," resulting in a new "uncertainty or anxiety over authorship and ownership" that played out in the attempts of auteur directors to assert and allegorize their independence ("Remapping *The Conversation*: Urban Design and Industrial Reflexivity in Seventies San Francisco," *Post45: Peer*

*Reviewed,* June 22, 2014, http://post45.research.yale.edu/2014/06/remapping-the-con versation-urban-design-and-industrial-reflexivity-in-seventies-san-francisco/).

61. On the work of selling *The Searchers* to Warner Brothers and on the studio's decision to delay the film's release, see Frankel, *Searchers,* 245–46, 304–5; and Buscombe, *BFI Film Classics,* 48–49.

62. Bill McKibben, *The End of Nature,* Tenth Anniversary Edition (New York: Anchor Books, 1999), 29.

63. Ibid., 47, xvii.

64. Ibid., xvi.

65. Quoted in ibid., xvii.

66. Quentin Tarantino, "Quentin Tarantino Tackles Old Dixie by Way of the Old West (by Way of Italy)," *New York Times Magazine,* September 27, 2012, http://www .nytimes.com/2012/09/30/magazine/quentin-tarantino-django.html.

67. On seasons as a way of marking time, see Benjamin S. Orlove, "How People Name Seasons," in *Weather, Climate, Culture,* ed. Sarah Strauss and Benjamin S. Orlove (Oxford: Berg, 2003), 121–40.

68. Wood, "Constable, Clouds, Climate Change," 31.

69. Parr, *Wrath of Capital,* 7.

70. McKibben, *End of Nature,* xvi, italics in original.

71. Cullen, *Weather of the Future,* 143.

72. Robert Capps, "Leonardo DiCaprio: The *WIRED* Interview," *WIRED,* December 14, 2015, http://www.wired.com/2015/12/leonardo-dicaprio-interview-revenant -climate-change/.

73. Wood, "Constable, Clouds, Climate Change," 31.

74. National Weather Service Weather Forecast Office, "May 2–3, 2013: Snow Event," http://www.srh.noaa.gov/tsa/?n=weather-event_2013may2.

75. Tobias Boes and Kate Marshall, "Writing the Anthropocene: An Introduction," *Minnesota Review* 83 (2014): 61.

76. André Bazin, "The Western, or the American Film *par excellence,*" in *What Is Cinema?* trans. and ed. Hugh Gray (Berkeley: University of California Press, 1971), 2:140–48.

77. See, for instance, MaryEllen Higgins, Rita Keresztesi, and Dayna Oscherwitz, eds., *The Western in the Global South* (London: Routledge, 2015), which includes essays on the Western in Asia, Australia, South America, Sub-Saharan Africa, and the Caribbean, among other places.

78. According to Frayling, Kurosawa was "compensated for the obvious resemblance between" *Yojimbo* and *A Fistful of Dollars* "by being granted exclusive rights to distribute *A Fistful of Dollars* in Japan, Formosa and South Korea, plus 15 per cent of the worldwide box-office takings" (*Spaghetti Westerns,* 147).

79. Hughes, *Once Upon a Time in the Italian West,* 5.

80. Ibid., 194. In this way, you could say that the spaghetti Western is an early example of the phenomenon that Rebecca Walkowitz terms "born translated," which describes artworks that "do not simply appear in translation" but "have been written for translation from the start" (*Born Translated: The Contemporary Novel in the Age of World Literature* [New York: Columbia University Press, 2015], 3).

81. Frayling, *Spaghetti Westerns,* 82–86.

82. Hughes, *Once Upon a Time in the Italian West*, 66.

83. Ibid., 60, 61.

84. Ingram and Malamud-Roam, *West Without Water*, 193.

85. A study published in the journal *Nature Climate Change* used statistical modeling to argue that the 2015 snowpack level was not the lowest level in 50 years but the lowest in 500 years. See Soumaya Belmecheri et al., "Multi-Century Evaluation of Sierra Nevada Snowpack," *Nature Climate Change*, September 14, 2015, doi:10.1038/nclimate2809.

86. Given that the dust bowl was still very much a recent memory in the 1940s and 1950s, drought also played an important role in the meteorological imaginary of the midcentury Western. For an extended discussion of water rights in the Western, see Murray and Heumann, *Gunfight at the Eco-Corral*, 81–107.

87. Elena Gorfinkel, "Exhausted Drift: Austerity, Dispossession and the Politics of Slow in Kelly Reichardt's *Meek's Cutoff*," in *Slow Cinema*, ed. Tiago de Luca and Nuno Barrados Jorge (Edinburgh: University of Edinburgh Press, 2015), 129.

88. Gorfinkel, "Exhausted Drift," 124.

89. Ingram and Malamud-Roam, *West Without Water*, 121.


## 5. SURVIVAL

1. The problem of narrating after the end of the world—specifically, after the nuclear annihilation of the world—is one that Daniel Grausam sees as central to the development of postmodern aesthetics, in *On Endings: American Postmodern Fiction and the Cold War* (Charlottesville: University of Virginia Press, 2011).

2. Lauren Berlant, *Cruel Optimism* (Durham, N.C.: Duke University Press, 2011), 169, italics in original.

3. Peter Y. Paik, *From Utopia to Apocalypse: Science Fiction and the Politics of Catastrophe* (Minneapolis: University of Minnesota Press, 2010), 123.

4. Phillip Wegner, for instance, reads twentieth-century dystopian fiction as "desiring a radical change of affairs, but pulling short of endorsing any mechanism or agency by which such a change might come about" (*Life Between Two Deaths, 1989–2001: U.S. Culture in the Long Nineties* [Durham, N.C.: Duke University Press, 2009], 124).

5. Caren Irr, *Toward the Geopolitical Novel: U.S. Fiction in the Twenty-First Century* (New York: Columbia University Press, 2014), 170, 169.

6. Kathi Weeks, *The Problem with Work: Feminism, Marxism, Antiwork Politics, and Postwork Imaginaries* (Durham, N.C.: Duke University Press, 2011), 2.

7. John Lanchester, "When Fiction Breaks Down," *Telegraph* (London), January 29, 2010, http://www.telegraph.co.uk/culture/books/7093699/When-fiction-breaks-down.html.

8. Franco Moretti, *The Bourgeois: Between History and Literature* (London: Verso, 2013), 30. Moretti argues that the rise of the modern novel in the eighteenth century was founded on a prose style that valued "productivity" over "meaning": "the better prose becomes at multiplying the concrete details that enrich our perception of the world—the better it becomes at *doing its work*—the more elusive is the reason for doing so" (66, italics in original). That is, novels learned to do their work at the cost of

explaining the deeper social meaning of how and why people work in the first place. The modern novel's commitment to its own work of detailed description, Moretti claims, paradoxically entails a diminished capacity to depict or assess the actual world of work.

9. For more on the ideology of individualized "vocation," see Sean McCann, "Training and Vision: Roth, DeLillo, Banks, Peck, and the Postmodern Aesthetics of Vocation," *Twentieth-Century Literature* 53, no. 3 (2007): 298–326.

10. Weeks, *Problem with Work*, 18.

11. Cormac McCarthy, *The Road* (New York: Vintage, 2006), 17, 96. Subsequent references are cited in the text.

12. Amy Hungerford, *Postmodern Belief: American Literature and Religion Since 1960* (Princeton, N.J.: Princeton University Press, 2010), 132–40.

13. Evan Calder Williams, *Combined and Uneven Apocalypse* (Winchester: Zero Books, 2010), 8.

14. Karl Marx, "Comments on James Mill," trans. Clemens Dutt, http://www.marxists.org/archive/marx/works/1844/james-mill/, italics in original.

15. Karl Marx, *Capital: A Critique of Political Economy*, trans. Ben Fowkes (London: Penguin, 1976), 1:284.

16. Wegner describes this as "the persistence of primitivist nostalgia in the dystopian narrative" (*Life Between Two Deaths*, 125).

17. Alan Liu, *The Laws of Cool: Knowledge Work and the Culture of Information* (Chicago: University of Chicago Press, 2004), 41–42.

18. John Maynard Keynes, "Economic Possibilities for Our Grandchildren (1930)," in *Revisiting Keynes: Economic Possibilities for Our Grandchildren*, ed. Lorenzo Pecchi and Gustavo Piga (Cambridge, Mass.: MIT Press, 2008), 22.

19. Jasper Bernes, "Art, Work, Endlessness: Flarf and Conceptual Poetry Among the Trolls," *Critical Inquiry* 42, no. 4 (2016): 764.

20. Ibid., 777.

21. *Neoliberalism* is now a common yet hotly contested term for changes in capitalist ideology at the end of the twentieth century. In this chapter, I have limited my infrequent use of the term to descriptions of changing labor practices and the new discourses of work used to enforce or justify those practices.

22. Irr, *Toward the Geopolitical Novel*, 169.

23. Weeks, *Problem with Work*, 3.

24. In emphasizing the specific relationship between post-apocalyptic survival and contemporary work, I am stopping short of suggesting that a novel like *The Road* "reflects . . . neoliberalism" in a broader ideological sense (45). For that reading of *The Road*, see Rachel Greenwald Smith, *Affect and American Literature in the Age of Neoliberalism* (Cambridge: Cambridge University Press, 2015), 42–48.

25. Franco "Bifo" Berardi, *The Soul at Work: From Alienation to Autonomy*, trans. Francesca Cadel and Mecchia Giuseppina (Los Angeles: Semiotext(e), 2009), 83.

26. Luc Boltanski and Eve Chiapello, *The New Spirit of Capitalism* (London: Verso, 2005), 82, 244, 71, italics in original.

27. Marx, *Capital*, 1:416.

28. Bernes, "Art, Work, and Endlessness," 766, italics in original. For more on 24/7 work and the increasing "indistinction between the times of work and of leisure" (58), see Jonathan Crary, *24/7: Late Capitalism and the Ends of Sleep* (London: Verso, 2013).

29. Sarah Brouillette, *Literature and the Creative Economy* (Stanford, Calif.: Stanford University Press, 2014), 36–37.

30. The question becomes all the more vexed as the hobby of "survivalism" becomes increasingly popular as both a right-wing fantasy (in which personal stockpiling becomes a way to free oneself from dependence on government services) and a lucrative business. Surveying the emerging landscape of survivalist stores, survivalist retreats, and survivalist products, Amanda Shapiro concludes: "For those with means, survivalism can look a lot like planning for a very comfortable retirement" ("Power Loss," *New Inquiry*, May 13, 2013, http://thenewinquiry.com/essays/power-loss/).

31. Brouillette, *Literature and the Creative Economy*, 54.

32. Fredric Jameson, "Marxism and Historicism," in *Ideologies of Theory* (London: Verso, 2008), 465.

33. Ben Marcus, *The Flame Alphabet* (New York: Vintage, 2012), 51, 44, 77, 98. Subsequent references are cited in the text.

34. Sianne Ngai, *Our Aesthetic Categories: Zany, Cute, Interesting* (Cambridge, Mass.: Harvard University Press, 2012), 196–97. On domestic or "women's work" as a paradigm for "the erosion of the line between paid and unpaid labor" and the consequent "feminization of postindustrial work," see 206–22, esp. 207 and 215.

35. Lee Konstantinou, "Anti-Comprehension Pills," *Los Angeles Review of Books*, March 28, 2012, https://lareviewofbooks.org/article/anti-comprehension-pills/.

36. Moretti, *Bourgeois*, 43, italics in original.

37. Ibid., 55.

38. Andy Kroll, "What's Happening in Wisconsin Explained," *Mother Jones*, March 17, 2011, http://www.motherjones.com/mojo/2011/02/whats-happening-wisconsin-explained.

39. Colson Whitehead, *Zone One* (New York: Anchor Books, 2011), 14, 21, 20, 20–21. Subsequent references are cited in the text.

40. Zombies tend to be distinguished by their obvious allegorical dimension: the zombie as hollow-eyed consumer (as in George A. Romero's *Dawn of the Dead*, which is set—a bit on the nose—in a shopping mall); as "plague of suspended agency" (Mark McGurl, "The Zombie Renaissance," *n +1* 9 [2010]: 168); or as "crisis of human embodiment" (Sarah Juliet Lauro and Karen Embry, "A Zombie Manifesto: The Nonhuman Condition in the Era of Advanced Capitalism," *boundary 2* 35, no. 1 [2008]: 87). But what do the zombies of *Zone One* mean? Frankly, it's hard to say. As Andrew Hoberek observes in his review of the novel, "Whitehead analogizes his zombies to all these threatening figures along the way" and, in doing so, appears to undermine the very process of allegorization ("Living with PASD," *Contemporary Literature* 53, no. 2 [2012]: 411). Whitehead's zombies are less identifiable allegories than empty references to the allegorical function that defines the genre itself.

41. The line—recently elevated to chapter title in Mark Fisher's *Capitalist Realism* (Winchester: Zero Books, 2009)—is often attributed to Slavoj Žižek, who seems to have lifted it from Fredric Jameson. But in a fitting twist, Jameson also refuses to take full authorial credit: "Someone once said that it is easier to imagine the end of the world than to imagine the end of capitalism" ("Future City," *New Left Review* 21 [2003]: 76). So Jameson lifted it too, but from where? He can't remember. As a kind of unauthored template, the line turns out to be just as generic—just as conventional or unoriginal (literally, without origin)—as the apocalyptic narratives it presumes to comment on.

42. Lauro and Embry, "Zombie Manifesto," 91–92.

43. Derek Nystrom, "Haut-Bourgeois Precarity in Boston: *The Company Men*," *Post45: Contemporaries*, January 14, 2013, http://post45.research.yale.edu/2013/01/haut-bourgeois-precarity-in-boston-the-company-men/.

44. For a more radical perspective on the relation between literature and office work, see *Franz Kafka: The Office Writings* (Princeton, N.J.: Princeton University Press, 2008), a collection of the fantastically boring writing that Kafka produced during his day job at the Workmen's Accident Insurance Institute. The very existence of this collection seems to imply that there may be no point in trying to distinguish between literature and office work in the first place.

45. Joshua Ferris, *Then We Came to the End* (New York: Back Bay Books, 2007), 3, 178, 4. Subsequent references are cited in the text.

46. Though it was often written by them; Melville himself, bard of those "watery-world dwellers," was a bank clerk.

47. Moretti, *Bourgeois*, 16.

48. Andrew Hoberek, *The Twilight of the Middle Class: Post-World War II American Literature and White Collar Work* (Princeton, N.J.: Princeton University Press, 2005), 126.

49. Ngai, *Our Aesthetic Categories*, 202, 181, 185.

50. Ibid., 202.

51. Ibid., 188.

52. Brouillette, *Literature and the Creative Economy*, 46.

53. McCann, for instance, suggests that postmodern complaints about "bureaucracy" and "the perils of routinization" fetishize independence and personal freedom while ignoring "the reality of inequality" ("Training and Vision," 317).

54. Liu, *Laws of Cool*, 394.

55. Ibid.

56. Margaret Ronda, "'Not/One': The Poetics of Multitude in Great Recession-Era America," in *Class and the Making of American Literature: Created Unequal*, ed. Andrew Lawson (London: Routledge, 2014), 249.

57. Carl Cederström and Peter Fleming, *Dead Man Working* (Winchester: Zero Books, 2012), 12.

58. According to the New York State Department of Labor, "Local Area Unemployment Statistics Program," http://labor.ny.gov/stats/laus.asp.

# BIBLIOGRAPHY

Agacinski, Sylviane. *Time Passing: Modernity and Nostalgia*. Translated by Jody Gladding. New York: Columbia University Press, 2003.

Agamben, Giorgio. *Homo Sacer: Sovereign Power and Bare Life*. Translated by Daniel Heller-Roazen. Stanford, Calif.: Stanford University Press, 1998.

——. *State of Exception*. Translated by Kevin Attell. Chicago: University of Chicago Press, 2005.

——. "What Is the Contemporary?" In *What Is an Apparatus? and Other Essays*. Translated by David Kishik and Stefan Pedatella, 39–54. Stanford, Calif.: Stanford University Press, 2009.

Anderson, Amanda. *The Powers of Distance: Cosmopolitanism and the Cultivation of Detachment*. Princeton, N.J.: Princeton University Press, 2001.

Anderson, Benedict. *Imagined Communities: Reflections on the Origin and Spread of Nationalism*. London: Verso, 1983.

Anderson, Perry. *The Origins of Postmodernity*. London: Verso, 2002.

Apter, Emily, and Elaine Freedgood. Afterword to "The Way We Read Now," edited by Sharon Marcus and Stephen Best, with Emily Apter and Elaine Freedgood. Special issue, *Representations* 108, no. 1 (2009): 1–21.

Archer, David. *The Long Thaw: How Humans Are Changing the Next 100,000 Years of Earth's Climate*. Princeton, N.J.: Princeton University Press, 2009.

Auerbach, Erich. *Mimesis: The Representation of Reality in Western Literature*. Translated by Willard R. Trask. Fiftieth Anniversary Edition. Princeton, N.J.: Princeton University Press, 2003.

Auster, Paul. *The New York Trilogy: City of Glass, Ghosts, The Locked Room*. New York: Penguin, 1990.

Balasopoulos, Antonis. "Ghosts of the Future: Marxism, Deconstruction, and the Afterlife of Utopia." *Theory and Event* 12, no. 3 (2009): 1–19.

Barthes, Roland. "The Reality Effect." In *The Novel: An Anthology of Criticism and Theory 1900–2000*, edited by Dorothy J. Hale, 229–34. Malden, Mass.: Blackwell, 2006.

———. "To Write: An Intransitive Verb?" In *The Structuralist Controversy: The Languages of Criticism and the Sciences of Man*, edited by Richard Macksey and Eugenio Donato, 134–45. Baltimore: Johns Hopkins University Press, 1970.

Baucom, Ian. *Specters of the Atlantic: Finance Capital, Slavery, and the Philosophy of History*. Durham, N.C.: Duke University Press, 2005.

Bazin, André. *What Is Cinema?* Vol. 2. Edited and translated by Hugh Gray. Berkeley: University of California Press, 1971.

Beck, Ulrich. *Risk Society: Towards a New Modernity*. Translated by Mark Ritter. London: Sage, 1992.

Beck, Ulrich, Anthony Giddens, and Scott Lash. *Reflexive Modernization: Politics, Tradition and Aesthetics in the Modern Social Order*. Stanford, Calif.: Stanford University Press, 1994.

Belmecheri, Soumaya, Flurin Babst, Eugene R. Wahl, David W. Stahle, and Valerie Trouet. "Multi-Century Evaluation of Sierra Nevada Snowpack." *Nature Climate Change* 6 (2016): 2–3.

Benjamin, Walter. *The Arcades Project*. Translated by Howard Eiland and Kevin McLaughlin. Cambridge, Mass.: Belknap Press of Harvard University, 1999.

———. *Illuminations: Essays and Reflections*. Translated by Harry Zohn. Edited by Hannah Arendt. New York: Schocken Books, 1968.

Bennett, Alice. *Afterlife and Narrative in Contemporary Fiction*. New York: Palgrave Macmillan, 2012.

Bentley, Nancy. *The Ethnography of Manners: Hawthorne, James, Wharton*. Cambridge: Cambridge University Press, 1995.

Berardi, Franco "Bifo." *The Soul at Work: From Alienation to Autonomy*. Translated by Francesca Cadel and Mecchia Giuseppina. Los Angeles: Semiotext(e), 2009.

Berlant, Lauren. "Critical Inquiry, Affirmative Culture." *Critical Inquiry* 30, no. 2 (2004): 445–51.

———. *Cruel Optimism*. Durham, N.C.: Duke University Press, 2011.

Bernes, Jasper. "Art, Work, Endlessness: Flarf and Conceptual Poetry Among the Trolls." *Critical Inquiry* 42, no. 4 (2016): 760–82.

Bertens, Hans. *The Idea of the Postmodern: A History*. London: Routledge, 1995.

Best, Stephen, and Sharon Marcus. "Surface Reading: An Introduction." In "The Way We Read Now," edited by Sharon Marcus and Stephen Best, with Emily Apter and Elaine Freedgood. Special issue, *Representations* 108, no. 1 (2009): 1–21.

Biel, Steven. "Lewis Allen's 'Only Yesterday' and the Idea of the Decade." *Journal of American Studies* 25, no. 2 (1991): 259–66.

Blackburn, Robin. "Finance and the Fourth Dimension." *New Left Review*, May–June 2006, 39–70.

Boes, Tobias, and Kate Marshall. "Writing the Anthropocene: An Introduction." *Minnesota Review* 83 (2014): 60–72.

Boltanski, Luc, and Eve Chiapello. *The New Spirit of Capitalism*. London: Verso, 2005.

Braudel, Fernand. *The Mediterranean and the Mediterranean World in the Age of Philip II*. Vol. 1. Translated by Siân Reynolds. Berkeley: University of California Press, 1995.

———. *On History.* Translated by Sarah Matthews. Chicago: University of Chicago Press, 1980.

Brooks, Peter. *Reading for the Plot: Design and Intention in Narrative.* Cambridge, Mass.: Harvard University Press, 1984.

Brouillette, Sarah. *Literature and the Creative Economy.* Stanford, Calif.: Stanford University Press, 2014.

Brown, Marshall. "Periods and Resistances." In "Periodization: Cutting Up the Past." Special issue, *Modern Language Quarterly* 62, no. 4 (2001): 309–16.

Brown, Nicholas. "The Work of Art in the Age of Its Real Subsumption by Capital," *nonsite.org*, March 13, 2012.

Buscombe, Edward. *The Searchers.* London: British Film Institute, 2000.

———. "Inventing Monument Valley: Nineteenth-Century Landscape Photography and the Western Film." In *The Western Reader*, edited by Jim Kitses and Gregg Rickman, 115–31. New York: Limelight, 1998.

Cain, James M. *The Postman Always Rings Twice.* New York: Vintage, 1992.

Capps, Robert. "Leonardo DiCaprio: The *WIRED* Interview." *WIRED*, December 14, 2015.

Carmichael, Deborah A. "The Living Presence of Monument Valley in John Ford's *Stagecoach* (1939)." In *The Landscape of Hollywood Westerns: Ecocriticism in an American Film Genre*, edited by Deborah A. Carmichael, 212–28. Salt Lake City: University of Utah Press, 2006.

Cazdyn, Eric. *The Already Dead: The New Time of Politics, Culture, and Illness.* Durham, N.C.: Duke University Press, 2012.

Cederström, Carl, and Peter Fleming. *Dead Man Working.* Winchester: Zero Books, 2012.

Chabon, Michael. *The Yiddish Policemen's Union.* New York: Harper Perennial, 2007.

Chakrabarty, Dipesh. "Climate and Capital: On Conjoined Histories." *Critical Inquiry* 41, no. 1 (2014): 1–23.

———. "The Climate of History: Four Theses." *Critical Inquiry* 35, no. 2 (2009): 197–222.

Challakere, Padmaja. "Aesthetics of Globalization in Contemporary Fiction: The Function of the Fall of the Berlin Wall in Zadie Smith's *White Teeth* (2000), Nicholas Royle's *Counterparts* (1996), and Philip Hensher's *Pleasured* (1998)." *Theory and Event*, 10, no. 1 (2007).

Chandler, James. *England in 1819: The Politics of Literary Culture and the Case of Romantic Historicism.* Chicago: University of Chicago Press, 1998.

Chandler, Raymond. *The Big Sleep.* New York: Vintage, 1992.

Chandra, Vikram. *Sacred Games.* New York: Harper Perennial, 2007.

Chion, Michel. *Audio-Vision: Sound on Screen.* Edited and translated by Claudio Gorbman. New York: Columbia University Press, 1994.

———. "The Three Listening Modes." In *The Sound Studies Reader*, edited by Jonathan Sterne, 48–53. London: Routledge, 2012.

Christensen, Jerome. *America's Corporate Art: The Studio Authorship of Hollywood Motion Pictures.* Stanford, Calif.: Stanford University Press, 2012.

Climate Central. *Global Weirdness: Severe Storms, Deadly Heat Waves, Relentless Drought, Rising Seas, and the Weather of the Future.* New York: Vintage, 2012.

Clover, Joshua. *1989: Bob Dylan Didn't Have This to Sing About*. Berkeley: University of California Press, 2009.

Cohen, Samuel. *After the End of History: American Fiction in the 1990s*. Iowa City: University of Iowa Press, 2009.

Connor, J. D. *The Studios After the Studios: Neoclassical Hollywood (1970–2010)*. Stanford, Calif.: Stanford University Press, 2015.

Cooppan, Vilashini. "Hauntologies of Form: Race, Genre, and the Literary World System." *Gramma: Journal of Theory and Criticism* 13 (2005): 71–86.

Copjec, Joan. *Imagine There's No Woman: Ethics and Sublimation*. Cambridge, Mass.: MIT Press, 2004.

———. "The Phenomenal Nonphenomenal: Private Space in *Film Noir*." In *Shades of Noir*, edited by Joan Copjec, 167–97. London: Verso, 1993.

Corkin, Stanley. *Cowboys as Cold Warriors: The Western and U.S. History*. Philadelphia: Temple University Press, 2004.

Crary, Jonathan. *24/7: Late Capitalism and the Ends of Sleep*. London: Verso, 2013.

Crutzen, Paul J. "Geology of Mankind." *Nature*, January 3, 2002, 23.

Crutzen, Paul J., and Eugene F. Stoermer. "The 'Anthropocene.'" *Global Change Newsletter*, May 2000, 17–18.

Cullen, Heidi. *The Weather of the Future: Heat Waves, Extreme Storms, and Other Scenes from a Climate-Changed Planet*. New York: Harper, 2010.

Dawson, Ashley. *Mongrel Nation: Diasporic Culture and the Making of Postcolonial Britain*. Ann Arbor: University of Michigan Press, 2007.

DeLillo, Don. *White Noise*. New York: Viking, 1985.

Derrida, Jacques. *Acts of Religion*. Edited by Gil Anidjar. New York: Routledge, 2002.

———. *Rogues: Two Essays on Reason*. Translated by Pascale-Anne Brault and Michael Naas. Stanford, Calif.: Stanford University Press, 2005.

De Toth, André. *De Toth on De Toth: Putting the Drama in Front of the Camera*. Edited by Anthony Slide. London: Faber & Faber, 1996.

Dietrich, Joy. "O Pioneers! Kelly Reichardt's Anti-Western." *T: New York Times Style Magazine*, April 7, 2011.

Dimendberg, Edward. *Film Noir and the Spaces of Modernity*. Cambridge, Mass.: Harvard University Press, 2004.

Dimock, Wai Chee. *Through Other Continents: American Literature Across Deep Time*. Princeton, N.J.: Princeton University Press, 2006.

Dinshaw, Carolyn, Lee Edelman, Roderick A. Ferguson, Carla Freccero, Elizabeth Freeman, Judith Halberstam, Annamarie Jagose, Christopher S. Nealon, and Tan Hoang Nguyen. "Theorizing Queer Temporalities: A Roundtable Discussion." In "Queer Temporalities," edited by Elizabeth Freeman. Special issue, *GLQ: A Journal of Lesbian and Gay Studies* 13, nos. 2–3 (2007): 177–95.

"Discussion: Barthes–Todorov." In *The Structuralist Controversy: The Languages of Criticism and the Sciences of Man*, edited by Richard Macksey and Eugenio Donato, 145–56. Baltimore: Johns Hopkins University Press, 1970.

Doane, Mary Ann. *The Emergence of Cinematic Time: Modernity, Contingency, the Archive*. Cambridge, Mass.: Harvard University Press, 2002.

Dolar, Mladen. *A Voice and Nothing More*. Cambridge, Mass.: MIT Press, 2006.

Doyle, Sir Arthur Conan. *Sherlock Holmes: The Complete Novels and Stories*. Vol. 1. New York: Bantam, 1986.

Eagleton, Terry. "Marxism Without Marxism." In *Ghostly Demarcations: A Symposium on Jacques Derrida's Specters of Marx*, edited by Michael Sprinker, 83–87. London: Verso, 1999.

Ellis, Bret Easton. *American Psycho*. New York: Vintage, 1991.

———. *Glamorama*. New York: Vintage, 1998.

English, James F. "Everywhere and Nowhere: The Sociology of Literature After 'the Sociology of Literature.'" *New Literary History* 41, no. 2 (2010): v–xxiii.

Eshel, Amir. *Futurity: Contemporary Literature and the Quest for the Past*. Chicago: University of Chicago Press, 2013.

Esty, Jed, and Colleen Lye. "Peripheral Realisms Now." In "Peripheral Realisms," edited by Joseph Clearly, Jed Esty, and Colleen Lye. Special issue, *Modern Language Quarterly* 73, no. 3 (2012): 269–88.

Felman, Shoshana. "Turning the Screw of Interpretation." *Yale French Studies* 52 (1975): 94–207.

Felski, Rita. "'Context Stinks!'" *New Literary History* 42, no. 4 (2011): 573–91.

Ferguson, Frances. "Climate Change and Us." *diacritics* 41, no. 3 (2013): 32–38.

———. *Pornography, the Theory: What Utilitarianism Did to Action*. Chicago: University of Chicago Press, 2004.

Ferris, Joshua. *Then We Came to the End*. New York: Little, Brown, 2007.

Fisher, Mark. *Capitalist Realism: Is There No Alternative?* Winchester: Zero Books, 2009.

Foucault, Michel. *Discipline and Punish: The Birth of the Prison*. Translated by Alan Sheridan. New York: Vintage, 1995.

Frankel, Glenn. *The Searchers: The Making of an American Legend*. New York: Bloomsbury, 2013.

Frayling, Christopher. *Spaghetti Westerns: Cowboys and Europeans from Karl May to Sergio Leone*. London: Tauris, 1998.

Fukuyama, Francis. "The End of History?" In *Globalization and the Challenges of a New Century: A Reader*, edited by Patrick O'Meara, Howard D. Mehlinger, and Matthew Krain, 161–80. Bloomington: Indiana University Press, 2000.

———. *The End of History and the Last Man*. New York: Avon Books, 1992.

Goodman, Kevis. *Georgic Modernity and British Romanticism: Poetry and the Mediation of History*. Cambridge: Cambridge University Press, 2004.

Gorfinkel, Elena. "Exhausted Drift: Austerity, Dispossession and the Politics of Slow in Kelly Reichardt's *Meek's Cutoff*." In *Slow Cinema*, edited by Tiago de Luca and Nuno Barrados Jorge, 123–36. Edinburgh: Edinburgh University Press, 2015.

Graff, Gerald. *Professing Literature: An Institutional History*. Chicago: University of Chicago Press, 1987.

Grausam, Daniel. *On Endings: American Postmodern Fiction and the Cold War*. Charlottesville: University of Virginia Press, 2011.

Green, Jeremy. *Late Postmodernism: American Fiction at the Millennium*. New York: Palgrave Macmillan, 2005.

Greenblatt, Stephen. *Shakespearean Negotiations: The Circulation of Social Energy in Renaissance England*. Berkeley: University of California Press, 1988.

Grusin, Richard. *Premediation: Affect and Mediality After 9/11*. New York: Palgrave Macmillan, 2010.

Hale, Dorothy J. "Aesthetics and the New Ethics: Theorizing the Novel in the Twenty-First Century." *PMLA* 124, no. 3 (2009): 896–905.

Harzewski, Stephanie. *Chick Lit and Postfeminism*. Charlottesville: University of Virginia Press, 2011.

Hayot, Eric. *On Literary Worlds*. New York: Oxford University Press, 2012.

Hegel, Georg Wilhelm Friedrich. *The Philosophy of Right*. Translated by S. W. Dyde. London: Bell, 1896.

Hensely, Nathan K. "Allegories of the Contemporary." In "The Contemporary Novel: Imagining the Twenty-First Century," edited by Tim Bewes. Special issue, *Novel: A Forum on Fiction* 45, no. 2 (2012): 276–300.

Higgins, Mary Ellen, Rita Keresztesi, and Dayna Oscherwitz, eds. *The Western in the Global South*. London: Routledge, 2015.

Hoberek, Andrew. "Introduction: After Postmodernism." In "After Postmodernism: Form and History in Contemporary American Fiction," edited by Andrew Hoberek. Special issue, *Twentieth-Century Literature* 53, no. 3 (2007): 233–47.

——. "Living with PASD." *Contemporary Literature* 53, no. 2 (2012): 406–13.

——. *The Twilight of the Middle Class: Post–World War II American Literature and White Collar Work*. Princeton, N.J.: Princeton University Press, 2005.

Hoberman, J. *An Army of Phantoms: American Movies and the Making of the Cold War*. New York: New Press, 2011.

——. "Dark Night Returns." Review of *Sin City*, Dimension Films. *Village Voice*, March 22, 2005.

Hoyos, Héctor, and Marília Librandi-Roch, eds. "Diálogo Crítico: Theories of the Contemporary in South America." Special issue, *Revista de Estudios Hispánicos* 48, no. 2 (2014).

Hughes, Howard C. *Once upon a Time in the Italian West: The Filmgoer's Guide to Spaghetti Westerns*. London: Tauris, 2005.

Hungerford, Amy. "On the Period Formerly Known as Contemporary." *American Literary History* 20, nos. 1–2 (2008): 410–19.

——. *Postmodern Belief: American Literature and Religion Since 1960*. Princeton, N.J.: Princeton University Press, 2010.

Hutner, Gordon. "Historicizing the Contemporary: A Response to Amy Hungerford." *American Literary History* 20, nos. 1–2 (2008): 420–24.

Ingram, B. Lynn, and Frances Malamud-Roam. *The West Without Water: What Past Floods, Droughts, and Other Climatic Clues Tell Us About Tomorrow*. Berkeley: University of California Press, 2013.

Irr, Caren. *Toward the Geopolitical Novel: U.S. Fiction in the Twenty-First Century*. New York: Columbia University Press, 2014.

Jackson, Virginia. "The Function of Criticism at the Present Time." *Los Angeles Review of Books*, April 12, 2015.

——. "Introduction: On Periodization and Its Discontents." In *On Periodization: Selected Essays from the English Institute*, edited by Virginia Jackson. ACLS Humanities E-Book, 2010.

James, P. D. *Talking About Detective Fiction*. New York: Knopf, 2009.

Jameson, Fredric. "Afterword: A Note on Literary Realism." In *A Concise Companion to Realism*, edited by Matthew Beaumont, 279–89. Chichester: Wiley-Blackwell, 2010.

——. *The Ideologies of Theory*. London: Verso, 2008.

——. *Postmodernism, or, The Cultural Logic of Late Capitalism.* Durham, N.C.: Duke University Press, 1991.

——. "Postmodernism and Consumer Society." In *The Anti-Aesthetic: Essays on Postmodern Culture,* edited by Hal Foster, 127–44. New York: New Press, 1998.

——. *A Singular Modernity: Essay on the Ontology of the Present.* London: Verso, 2002.

——. "The Synoptic Chandler." In *Shades of Noir,* edited by Joan Copjec, 33–56. London: Verso, 1993.

Jarlett, Franklin. *Robert Ryan: A Biography and Critical Filmography.* Jefferson, N.C.: McFarland, 1990.

Jencks, Charles. *The New Paradigm in Architecture: The Language of Postmodernism.* New Haven, Conn.: Yale University Press, 2002.

Jennison, Ruth. *The Zukofsky Era: Modernity, Margins, and the Avant-Garde.* Baltimore: Johns Hopkins University Press, 2012.

Jockers, Matthew. *Macroanalysis: Digital Methods and Literary History.* Urbana: University of Illinois Press, 2013.

Kaplan, Amy. *The Social Construction of American Realism.* Chicago: University of Chicago Press, 1988.

Kelly, Adam. *American Fiction in Transition: Observer-Hero Narrative, the 1990s, and Postmodernism.* London: Bloomsbury, 2013.

Kermode, Frank. *The Art of Telling: Essays on Fiction.* Cambridge, Mass.: Harvard University Press, 1983.

Keynes, John Maynard. "Economic Possibilities for Our Grandchildren (1930)." In *Revisiting Keynes: Economic Possibilities for Our Grandchildren,* edited by Lorenzo Pecchi and Gustavo Piga, 17–26. Cambridge, Mass.: MIT Press, 2008.

Kittler, Friedrich A. *Discourse Networks, 1800/1900.*Translated by Michael Metteer, with Chris Cullens. Stanford, Calif.: Stanford University Press, 1990.

——. *Gramophone, Film, Typewriter.* Translated by Geoffrey Winthrop-Young and Michael Wutz. Stanford, Calif.: Stanford University Press, 1999.

Klein, Naomi. *This Changes Everything: Capitalism vs. the Climate.* New York: Simon and Schuster, 2014.

Klinkowitz, Jerome. *The New American Novel of Manners: The Fiction of Richard Yates, Dan Wakefield, and Thomas McGuane.* Athens: University of Georgia Press, 1986.

Koepnick, Lutz. *On Slowness: Toward an Aesthetic of the Contemporary.* New York: Columbia University Press, 2014.

Konstantinou, Lee. "Anti-Comprehension Pills." *Los Angeles Review of Books,* March 28, 2012.

Kozloff, Sarah. *Invisible Storytellers: Voice-Over Narration in American Fiction Film.* Berkeley: University of California Press, 1988.

Kracauer, Siegfried. *The Mass Ornament: Weimar Essays.* Translated and edited by Thomas Y. Levin. Cambridge, Mass.: Harvard University Press, 1995.

Kroll, Andy. "What's Happening in Wisconsin Explained." *Mother Jones,* March 17, 2011.

La Berge, Leigh Claire. *Scandals and Abstraction: Financial Fiction of the Long 1980s.* New York: Oxford University Press, 2015.

Lanchester, John. "When Fiction Breaks Down." *Telegraph* (London), January 29, 2010.

Latour, Bruno. "Why Has Critique Run Out of Steam? From Matters of Fact to Matters of Concern." *Critical Inquiry* 30, no. 2 (2004): 225–48.

Lauro, Sarah Juliet, and Karen Embry. "A Zombie Manifesto: The Nonhuman Condition in the Era of Advanced Capitalism." *boundary 2* 35, no. 1 (2008): 85–108.

Lawrence, John Shelton. "Western Ecological Films: The Subgenre with No Name." In *The Landscape of Hollywood Westerns: Ecocriticism in an American Film Genre*, edited by Deborah A. Carmichael, 19–50. Salt Lake City: University of Utah Press, 2006.

Lefebvre, Henri. *Critique of Everyday Life*. Vol. 3, *From Modernity to Modernism (Towards a Metaphilosophy of Daily Life)*. Translated by Gregory Elliott. London: Verso, 2005.

Lim, Bliss Cua. *Translating Time: Cinema, the Fantastic, and Temporal Critique*. Durham, N.C.: Duke University Press, 2009.

Liu, Alan. *The Laws of Cool: Knowledge Work and the Culture of Information*. Chicago: University of Chicago Press, 2004.

———. *Local Transcendence: Essays on Postmodern Historicism and the Database*. Chicago: University of Chicago Press, 2008.

Love, Heather. "Close but Not Deep: Literary Ethics and the Descriptive Turn." *New Literary History* 41, no. 2 (2010): 371–91.

Luckhurst, Roger, and Peter Marks, eds. *Literature and the Contemporary: Fictions and Theories of the Present*. London: Longman, 1999.

MacLean, Robert. "The Big-Bang Hypothesis: Blowing Up the Image." *Film Quarterly* 32, no. 2 (1978–1979): 2–7.

Malm, Andreas. "The Anthropocene Myth." *Jacobin*, March 30, 2015.

———. "The Origins of Fossil Capital: From Water to Steam in the British Cotton Industry." *Historical Materialism* 21, no. 1 (2013): 15–68.

Mandel, Naomi, ed. *Bret Easton Ellis: American Psycho, Glamorama, Lunar Park*. New York: Continuum, 2011.

Marcus, Ben. *The Flame Alphabet*. New York: Vintage, 2012.

Martin, Theodore. "The Long Wait: Timely Secrets of the Contemporary Detective Novel." In "The Contemporary Novel: Imagining the Twenty-First Century," edited by Tim Bewes. Special issue, *Novel: A Forum on Fiction* 45, no. 2 (2012): 165–83.

———. "The Privilege of Contemporary Life: Periodization in the Bret Easton Ellis Decades." *Modern Language Quarterly* 71, no. 2 (2010): 153–74.

Marx, Karl. *Capital: A Critique of Political Economy*. Vol. 1. Translated by Ben Fowkes. London: Penguin, 1976

———. "Comments on James Mill, *Éléments d'économie politique*." Translated by Clemens Dutt. http://www.marxists.org/archive/marx/works/1844/james-mill/.

Marx, Karl, and Friedrich Engels. *The Marx-Engels Reader*. Edited by Robert C. Tucker. 2nd ed. New York: Norton, 1978.

Massumi, Brian. "The Future of the Affective Fact: The Political Ontology of Threat." In *The Affect Theory Reader*, edited by Melissa Gregg and Gregory J. Seigworth, 52–70. Durham, N.C.: Duke University Press, 2010.

———. "Potential Politics and the Primacy of Preemption." *Theory and Event* 10, no. 2 (2007).

McCann, Sean. *Gumshoe America: Hard-Boiled Crime Fiction and the Rise and Fall of New Deal Liberalism*. Durham, N.C.: Duke University Press, 2000.

——. "Training and Vision: Roth, DeLillo, Banks, Peck, and the Postmodern Aesthetics of Vocation." *Twentieth-Century Literature* 53, no. 3 (2007): 298–326.

McCann, Sean, and Michael Szalay. "Do You Believe in Magic? Literary Thinking After the New Left." *Yale Journal of Criticism* 18, no. 2 (2005): 435–68.

McCarthy, Cormac. *The Road*. New York: Vintage, 2006.

McClanahan, Annie. "Future's Shock: Plausibility, Preemption, and the Fiction of 9/11." *symploke* 17, nos. 1–2 (2009): 41–62.

McGurl, Mark. "The New Cultural Geology." In "Postmodernism, Then," edited by Jason Gladstone and Daniel Worden. Special issue, *Twentieth-Century Literature* 57, nos. 3–4 (2011): 380–90.

——. "Ordinary Doom: Literary Studies in the Waste Land of the Present." *New Literary History* 41, no. 2 (2010): 329–49.

——. *The Program Era: Postwar Fiction and the Rise of the Creative Writing Program*. Cambridge, Mass.: Harvard University Press, 2009.

——. "The Zombie Renaissance." *n +1*, no. 9 (2010): 167–76.

McHale, Brian. "What Was Postmodernism?" *Electronic Book Review*, December 20, 2007.

McKibben, Bill. *The End of Nature*. Tenth Anniversary Edition. New York: Anchor Books, 1999.

McKim, Kristi. *Cinema as Weather: Stylistic Screens and Atmospheric Change*. London: Routledge, 2013.

Mendelsohn, Daniel. "Lesser Than Zero." Review of *Glamorama*, by Bret Easton Ellis. *New York Times*, January 24, 1999.

Meyer, Richard. *What Was Contemporary Art?* Cambridge, Mass.: MIT Press, 2013.

Michaels, Walter Benn. *The Shape of the Signifier: 1967 to the End of History*. Princeton, N.J.: Princeton University Press, 2004.

Miéville, China. *Between Equal Rights: A Marxist Theory of International Law*. Chicago: Haymarket, 2006.

——. *The City and the City*. New York: Del Rey, 2009.

Miller, D. A. *The Novel and the Police*. Berkeley: University of California Press, 1988.

Miller, Frank. *Frank Miller's Sin City*. Vol. 4, *That Yellow Bastard*. Milwaukie, Ore.: Dark Horse Books, 2005.

Modleski, Tania. *Loving with a Vengeance: Mass Produced Fantasies for Women*. 2nd ed. New York: Routledge, 2008.

Moore, Jason W. *Capitalism in the Web of Life: Ecology and the Accumulation of Capital*. London: Verso, 2015.

Morawski, Stefan. *The Troubles with Postmodernism*. London: Routledge, 1996.

Moretti, Franco. *The Bourgeois: Between History and Literature*. London: Verso, 2013.

——. *Graphs, Maps, Trees: Abstract Models for Literary History*. London: Verso, 2007.

——. *Signs Taken for Wonders: Essays in the Sociology of Literary Forms*. Translated by Susan Fischer, David Forgacs, and David Miller. Rev. ed. London: Verso, 1988.

Morton, Timothy. "Ecology Without the Present." *Oxford Literary Review* 34, no. 2 (2012): 229–38.

Murray, Robin L., and Joseph K. Heumann. *Gunfight at the Eco-Corral: Western Cinema and the Environment*. Norman: University of Oklahoma Press, 2012.

Naremore, James. *More Than Night: Film Noir in Its Contexts*. Berkeley: University of California Press, 1998.

Nealon, Christopher. "Reading on the Left." In "The Way We Read Now," edited by Sharon Marcus and Stephen Best, with Emily Apter and Elaine Freedgood. Special issue, *Representations* 108, no. 1 (2009): 22–50.

Nealon, Jeffrey T. *Post-Postmodernism, or, The Cultural Logic of Just-in-Time Capitalism.* Stanford, Calif.: Stanford University Press, 2012.

Nelson, Andrew Patrick, ed. *Contemporary Westerns: Film and Television Since 1990.* Lanham, Md.: Scarecrow Press, 2013.

Newman, Michael Z., and Elena Levine. *Legitimating Television: Media Convergence and Cultural Status.* New York: Routledge, 2012.

Ngai, Sianne. *Our Aesthetic Categories: Zany, Cute, Interesting.* Cambridge, Mass.: Harvard University Press, 2012.

——. *Ugly Feelings.* Cambridge, Mass.: Harvard University Press, 2005.

Nicol, Bran, ed. *Postmodernism and the Contemporary Novel: A Reader.* Edinburgh: Edinburgh University Press, 2003.

North, Michael. "Virtual Histories: The Year as Literary History." In "Periodization: Cutting Up the Past." Special issue, *Modern Language Quarterly* 62, no. 4 (2001): 407–24.

Nystrom, Derek. "Haut-Bourgeois Precarity in Boston: *The Company Men.*" *Post45: Contemporaries,* January 14, 2013.

O'Meara, Patrick, Howard D. Mehlinger, and Matthew Krain, eds. *Globalization and the Challenges of a New Century: A Reader.* Bloomington: Indiana University Press, 2000.

Oreskes, Naomi, and Erik M. Conway. *Merchants of Doubt: How a Handful of Scientists Obscured the Truth on Issues from Tobacco Smoke to Global Warming.* New York: Bloomsbury, 2010.

Orlove, Benjamin S. "How People Name Seasons." In *Weather, Climate, Culture,* edited by Sarah Strauss and Benjamin S. Orlove, 121–40. Oxford: Berg, 2003.

Osborne, Peter. *Anywhere or Not at All: Philosophy of Contemporary Art.* London: Verso, 2013.

Paik, Peter Y. *From Utopia to Apocalypse: Science Fiction and the Politics of Catastrophe.* Minneapolis: University of Minnesota Press, 2010.

Parr, Adrian. *The Wrath of Capital: Neoliberalism and Climate Change Politics.* New York: Columbia University Press, 2013.

Pfeil, Fred. "Home Fires Burning: Family *Noir* in *Blue Velvet* and *Terminator 2.*" In *Shades of Noir,* edited by Joan Copjec, 227–59. London: Verso, 1993.

Phelps, William Lyon. *Essays on Modern Novelists.* New York: Macmillan, 1910.

Pippin, Robert. *Fatalism in American Film Noir: Some Cinematic Philosophy.* Charlottesville: University of Virginia Press, 2012.

——. "What Is a Western? Politics and Self-Knowledge in John Ford's *The Searchers.*" *Critical Inquiry* 35, no. 2 (2009): 223–53.

Poe, Edgar Allan. *The Murders in the Rue Morgue: The Dupin Stories.* New York: Modern Library, 2006.

——. *The Portable Poe.* Edited by Philip Van Doren Stern. New York: Penguin, 1977.

Porter, Dennis. *The Pursuit of Crime: Art and Ideology in Detective Fiction.* New Haven, Conn.: Yale University Press, 1981.

Prosser, Jay, ed. *American Fiction of the 1990s: Reflections of History and Culture.* London: Routledge, 2008.

Puckett, Kent. *Bad Form: Social Mistakes and the Nineteenth-Century Novel*. Oxford: Oxford University Press, 2008.

Pynchon, Thomas. *The Crying of Lot 49*. New York: Harper Perennial, 1966.

Rabinow, Paul. *Marking Time: On the Anthropology of the Contemporary*. Princeton, N.J.: Princeton University Press, 2008.

Ransom, John Crowe. "Criticism, Inc." *Virginia Quarterly Review* 13, no. 4 (1937).

Richardson, Brian. *Unnatural Voices: Extreme Narration in Modern and Contemporary Fiction*. Columbus: Ohio State University Press, 2006.

Roach, Kent. *The 9/11 Effect: Comparative Counter-Terrorism*. Cambridge: Cambridge University Press, 2011.

Ronda, Margaret. "Mourning and Melancholia in the Anthropocene." *Post45: Peer Reviewed*, June 10, 2013.

——. "'Not/One': The Poetics of Multitude in Great Recession-Era America." In *Class and the Making of American Literature: Created Unequal*, edited by Andrew Lawson, 245–62. London: Routledge, 2014.

Rosa, Hartmut. *Social Acceleration: A New Theory of Modernity*. Translated by Jonathan Trejoy-Mathys. New York: Columbia University Press, 2013.

Rushing, Robert A. *Resisting Arrest: Detective Fiction and Popular Culture*. New York: Other Press, 2007.

——. "Traveling Detectives: The 'Logic of Arrest' and the Pleasures of (Avoiding) the Real." *Yale French Studies* 108 (2005): 89–101.

Saint-Amour, Paul K. *Tense Future: Modernism, Total War, Encyclopedic Form*. Oxford: Oxford University Press, 2015.

Sartre, Jean-Paul. *Being and Nothingness*. Translated by Hazel E. Barnes. New York: Washington Square Press, 1984.

——. *Search for a Method*. Translated by Hazel E. Barnes. New York: Vintage, 1963.

Self, Robert T. *Robert Altman's "McCabe & Mrs. Miller": Reframing the American West*. Lawrence: University Press of Kansas, 2007.

Serpell, C. Namwali. *Seven Modes of Uncertainty*. Cambridge, Mass.: Harvard University Press, 2014.

Shapiro, Amanda. "Power Loss." *New Inquiry*, May 13, 2013.

Sikov, Ed. *On Sunset Boulevard: The Life and Times of Billy Wilder*. New York: Hyperion, 1998.

Silverman, Kaja. *The Acoustic Mirror: The Female Voice in Psychoanalysis and Cinema*. Bloomington: Indiana University Press, 1988.

Simmon, Scott. *The Invention of the Western Film: A Cultural History of the Genre's First Half-Century*. Cambridge: Cambridge University Press, 2003.

Simpson, David. *The Academic Postmodern and the Rule of Literature: A Report on Half-Knowledge*. Chicago: University of Chicago Press, 1995.

——. *Situatedness, or, Why We Keep Saying Where We're Coming From*. Durham, N.C.: Duke University Press, 2002.

Slotkin, Richard. *Gunfighter Nation: The Myth of the Frontier in Twentieth-Century America*. New York: Harper Perennial, 1992.

Smith, Rachel Greenwald. *Affect and American Literature in the Age of Neoliberalism*. Cambridge: Cambridge University Press, 2015.

Smith, Terry. *What Is Contemporary Art?* Chicago: University of Chicago Press, 2009.

Smith, Terry, Okwui Enwezor, and Nancy Condee, eds. *Antinomies of Art and Culture: Modernity, Postmodernity, Contemporaneity*. Durham, N.C.: Duke University Press, 2008.

Smith, Zadie. *White Teeth*. New York: Vintage, 2000.

Spinks, Lee. "Except for Law: Raymond Chandler, James Ellroy, and the Politics of Exception." *South Atlantic Quarterly* 107, no. 1 (2008): 121–43.

Sprinker, Michael, ed. *Ghostly Demarcations: A Symposium on Jacques Derrida's Specters of Marx*. London: Verso, 1999.

Stewart, Garrett. *Framed Time: Toward a Postfilmic Cinema*. Chicago: University of Chicago Press, 2007.

Sturrock, John ed. *The Oxford Guide to Contemporary Writing*. Oxford: Oxford University Press, 1996.

Tarantino, Quentin. "Quentin Tarantino Tackles Old Dixie by Way of the Old West (by Way of Italy)." *New York Times Magazine*, September 27, 2012.

Telotte, J. P. *Voices in the Dark: The Narrative Patterns of Film Noir*. Urbana: University of Illinois Press, 1989.

Thomas, Ronald R. *Detective Fiction and the Rise of Forensic Science*. Cambridge: Cambridge University Press, 1999.

Thompson, Graham. "Periodizing the '80s: The 'Differential of History' in Nicholson Baker's *The Mezzanine*." *Modern Fiction Studies* 57, no. 2 (2011): 300–317.

Todorov, Tzvetan. *The Poetics of Prose*. Translated by Richard Howard. Ithaca, N.Y.: Cornell University Press, 1977.

Tomkins, Jane. *West of Everything: The Inner Life of Westerns*. New York: Oxford University Press, 1992.

Tong, Allan. "Old, Faded Pictures: Vilmos Zsigmond on *McCabe & Mrs. Miller*." *Filmmaker Magazine*, August 12, 2014.

Underwood, Ted. *Why Literary Periods Mattered: Historical Contrast and the Prestige of English Studies*. Stanford, Calif.: Stanford University Press, 2013.

Van Dine, S. S. "Twenty Rules for Writing Detective Stories." *American Magazine*, September 1928.

Vernet, Marc. "*Film Noir* on the Edge of Doom." In *Shades of Noir*, edited by Joan Copjec, 1–31. London: Verso, 1993.

Wajcman, Judy. *Pressed for Time: The Acceleration of Life in Digital Capitalism*. Chicago: University of Chicago Press, 2015.

Walkowitz, Rebecca. *Born Translated: The Contemporary Novel in the Age of World Literature*. New York: Columbia University Press, 2015.

Webb, Lawrence. "Remapping *The Conversation*: Urban Design and Industrial Reflexivity in Seventies San Francisco." *Post45: Peer Reviewed*, June 22, 2014.

Weeks, Kathi. *The Problem with Work: Feminism, Marxism, Antiwork Politics, and Postwork Imaginaries*. Durham, N.C.: Duke University Press, 2011.

Wegner, Phillip E. *Life Between Two Deaths, 1989–2001: U.S. Culture in the Long Nineties*. Durham, N.C.: Duke University Press, 2009.

Whitehead, Colson. *Zone One*. New York: Anchor Books, 2011.

Wilkins, Matthew. "Contemporary Fiction by the Numbers." *Post45: Contemporaries*, March 11, 2011.

Williams, Evan Calder. *Combined and Uneven Apocalypse: Luciferian Marxism*. Winchester: Zero Books, 2010.

Wood, Gillen D'Arcy. "Constable, Clouds, Climate Change." *Wordsworth Circle* 38, nos. 1–2 (2007): 25–38.

Wood, James. "Human, All Too Inhuman." Review of *White Teeth*, by Zadie Smith. *New Republic*, July 24, 2000.

Woolf, Virginia. "Mr. Bennett and Mrs. Brown." In *Essentials of the Theory of Fiction*, edited by Michael J. Hoffman and Patrick D. Murphy, 21–34. 3rd ed. Durham, N.C.: Duke University Press, 2005.

Žižek, Slavoj. *Looking Awry: An Introduction to Jacques Lacan Through Popular Culture*. Cambridge, Mass.: MIT Press, 1991.

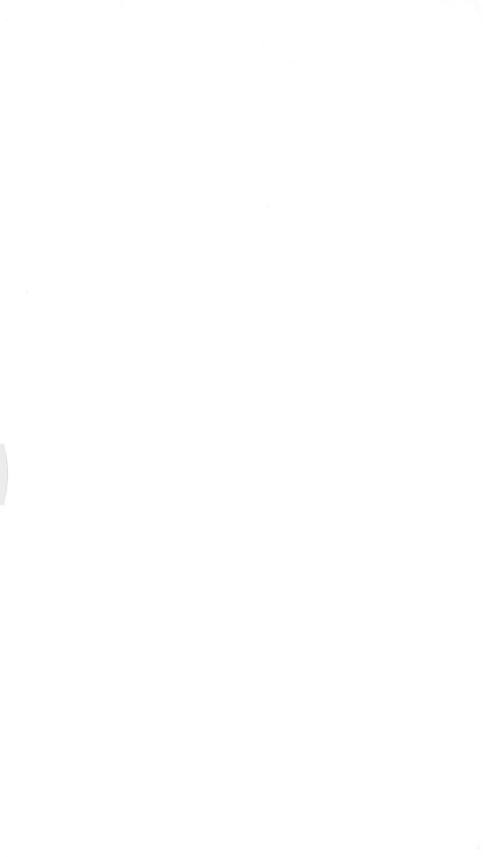

# INDEX